Neighbors to the Presidents

1. **Van Ness House**
John and Marcia Van Ness
Columbian University
O.A.S

2. **Carbery House**
Thomas Carbery
Ruth and Catherine Carbery
D.A.R.

3. **Red Cross**

4. **New Corcoran Gallery of Art**

5. **Octagon House**
John Tayloe
President Madison
St. Rose Technical Institute
AIA

6. **Grant Building**
Nathan Towson
Gen. U.S. Grant (office)
State Department (division)

7. **Winder Building**

8. **Seven Buildings**
Martin Van Buren
President Madison
Stephen Decatur
Peoples Drug Store
Mexican Embassy

9. **Franklin House**
William O'Neale
Peggy O'Neale Eaton

10. **Old Corcoran Gallery of Art**

11. **Blair House**
Dr. Joseph Lovell
Francis P. Blair
George Bancroft
Thomas Ewing
Montgomery Blair
U.S. Government

12. **700 Jackson Place**
Dr. Peter Parker
Carnegie Peace Endowment
Pan American Union

13. **704 Jackson Place**
Gen. Townsend
Franklin Dick
Carnegie Peace Endowment
Pan American Union
Mellon Trust

14. **708 Jackson Place**
Mr. Trowbridge
Mellon Trust

15. **712 Jackson Place**
Henry Rathbone
Nicholas Anderson

16. **716 Jackson Place**
Mrs. Mary Jessup Blair (owner)
Senator Arthur Gorman
Mellon Trust

17. **718 Jackson Place**
Mary Jessup Blair
Violet Blair Janin
C.I.O.

18. **722 Jackson Place (Ewell House)**
Dr. Thomas Ewell
Smith Thompson
Samuel Southard
Levi Woodbury
Francis Stockton
Daniel Sickles
Schuyler Colfax
Chilean Legation
Gen. D.B. Sacket
Spanish Legation
Washington McLean
William Boardman
Elihu Root
Brazilian Legation
National Women's Party
Brookings Institute

19. **726 Jackson Place**
Maj. Gen. J.G. Parker
International Bank Building
Brookings Institute

20. **730 Jackson Place**
William Murtaugh

21. **734 Jackson Place**
Charles Glover
Brookings Institute

22. **736 Jackson Place (Marcy House)**
William L. Marcy
James G. Blaine
William L. Scott
Richard Townsend
President Theodore Roosevelt

23. **740-44 Jackson Place**
Decatur House Gardens
Brookings Institute
National Grange

Baron Hyde de Neuville
Baron Tuyll
Henry Clay
Martin Van Buren
Edward Livingston
Charles Vaughn
John Gadsby
George M. Dallas
Joseph Gales
Howell Cobb
Judah Benjamin
U.S. Military
Edward F. Beale
Truxton Beale
Marie Beale
National Trust for Historic Preservation

25. **Metropolitan Club**

26. **Shubrick and Bancroft Houses**
Adm. William B. Shubrick
Dr. George Clymer
Mrs. Thomas Bayard, Jr.
George Bancroft

27. **Tracy House**
Don Dickson
Benjamin Tracy
Augustus Tyler
Count Cassini
Men's City Club
A.A.U.W.

28. **Corcoran House**
Thomas Swann
Baron Krudener
Daniel Webster
Sir Richard Parkenham
W. W. Corcoran
Calvin Brice
Chauncey Depew
William Corcoran Eustis
U.S. Chamber of Commerce

29. **Slidell House**
Thomas Ritchie
John Slidell
Gideon Wells
John P. Stockton
Henry and Clover Adams
Russell Alger
U.S. Chamber of Commerce

PROXIMITY

TO

POWER

Neighbors to the Presidents near Lafayette Square

Jeanne Fogle
2003

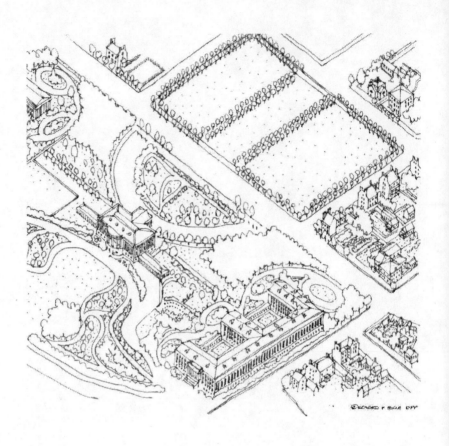

PROXIMITY

TO

POWER

Neighbors to the Presidents near Lafayette Square

by Jeanne Fogle

Illustrations by
Edward F. Fogle

A TOUR
DE FORCE
PUBLICATIONS

About the Author

Jeanne Fogle is a local historian who was born in Washington, D.C. where her family has lived for over 150 years. Washington's premier raconteur, Jeanne is "the keeper of a vast store of historical anecdotes and legends about the great, near great, good and bad, the sad and funny, the rich and poor who have made their homes in Washington," noted *The Smithsonian Associate.* Kevin McManus, of the *Washington Post,* wrote, "Jeanne Fogle is a teacher, the history teacher you wish you'd had every year in high school. When she lectures, all the essential dates, names, and facts get blended into appetizing little tales and character sketches."

After graduating from Valparaiso University and traveling for several years through Europe and to Hawaii, she returned home to Washington and fell in love with the city. That love affair is going strong. In 1984, Jeanne founded her tour company, **A Tour de Force**, which specializes in unusual, historical tours of Washington. In 1991, she began teaching local history and regional tour guiding as an adjunct professor at Northern Virginia Community College. That same year, Jeanne's first book, *Two Hundred Years, Stories of the Nation's Capital*, was published. Woody West of the *Washington Times* described her book as "a breezy, anecdotal tour, past and present, of this absurd and enchanting city."

Edward F. Fogle, the illustrator of the book, is the author's brother. Their great-grandfather, George F. W. Strieby, worked as a fresco and mural artist at the U.S. Capitol for nearly twenty-five years with Constantino Brumidi. Like his great-grandfather, Ed's artistic and architectural talents led him to a career at the Capitol. Ed graduated from The Catholic University of America in Washington with a degree in Architecture and has been employed with the Office of the Architect of the Capitol since 1983.

Acknowledgments

My heartfelt thanks to my brother, Edward F. Fogle, who makes dull buildings appear to dance on the page. To my friend, Linda Ferrall, I owe a huge debt of gratitude for going far beyond the call of duty in editing the book's content, reading and rereading every paragraph with pink pen in hand. My very special thanks to Nicole Lubar, whose computer knowledge coupled with her calming disposition, made the logistics of formatting this book a joy. I am indebted to my copyeditor, Pam Leigh, for her dogged perseverance in trying to track every comma, capitalization, and redundant phrase. Thanks to Donald Tyler and the staff at TechniGrafix, whose state-of-the-art printing company made the actual production of the book almost effortless. Most of all, I'm indebted to my liaison to reality — my husband, Tom Lyons, for his patience, kindness, support, and occasional bouquets of flowers, during the months I spent lost in a cloud of research and word-crafting.

— *JF*

Published by
A Tour de Force Publications
P.O. Box 2782
Washington, DC 20013

Copyright 1999 by A Tour de Force Publications

ISBN 0-9676095-7-7

Library of Congress Catalog Number
99 96928

Manufactured in the United States of America. This book was printed by
TechniGraphix, A Division of Phoenix Color, Hagerstown, Maryland.

Table of Contents

1

Stag Parties, Afternoon Levees, & the Big Cheese

Neighbors to the Presidents :   John Adams - Andrew Jackson (1797-1837)

Proximity to power is power. For that reason, power-seekers followed the government in 1800, when the capital city relocated from Philadelphia to Washington, D.C. A small but dynamic group of people arrived in the largely undeveloped new federal city to find few homes and no established communities, so they set to work to create what they needed.

The wealthy and influential chose to live as close as possible to their perceived center of power, the President's House. A new society evolved from a rush of unacquainted, upper-class citizens who shared no common ancestors, origins, politics, or religion. The one interest they did share was government, the business of the emerging federal city. Most members of this new community also shared optimism in the potential of the new utopia and in the experiment of self-government. Military heroes, high government officials, diplomats, bankers, philanthropists, historians, lobbyists, newspaper editors, men of independent means, and wealthy socialites were among the new Washington residents who wished to become neighbors of the president. They quickly established churches, charities, and civic associations. They invested their time and money in creating a dream.

Not everyone who was sent to the new Capital saw the promise of the future. Treasury Secretary Oliver Wolcott saw only the worst. He wrote to his wife on July 4, 1800, "No stranger can be here a day and converse with the proprietors, without conceiving himself in the company of crazy people. Their ignorance of the rest of the world and their delusions with respect to their own prospects are without parallel."[1] Washington was not a place to which politicians and diplomats could bring their wives or families in the early 19th century. Foreign governments considered Washington a hardship post and sent mostly bachelors as foreign ministers. All the same, the diplomatic community added a dimension of sophistication to society in Washington that no other city in the country could claim.

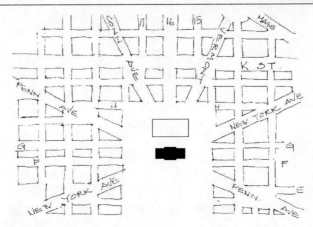

President's Park & President's House — *the first story*—

Lafayette Square and The White House

In 1790, Congress created a new 100-square-mile federal territory on the Potomac River called the District of Columbia, to honor Christopher Columbus. Within the territory a new city was planned and called Washington, to honor George Washington. In the heart of the new city, on a small hill, a site was chosen where the President's House was to be built. The high ground to the north of the site was the Pearce family farm, a portion of which was designated as the site for the President's Park.

A newly arrived land speculator from Scotland named Samuel Davidson purchased Pearce's property in 1791 before the government could purchase it. Davidson understood the value of real estate located opposite the site designated for the President's House. He became embroiled in a fierce and prolonged controversy with the city commissioners concerning his assumed right to plat and sell part of his newly purchased property. The commissioners fought hard to save all the land directly north of the President's House for a park. The drawn out dispute had the effect of retarding any building or landscaping on or near the President's Park (Lafayette Square) for almost twenty years. Eventually, however, the commissioners were forced to compromise with Davidson.

The design for the new Capital City was grand and ambitious. Pierre L'Enfant, who had planned the city in 1791, designated the property surrounding the "President's Palace" (the White House) to be 1,800-feet wide and over one-half of a mile long, stretching from Tiber Creek on the south (Constitution Avenue), northward and upward to the Old Ferry Road (H Street). The lawn to the south of the White House was called the Ellipse because of the elliptical-shaped drive that circled the lawn. The lawn to the north was called President's Park. Botanical gardens were planned for the expansive north lawn, emulating the popular Pleasure Gardens of Europe. The President's Park was separated from the rest of the property in the early 1800s when a street (Pennsylvania Avenue) was cut through. However, the President's Park was not cleared, graded, fenced, planted, or renamed (Lafayette Square) until twenty-five years later. Five spacious avenues radiated outward from the park, like rays of the sun; they were Pennsylvania Avenue, Connecticut Avenue, Vermont Avenue, New York Avenue, and 16th Street, NW.

Pierre L'Enfant planned the President's House to be like a palace, grander by five times than the house that was finally built. Unfortunately by early 1792, L'Enfant had been removed from the project of planning the city, and a competition was held for the design of the "President's Palace." George Washington chose the exact site where the house was to be built and he made a decision to radically reduce its size. The winning design for the President's House was submitted by an optimistic young architect named James Hoban, who was undeterred by the gloomy scene he observed of the surrounding, undeveloped, muddy farmland.

In 1797, five years after the construction of the President's House was started, George Washington paid a visit to the new federal city. In honor of his visit, a 16-gun salute was staged on the commons north of the house. James Hoban, who was acting in the capacity of newly elected captain of the volunteer militia, presided over this event, which was the first ceremony held in the President's Park (Lafayette Square) and the only one the first president would attend in his namesake city. When George Washington returned home to Mount Vernon, he was disappointed with what he had seen, and he carried with him serious doubts about his once grand vision for the new Nation's Capital.

The President's House was not commonly called the "White House" until 1817, when the exterior walls were covered with white paint. Prior to 1817, the house glowed with a pinkish tint from the ferrous content of the Aquia Creek sandstone used in its construction. The white paint was applied to hide the scorch marks left by the fire of 1814, which was started by the invading British troops during the War of 1812. The first *official* use of the name "White House" was instituted by the President Theodore Roosevelt, in the beginning of the 20th century, when he insisted on having the presidential letterhead printed to read, "The White House, Washington, D.C."

John Adams, the 2nd President, 1797-1801

Presidents and their first ladies became the leaders of society in the Nation's Capital, beginning with John and Abigail Adams in 1800. Each new administration set the tone and the trends in formal entertaining of the powerful and the power-seekers. Any new resident to Washington realized that establishing oneself in the newly created society was one way to secure a powerful position in the new government.

President John Adams arrived in the new capital in December 1800 as a lame duck president, having lost the recent election to Thomas Jefferson. Although Adams lived in the President's House for only four months, he set a precedent by holding the first public reception on New Year's Day in 1801. Though the President's House was unfinished and unfurnished, diplomats, military officers, cabinet officials, members of Congress, and esteemed citizens flocked to pay their respects. All came to see and be seen, and the President's Park across from the President's House became the gathering place for major public celebrations in Washington.

When Adams moved out of the President's House in March 1801, he was embittered by the overwhelming victory of Jefferson's Democratic-Republicans over his Federalist Party. If the future of the country looked dim to Adams, his view was reflected in what he saw in the new federal city he left behind. The spacious north lawn of the President's Park was littered with mounds of broken stones, bricks, logs, and lumber. Rows of roughhewn wooden workmen's sheds lined the top of the park. Below the sheds were brickyard kilns, storehouses, stonecutters' lodges, a cookhouse, and a large carpenter's hall that also served as the Masonic lodge and the local church. The remnants of the former proprietors' agrarian past had yet to be removed, including an apple orchard, a deserted farmhouse, a tobacco barn, and the little fenced-in Pearce family graveyard. A racetrack cut across the southwest corner of the park and a farmer's market borrowed space in the carpenter's lodge. Nothing pleasant or refined lay within view of the President's House in 1801. The president could see no other homes and he had no neighbors on Lafayette Square.

Thomas Jefferson, the 3rd President, 1801-1809

President Thomas Jefferson had the capacity to see far beyond the reality that greeted him when he moved into the new Executive Mansion in 1801. Jefferson had spent a good part of his life designing, building, and rebuilding his own home in Virginia. The imperfect character of the new President's House did not disturb him. His chief complaint centered on the immense size of the house and the vast expanse of the grounds, which Jefferson felt were much too grand for the leader of a democracy. Unable to alter the mansion, he filled it with his working staff, a gardener, a cook, two sons-in-law, and his private secretary, Merriwether Lewis. Jefferson's many grandchildren were often in residence, and one grandson, James Madison Randolph, was the first child born in the President's House.

Jefferson was able to reduce the size of the grounds in front of the President's House by requesting that a road, called Executive Way, be cut through the lawn to the north. (This road later became the extension of Pennsylvania Avenue.) Jefferson severed seven acres of land in front of the house, including part of the disputed Davidson property. He then requested that the seven acres be converted into a public park, which was simply called the "President's Park" until 1924. Jefferson suggested leveling and landscaping the park. However, he was unable to convince Congress to appropriate the funds.

Each year, President Jefferson held two public events at the President's House: a New Year's Day reception and an Independence Day, outdoor celebration. Jefferson's old nemesis, John Adams, set the example in 1801 for the New Year's Day reception. Adams also suggested observing Independence

Day, saying, "The day ought to be solemnized with pomp and parades, by solemn acts of devotion to Almighty God."[2]

Jefferson wanted the observance of Independence Day to be anything but a somber event. On the Fourth of July 1801, the President's Park came alive. The celebration began with a gun salute at dawn. Tents were raised, crowds came, and a fair was held where all sorts of "cottage products" could be purchased. At noon the president held an official reception for high-ranking government officials, civic and military leaders, diplomats, respected citizens of the city, "strangers of distinction," and Cherokee chiefs. The militia drilled in the middle of the square and fired gun salutes, while sideline activities included cockfights and dogfights. The Marine Band played at intervals throughout the day and into the evening. The first Independence Day celebration in Washington was a great success.

The next year, the city's residents anxiously anticipated the Fourth of July celebration of 1802. A surprise gift added to the entertainment of the day: a 1,200-pound cheese was sent to the president by the Republican Ladies of Cheshire, Massachusetts. The press reported that "the cheese arrived in a wagon, drawn by six horses handsomely decorated with ribbons. It measured 4 feet 6 inches in diameter and was one foot six inches thick."[3] Sending giant American cheeses as gifts to presidents became a fad that lasted for years.

Because Jefferson was a widower, no first lady regularly presided over the receptions, and a hostess was required in order to entertain in the presence of ladies. Consequently, many of Jefferson's parties were stag. However, Dolley Madison, the wife of the secretary of state, relished the duty of serving as President Jefferson's first lady when called upon. Occasionally Jefferson's daughter, Martha, reluctantly accepted the first lady's responsibilities.

The newly arrived residents in Washington jealously sought invitations to President Jefferson's intimate and informal round-table dinners. Fortunately for the power-seekers, Jefferson rarely dined alone. The number of dinner guests seldom exceeded twelve or fourteen, and often included a mix of politicians, intellectuals, scientists, and literary figures. Jefferson's informality was wildly popular with most individuals in Washington society. Members of the diplomatic community, however, found this form of entertaining insulting.

Jefferson claimed many accomplishments during his two terms in office, including the purchase and exploration of the Louisiana Territory. In the fall of 1803, Jefferson sent James Monroe and Robert Livingston to negotiate the purchase of New Orleans from the French. When Napoleon offered to sell the entire Louisiana territory (828,000 square miles of land stretching from New Orleans to Montana) for $15 million, Jefferson agreed to buy it and the size of the United States nearly doubled. The next year, in 1804, Jefferson sponsored the exploration of this newly acquired land for economic reasons and for political security, as well as to satisfy his scientific curiosity. Jefferson's secretary, Merriwether Lewis, and Army officer William Clark led the two-year expedition "which opened the door to the heart of the Far West,"[4] as Theodore Roosevelt noted a century later.

Octagon House — the first story —

18th Street and New York Avenue, NW — northeast corner

©EDWARD F POGUE ᴇғғ

President Jefferson's nearest neighbor was the wealthy Virginia planter John Tayloe III. In 1799, at the age of twenty-nine, Tayloe recognized the potential of the new federal city. He built his distinguished home, the Octagon House, two blocks west of the President's House. He also purchased many small property lots nearby. His son, Benjamin Ogle Tayloe, spent nearly his entire life in Washington, and he kept a detailed journal that was published years later under the title, *Our Neighbors on LaFayette Square*. He met all the presidents from Thomas Jefferson through Andrew Johnson, and he recorded his opinions of each one. Tayloe described President Jefferson this way: "His appearance was in every way plain, his hair was reddish, his face freckled. . . . Mr. Jefferson was sprightly and intellectual, with much attractive information on a variety of subjects. He was highly accomplished in the ways of society, and he gave delightful *recherché* dinners, with French cookery, French wines, and everything French, well knowing how to select his company."[5]

Dr. William Thornton, a friend of John Tayloe, designed the elegant Octagon House. (Thornton had just designed the Capitol.) The house was planned for the triangular lot at the northeast corner of New York Avenue and 18th Street, NW. It was large, stylish, multi-sided house built of bricks made at Sam Davidson's brick kilns, which were located on the President's Park. The first cost estimate for the Octagon House was $13,000; years later, the final investment was calculated at $35,000. The grandeur of Tayloe's Octagon House seemed to affirm a belief in the future of the new capital city; its presence inspired the building of many more impressive private residences nearby.

The Tayloes played a major role in the development of Washington's early social life. Winter was Washington's social season because during the winter months Congress was in session. At first, the Octagon House was used by the Tayloe family as just a winter residence. The Tayloes arrived in Washington in late November and left by early April. They entertained freely, hosting many dinners and dances purely for amusement. Other entertainments, however, were closely allied with business and political interests.

The Octagon House became legendary when the British invaded Washington and set fire to the President's House in August 1814. According to Benjamin Tayloe, his mother had just vacated the Octagon House and "induced Mons. Serrurier, the French minister, to occupy it, with a view to its protection."[6] Dolley Madison, who had made her escape just ahead of the invading British (taking with her many important government documents), entrusted her parrot to the new occupant of the Octagon. The parrot was delivered by her steward, French John, while Dolley Madison fled from the burning city. Meanwhile, Louis Serrurier sent a message to British General Robert Ross to spare the Octagon House because it served as the French legation. Ross respected the request and the Octagon House was untouched.

The President's House was in ruins when President and Mrs. Madison returned to Washington soon after the British troops withdrew from the city. The Tayloes generously offered the use of the Octagon House to the Madisons, making it the first official temporary presidential residence. In 1815, in the second floor circular study of the Octagon House, President Madison signed the Treaty of Ghent, brought to him by John Quincy Adams from Ghent, Belgium, which ended the War of 1812.

In the fall of 1815, the Tayloes moved back to the Octagon House, and for the next thirty-seven years various members of the family occupied the home. When John Tayloe III died in 1828, eleven of his fifteen children survived him. In that same year, Tayloe's son, Benjamin Ogle Tayloe, moved into his own new house which he built facing Lafayette Square; he continued to live there for the rest of his life.

F Street Row Houses — *the first story* —

F Street between 13th and 15th Streets, NW — north side

A few blocks to the east of the President's House, an outstanding row of large, brick, colonial-style houses were built on F Street, NW, in the 1790s. Dr. William Thornton, architect of the Capitol, and his wife, Anna Maria, purchased one of the F Street Row Houses soon after they were built. Their home (later numbered 1331 F Street) became a center of Washington social life in the early years of the city.

Thornton was a man of independent means, having inherited his wealth at an early age. He possessed a fine sense of humor and was once described as "an antidote to dullness." Although trained as a physician, Thornton proved to be a multi-talented man, fond of poetry, art, music, astronomy, philosophy, and all of the sciences. He loved fine racehorses and bred them on his nearby farm, often racing them against those of his friend John Tayloe. Thornton was a self-trained architect who designed not only the Octagon House in Washington, and the Capitol, but also Tudor Place in Georgetown for Martha Washington's granddaughter. His wife's legacy is the wonderful diary she kept for nearly forty years, beginning January 1, 1800. Anna Maria Thornton was one of the finest chroniclers of early Washington social life.

James and Dolley Madison were neighbors to the Thorntons when they lived on F Street, NW. They resided in one of the fine row houses while Madison served as President Jefferson's secretary of state. Their home (later numbered 1333-35 F Street) was called the "stepping-stone to the White House." On March 4, 1809, the Madisons moved from the F Street Row House to the President's House, a few blocks away. Sixteen years later to the day, John Quincy Adams, President's Monroe's secretary of state, moved from the same house into the White House. In the interim, Dolley Madison's sister and brother-in-law, Richard and Anna Payne Cutts, were living in the F Street home when the British burned the President's House in 1814. For ten days, the Madisons again resided in the F Street Row House, loaned to them by the Cutts, before moving to the Octagon House.

Rhodes Tavern — the first story —

15th and F Streets, NW — northeast corner

Rhodes Tavern was built in 1797, across from the Treasury Department near the west end of F Street where it meets 15th Street, NW. In 1800, the tavern building was leased as a hotel to William Rhodes, and later to John Semmes in 1804. During these early years, the tavern served as the unofficial town hall for the citizens of Washington. Local residents assembled at Rhodes Tavern in 1801 to demand representation in the government (which would not be granted, even in limited form, until 150 years later).

The building was sold in 1804 and the Bank of the Metropolis, one of the city's first private banks, occupied several rooms in the Rhodes Tavern. John Van Ness served as the bank's first president. Mrs. Barbara Suter operated a boardinghouse in Rhodes Tavern in the early 19th century. On August 24, 1814, the haughty, invading British military officers were said to have been feasting in Mrs. Sutter's second-floor dining room while watching the fire they had set at the President's House and the Treasury Department across the street.

Franklin House — a story —
Pennsylvania Avenue near 21st Street, NW — north side

In the early 19th century, operating a boardinghouse was considered to be one of the most respectable businesses in Washington. The Franklin House was one of the more popular boardinghouses with members of Congress because it was located not far from the President's House, on Pennsylvania Avenue at 21st Street, NW. Andrew Jackson was a friend of the owner, William O'Neale, and Jackson stayed at the Franklin House while serving in the Senate during Monroe's second term. Another resident was Congressman John Eaton, Jackson's friend from Tennessee. While residing at the Franklin House, both Jackson and Eaton were befriended by Peggy O'Neale, the owner's attractive and charming daughter.

Years later, Peggy O'Neale was blamed as the cause of the "petticoat wars" during Andrew Jackson's first administration. Peggy (O'Neale) Timberlake and John Eaton were often seen together during Peggy's husband's frequent absences. Only a few months after the untimely death at sea of her husband, Peggy married John Eaton on New Year's Day 1829. Three months later, Andrew Jackson was inaugurated as president. John Eaton was appointed as President Jackson's secretary of war. Society ladies snubbed Peggy, even though she was the wife of a cabinet member, however, Jackson supported her. The social wars continued among the cabinet officials' wives until the collapse of Jackson's cabinet in 1831, for which Peggy became the political scapegoat.

Seven Buildings — *the first story* —
Pennsylvania Avenue near 19th Street, NW — north side

The Seven Buildings were built on Pennsylvania Avenue at 19th Street, NW, near to the Franklin House. These tall, federal-style row houses served as one of the most prestigious addresses in the city. Erected in 1796 by Robert Morris and John Nicholson, on speculation, the buildings were distinguished architecturally by their doorway keystones decoratively carved with angelic, female faces. Diplomats and government officials resided in these handsome townhouses, including Elbridge Gerry, President Madison's second vice president and Martin Van Buren.

The largest of the Seven Buildings was the massive, rounded, corner building. In 1800, the State Department was accommodated there for a brief time. In the fall of 1815, President and Dolley Madison moved from the Octagon House to the corner house of the Seven Buildings, while the President's House was being rebuilt after the fire. The corner house became known as the "House of a Thousand Candles" because Dolley Madison filled the windows and rooms with glowing candles for evening receptions.

James Madison, the 4th President, 1809-1817

Serious problems challenged James Madison when he was elected president because of Jefferson's previous Embargo Acts. Great Britain and

France were at war, and each tried to stop the other from trading with the Americans by keeping American ships from entering each other's ports. Jefferson halted trade with all foreign countries in order to show the importance of U.S. products and markets. The unfortunate result of Jefferson's action was a stagnation of the U.S. economy by the time Madison was inaugurated president.

Three days before leaving office, Jefferson signed the Non-Intercourse Act and ended the embargo against all countries except Great Britain and France. In protest against the embargo, British war ships were stopping and boarding American commercial vessels, seizing cargo, and impressing (taking by force) any sailor suspected of being British by birth. The first ship stopped was Commodore Barron's frigate *Chesapeake* in 1807. Henry Clay and John Calhoun, the "War Hawks" of Congress, urged newly elected President Madison to declare war on Great Britain. In June 1812, at the request of the president, Congress voted for a declaration of war. This was just months before Madison was to run for reelection.

America was not prepared for the War of 1812. Many of her citizens did not support the war, and some actually favored the British in their fight against the French. William Henry Harrison and Andrew Jackson won victories and their reputations, in the War of 1812, but, generally, the war was fought poorly by the United States. The worst moment came when the British invaded Washington in 1814 and burned the federal buildings. After the 1815 Treaty of Ghent was signed ending the war, the peace that followed induced a surge of nationalism. The economy recovered and Americans were optimistic, making Madison's last two years in office successful ones. President James Madison was "so small in stature, but in every respect a Virginia gentleman, very hospitable and liberal in his entertainments, with great powers of conversation, replete with anecdotes and well constituted to shine in society,"[7] noted Benjamin Ogle Tayloe.

From the first moment the Madisons moved into the President's House, Dolley Madison led society and society lovingly followed her. No longer was the President's House considered a male-dominated abode. Unlike President Jefferson, Dolley delighted in giving large, formal dinner parties and weekly levees (small fashionable receptions). She set the trend in fashion, menus, and grace. Her contemporary, Margaret Bayard Smith, commented that "it would be absolutely impossible for anyone to behave with more perfect propriety than she did. Unassuming dignity, sweetness, grace."[8] Dolley Madison earned her reputation as the new lady of the new century at the first inaugural ball held in 1809. (She has been called the most highly regarded woman in Washington's 200-year history.) Her near-perfect memory for names and faces was as enviable as her remarkable ability to put people at ease. She had a smile and a kind word for everyone. Her courage and intelligence, coupled with her sensitive managerial style and strong will, were of great help to her rather aloof husband. Dolley's influence over official society lasted for half of a century, through eight administrations.

Dolley Madison wielded her influence to have the first structure built on the President's Park. In 1816, St. John's Episcopal Church, known as the "Church of the Presidents," was constructed. Three years later, Commodore Stephen Decatur built his attractive and expensive home near to St. John's, on a corner of the park. These two fine building were the anchors of the early neighborhood and of Washington's society.

St. John's Church — *the first story* —
16ᵗʰ and H Streets, NW — northeast corner

Among the president's neighbors were many Episcopalians. Before 1816, the only two episcopal churches were located several miles from the White House. One was in Georgetown and the other was near the Navy Yard. With the encouragement of Dolley Madison, a committee of highly respected citizens, including John Tayloe and John P. Van Ness, purchased property just to the north of the President's Park in anticipation of building St. John's Church upon it. The architectural services of the talented Benjamin Henry Latrobe were secured, and in 1816, St John's Church was dedicated. Dolley Madison, who was raised a Quaker, was baptized and confirmed in St. John's in 1836. Years later her funeral services would be held here.

"I have just completed a church that made many Washingtonians religious who had not been religious before,"[9] wrote Benjamin Latrobe, the church's architect who also served as St. John's organist. It was variously called "Church of the Establishment," "Church of Congress," "Church of the Diplomats," but most often "Church of the Presidents," because every president since Madison has attended services at St. John's, at least once. Pew 28 is permanently reserved as the President's Pew.

The St. John's design was simple and practical: a Greek cross without a nave and a central saucer-shaped dome with semi-lune windows. An unusual wineglass-shaped pulpit was installed on wheels set on tracks that bisected the brick floor. One Sunday the wheels came unclasped and the pulpit, with the bishop atop, glided away, gaining speed until it ended its journey with a crash into the wall. The moveable pulpit was permanently removed. The western nave entry and belfry were added in 1822. The thousand-pound steeple bell, a gift from President Monroe in 1822, was cast from a British cannon in Boston's Paul Revere foundry works.

Van Ness House — the first story —
Constitution Avenue between 17th and 18th Streets, NW

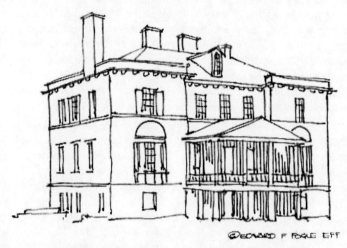

©LEONARD F FOGLE LFF

By late 1816, a postwar prosperity prompted real estate sales in Washington and Georgetown to increase by 500 percent over the prewar years. Row houses and fashionable boardinghouses were filling the president's neighborhood, though no homes had yet been built facing on the President's Park. To the southwest of the President's House, John and Marcia Van Ness built one of the finest private residences in the city. Benjamin Henry Latrobe designed the Van Ness House. He had just designed St. John's Church and was serving as the supervisory architect of government buildings. The Van Ness House was located on the bank of the Potomac River (later Constitution Avenue, NW) between 17th and 18th Streets, NW.

Situated near the elegant Van Ness House was the humble little Burnes' cottage where Marcia Burnes Van Ness grew up. Her father, Davey Burnes, was a tobacco farmer as well as a shrewd negotiator. The government paid him the highest price, in 1791, for a large portion of his 600-acre farm that extended eastward from 18th Street to 3rd Street, NW, and northward from the Tiber Creek (Constitution Avenue) to include the ground on which the President's House was built. Burnes' land was valued at $1.5 million and when Burnes died in 1799, his only daughter Marcia inherited his wealth. She was known as "the heiress of Washington." Marcia preserved the simple cottage and delighted in showing it to friends.

The Van Ness House was Greek Revival in style and was two stories tall with a raised basement. The house was built of brick covered with heavy stucco and was elegantly and elaborately furnished. The grounds were enclosed with a brick wall. From the front windows on the upper floor, ships from Europe could be seen moored to docks in Alexandria.

John Van Ness was considered dashing and brilliant. Marcia was well educated and generous. They gave the grandest entertainments in the city of Washington, which were considered the social sensations of the day. John and Marcia Burnes Van Ness became leaders in the community and did a great deal to advance the development of Washington. John was president of both the Bank of the United States and the Bank of the Metropolis. He supported the Washington Canal Company, the Washington Monument Society, and the Volunteer Fire Department. He also served as a vestryman at St. John's Church on Lafayette Square, and he became the mayor of Washington in 1830. Marcia devoted her life to their daughter and only child, Ann, and to charitable works. With Dolley Madison, Marcia helped to establish the City's Female Orphan Asylum and devoted much time to helping the orphaned children.

Ann Van Ness married Arthur Middleton of South Carolina in the late 1820s. Only two years after they were married, Ann died in childbirth, and the baby died a few days later. In order to overcome her grief at the loss of her only child and grandchild, Marcia devoted her time to assisting people in need. In 1832, a cholera epidemic seized Washington and Marcia nursed those who were afflicted. In September of that year she died a victim of cholera. Marcia was so well respected in Washington that Congress adjourned in tribute to her, thereby making her the only woman thus honored by Congress. John Van Ness continued to live in the mansion for another fourteen years until his death in 1846.

Decatur House — the first story —

748 Jackson Place, NW   (formerly 28 Lafayette Square)

Stephen Decatur, the hero of the Tripolitan Wars, became the champion of Washington society when he chose to spend his war prize money to build his home, Decatur House, near the White House facing the President's Park. Decatur won his fame and fortune in the naval war with Tripoli, which lasted from 1801 until 1805. The governments of Morocco, Algiers, Tunis, and Tripoli were extracting payments from American and European nations to protect their ships from the harassment of pirates operating off the Barbary Coast. Jefferson sent warships to the Mediterranean and defeated Tripoli in a naval war. Among the commodores sent to fight were Stephen Decatur, John Rodgers, and David D. Porter. Decatur exercised both daring and trickery when he entered enemy waters in his Moorish designed ketch, the *Intrepid,* on a mission to recapture the frigate *Philadelphia* from the Barbary pirates. Under orders to burn the *Philadelphia* rather than let her stay in enemy hands, Decatur managed at night to bring the *Intrepid* next to the captured *Philadelphia.* With an element of surprise, Decatur and his men boarded the captured ship, overpowered the pirate crew, and set the ship ablaze. In just twenty minutes, they had fulfilled their mission and escaped unharmed. Decatur's act of bravery brought him not only prize money, but praise from around the world. British Admiral Lord Nelson called Decatur's heroics "the boldest act of the age."

Ten years later, in 1815, Decatur moved to Washington as the newly appointed Navy Commissioner. The carefully chosen conspicuous site for his new home facing the President's Park mirrored Decatur's social aspirations. He was thirty-six years old when he purchased nineteen lots from Samuel Davidson on the west side of the park. Decatur and his beautiful wife Susan agreed to engage the most celebrated architect of the day, Benjamin H. Latrobe, to design a home in which they could entertain the socially elite. Decatur also purchased one of the Seven Buildings to serve as a residence while his new home was being designed and built.

The Decaturs moved into their charming residence in January 1819. They had no children of their own, but lavished their affections on Decatur's nieces, the daughters of his widowed sister. Decatur and his wife were a popular couple and their social life was very active. Though Decatur was not involved in politics, many of his friends were politicians, including Andrew Jackson. Decatur also had one enemy, Commodore James Barron, who had once been Decatur's mentor in his early naval career. Years earlier, Decatur had been a member of an inquiry board investigating the incident in which Commodore Barron was commanding the frigate *Chesapeake* when it was overpowered by the British frigate *Leopard.* The British captain demanded the surrender of three sailors who were alleged to be British deserters. Commodore Barron refused and the *Leopard* opened fire. Although Barron's ship should have been prepared to return fire, it was not and Barron surrendered the sailors. For this offence, the board on which Decatur served ordered a court-martial and suspended Barron from active duty for five years. Barron never forgave Decatur for his part in ordering the court-martial. By his own account, Barron was forced to remain in Europe during the War of 1812, due to financial difficulties.

Barron heard rumors that Decatur spoke poorly about him in society in 1819, soon after Decatur moved into his new home on Lafayette Square. He corresponded with Decatur, demanding satisfaction in a duel. Decatur responded that dueling was "a barbarous practice which ought to be exploded from civilized society."[10] The confrontations became more personal in late-January 1820, and finally a duel was arranged. The date was set for March 22 at dawn. The place was the Bladensburg, Maryland dueling grounds, just outside the city. On March 8, which was the Decatur's fourteenth wedding anniversary, they hosted a party in honor of President Monroe's daughter Maria, who was engaged to be married nine days later. Maria Monroe's wedding would be the first White House wedding of a president's daughter.

On the morning of the duel, Decatur was reported to have said to Barron, "I was never your enemy." Upon hearing Decatur's statement, either man's second could have assumed this was a gesture toward reconciliation and stopped the duel. Instead, Barron's second, Captain Jesse Elliott, immediately commanded, "Gentlemen, to your places."[11] The two men took their paces, turned, and fired simultaneously. Both were hit. Decatur had aimed low to hit Barron in the hip, but Barron had delivered a fatal shot to Decatur. Commodore Rodgers, Decatur's friend, was present at the duel. Rodgers accompanied the mortally wounded Decatur back to his home on the President's Park. Decatur died the next day with Commodore Rodgers at his side. Thousands attended the funeral. The *National Intelligencer* wrote of Decatur, "Mourn Columbia! For one of thy brightest stars has set, a son without fear and without reproach."[12]

Susan Decatur could not bear to live in her new house on Lafayette Square without her beloved husband, so the house stood empty for a period. In 1821, His Excellency Baron Jean Guillaume Hyde de Neuville, French Minister to the United States, secured a lease from Susan Decatur and the French flag was raised over Decatur House. Washington's Diplomatic Corps now included ministers from seven countries: France, Britain, Spain, the Netherlands, Portugal, Prussia, and Denmark. The French minister and his wife entertained extensively during their brief stay in Washington's exclusive neighborhood.

John Quincy Adams, speaking as secretary of state, described de Neuville as, "frank, candid, honorable, generous, benevolent, humane, adoring his country . . . He is flighty but not inconstant in his sentiments; accessible to reason . . . altogether a safe man with whom to transact business."[13] Mme. de Neuville was well loved by Washingtonians. She spoke English, using delightful, slightly twisted phrases; for example, she would greet her guests by saying, "I am charming to see you."[14] She was a watercolorist who painted some of the best-known depictions of early Washington scenes around President's Park. In 1822 Baron and Madame Hyde de Neuville returned to France.

Later the same year, in 1822, Decatur House became the Russian legation. Major General Baron Feodor Vasil'evich Teil'-fan-Seroskerken, the Russian minister, moved to Washington, leased Decatur House, and stayed for four years. To his American friends, he was known as Baron de Tuyll. As far as the Baron was concerned, entertaining was a means to a purposeful end. He wanted to involve the United States in the Holy Alliance, which was a combination of European powers under Czar Alexander. This international bloc of countries was called the Holy Alliance because they believed they were connected through mutual relations according to Christian principles. They wanted to return the Western Hemisphere colonies to the control of European nations. Spain's empire was crumbling and she wanted to reconquer her Latin American colonies. In order to encourage the United States to agree with this strategy, the witty epicure, Baron de Tuyll, attempted to cultivate the men in power through the small dinner parties he hosted at Decatur House.

The sentiment in 19th century Washington was strongly in favor of a policy of isolationism, which proved detrimental to the Baron's objective. Secretary of State Adams penned a tart but diplomatic reply to the Baron's proposals, expressing aversion to the Spanish action of colonial reconquest in Latin America. President Monroe announced this course of action in the final sentences of his seventh annual message to Congress in 1823. This policy, which became known as the Monroe Doctrine, asserts that the U.S. is against any attempt by European powers to colonize the Americas or interfere in the internal affairs of the Western Hemisphere. The Monroe Doctrine also declared that the U.S. would distance itself from European quarrels.

By 1823, Baron de Tuyll realized that his "Holy Alliance mission" had failed, and during the remainder of his stay in Washington, he claimed to be a "prisoner of gout" and entertained little. He also proved to be a disagreeable tenant at Decatur House. Susan Decatur complained that the Baron ruined her gardens when his servants dug up and sold the flowers; that his steward redecorated a parlor and sent her the bills; and, that when the Baron added a conservatory to the house, without her knowledge, her insurance was canceled. The Baron left Washington in 1826, making no retribution.

The next occupant of Decatur House was Henry Clay of Kentucky, while he was serving as John Quincy Adams' secretary of state. Clay and his family moved from their F Street Row House to Lafayette Square in 1827. He was then fifty years old, and half his life had been spent in public office. Clay had first served as a member of the Kentucky State Legislature at the age of twenty-six. Three years later he had been elected to the U.S. Senate. Next, in 1811, Clay was elected to the House of Representatives, where he was immediately chosen Speaker of the House, and served in that capacity for six consecutive terms. Clay advocated a strong international policy. As a War Hawk he promoted the tariff bill, which the Southern states felt should not apply to them.

As sectional feelings began to divide Congress, Clay exercised his strong belief in compromise in order to keep the country united. He labored for the successful passage of a congressional bill in 1820, which later became known as the Missouri Compromise. This compromise bill specified that Maine would enter the United States as a free state while Missouri would enter as a slave state, and that slavery was to be prohibited in the rest of the Louisiana Territory north of the latitude marked by the southern border of Missouri. After the passage of the Missouri Compromise, Henry Clay was called "The Great Compromiser."

Clay also started a movement that would not become reality until the end of the 19th century. He had great sympathy for the Latin American countries as they were struggling to achieve independence. In 1826, General Simon Bolivar, president of Columbia, called for a Congress of the American Nations. He hoped to form a confederation of the Western Hemisphere countries for protection against the threatening powers of Europe, known as the Holy Alliance. Clay secured the participation of the United States in Bolivar's plan. Although the actual conference was disappointing, it formed a basis of cooperation that would eventually lead to the establishment of the Pan American Union more than sixty years later.

Clay desperately wanted to be president but he did not want to be associated with the Federalists. John Quincy Adams worked with Clay to help establish the Whig Party. However, Clay's real talent was in Congress as a popular and eloquent orator, who could cleverly illustrate his opinions with entertaining stories. His patriotism was intense: "I owe a paramount allegiance to the whole Union–a subordinate one to my State,"[15] he said. Clay was endowed with a great ability to win friends whom he loved to entertain. He also loved to gamble, and his wife said she did not mind her husband's gambling because he usually won. Years before he moved to Decatur House, Clay had gambled and won several lots on the east side of Lafayette Square, which he traded to Commodore Rodgers for an imported jackass. On these lots Rodgers later built a grand, thirty-room home. Henry Clay took the imported jackass to his Kentucky farm to be bred, and it is said that many of the famous Kentucky mules claim their lineage to Clay's Andalusian jackass.

———

Decatur House did not prove to be a stepping-stone to the presidency for Henry Clay. However, it did serve that purpose for the next occupant, Martin Van Buren when he was Andrew Jackson's secretary of state. In 1829, Van Buren moved to Decatur House to be closer to the White House. He was a strategist with a sense of humor who was always cordial and courteous toward his political enemies. Van Buren took great pride in not committing himself on any issue and became known in Washington as the "Little Magician."

The traditional cabinet dinner was the first social event at Decatur House that Van Buren had the opportunity to manipulate. This dinner became a complicated affair because Peggy O'Neale Eaton, the new wife of Secretary of War John Eaton, was not accepted by society. Peggy was unfairly described as a woman without virtue, and John Eaton was criticized for having married her. Van Buren genuinely liked both Peggy and John. He proved that he could entertain them without embarrassment because he was a bachelor. (Those who felt compelled to snub Peggy Eaton were the *wives* of the cabinet officials.)

Peggy Eaton was given a cool reception at that cabinet dinner. Fortunately, no scandalous episodes occurred, nor were any insults exchanged. The Russian and British Ministers, Baron Krudener and Sir Charles Vaughan, were both bachelors. Van Buren encouraged them to entertain Peggy and John Eaton. Washington society began to split on the issue of whether or not to accept

Mrs. Eaton socially. The cabinet wives turned against her and also influenced their husbands' opinions concerning Peggy's husband, the secretary of war. The wives refused to invite her to their parties and they refused to attend any social events where Mrs. Eaton was present, including the president's receptions.

As secretary of state, Van Buren had one goal in mind during the Peggy Eaton affair: to masterfully maneuver himself into position for the presidency. Van Buren realized that President Jackson's cabinet members disagreed on nearly every issue and that Jackson was exasperated by the lack of accord. Arguments among the cabinet officials often digressed to the point of personal attacks, with total disregard to actual policy issues. Jackson was loyal to his secretary of war, John Eaton, causing Jackson to lose all control over the cabinet. The cabinet members, who were influenced by their wives negative opinions of Peggy Eaton, refused to support John Eaton on any issues. In order to facilitate the reorganization of the cabinet, Van Buren resigned as secretary of state, knowing that his resignation would induce the other cabinet members to follow. This allowed Jackson the freedom to choose those whom he wanted as replacements for the cabinet vacancies. Van Buren was later rewarded.

John Eaton resigned as secretary of war during the reorganization of President Jackson's cabinet. Jackson later offered Eaton the post of minister to Spain. When the Senate confirmed Eaton for this position, Peggy was delighted. Jackson also appointed Van Buren as minister to England. However, after Van Buren arrived in London, he learned that the Senate had refused to approve his appointment, so he returned to Washington. Jackson was also battling with his vice president, John Calhoun. Calhoun believed in the rights of states to ignore a federal law and the right of secession. President Jackson believed only in the Union. In disgust, Calhoun resigned as vice president two months before his term expired in 1832. No one was appointed to replace him. During Jackson's campaign for reelection, the vice presidency was offered to Van Buren. In 1832, Jackson was again elected president, with Van Buren as his vice president. Four years later, in 1836, Van Buren was elected president.

Van Buren's successor, as secretary of state under President Jackson and as occupant of Decatur House, was Edward Livingston. Jackson and Livingston had met in New Orleans in 1814 and remained lifelong friends. Livingston was seventy years old when he moved to Washington. As secretary of state, he was challenged by John Calhoun who led the state of South Carolina in refusing accept federal tariff laws, calling for the nullification of those laws, and threatening secession from the Union in order to form a separate government.

Edward Livingston drafted a proclamation in 1832 denying the rights of states to secede from the Union, reaffirming the principles of the Union, and stating it was the job of the judiciary, not the states, to check and restrict the federal government. The proclamation caused a sensation, but its purpose was accomplished. South Carolina stayed in the Union.

One year later, in 1833, Livingston was involved in a much more pleasant event at Decatur House – the wedding of his beautiful daughter Cora, who was called, "the queen of American society." Decatur House overflowed with guests. Cora's mother was Louise de Lassy, Livingston's second wife, whom Livingston had met in New Orleans in 1805. One year after the wedding, in 1834, Livingston was made minister to France and his new son-in-law, Thomas P. Barton of Philadelphia, became Livingston's secretary of Legation.

Upon the departure of Edward Livingston in 1834, Decatur House was occupied for a year by the British legation, headed by Sir Charles Vaughan. Vaughan first came to Washington on a diplomatic mission in 1825. He had acquired a reputation of being very capable and very charming. He also had a unique quality of freely using slang and profanity, which he believed was appropriate in a republic. This caused quite a stir in the local social circles.

Vaughn was an adventurous young man, having traveled extensively through Asia Minor and Russia. His first diplomatic post was in Spain in 1808. After accepting a series of lesser posts, he served in Paris and Switzerland before coming to the United States. While serving in the U.S., Vaughn's wanderlust took him on journeys throughout the country. His diplomatic duties while in Washington involved issues concerning the suppression of slave trade, the Canadian boundary question, and tariff problems. At Decatur House, Vaughan continued the tradition of lavish entertaining, and on one occasion he even invited Peggy O'Neale Eaton to a reception.

James Monroe, the 5th President, 1817-1825

Monroe was the last of the Revolutionary War officers to serve as president. He was sixty years old and still an adventurer when he was elected in 1816. He gained wide popularity when, two months after his first inaugural, in May of 1817, he set out on horseback to tour the country, wearing his Colonel's Revolutionary Army uniform. He rode as far east as Portland, Maine, and as far west as Detroit, covering 3,000 miles in four months. When he reached Boston, he received an enthusiastic reception, which was interpreted in a local newspaper as the beginning of a political "era of good feelings." "Mr. Monroe . . . was plain and awkward, and frequently at a loss for conversation," wrote Benjamin Ogle Tayloe in his journal; "His manner was kind and unpretending. Mrs. Monroe . . . was handsome and graceful, but so dignified and distant as to be thought haughty."[14]

Almost twenty-five years before Monroe became president, his wife, Elizabeth Monroe, proved to be a daring and brave young woman. She accompanied her husband to Paris in the late 1790s when he was sent to France as the American minister. At that time, Madame Lafayette, wife of the Marquis de Lafayette, was imprisoned and had been sentenced to death during the chaos following the French Revolution. With no assistance and by using diplomatic and political ploys, Elizabeth secured Madame Lafayette's freedom and ensured her safety.

Elizabeth Monroe had cultivated a sense of European formality while accompanying her husband on his several diplomatic missions overseas. Her behavior caused a "social revolution" when she moved into the White House as first lady. Local residents were outraged when Elizabeth announced that she would neither pay nor return social calls. When President James Monroe announced that he would receive foreign ministers only by appointment, the result was a near social boycott. Mrs. Monroe further enraged the citizenry by not extending mass invitations to the wedding of her daughter, Maria. President and Mrs. Monroe felt that official society had grown too large. Therefore, Monroe asked his secretary of state, John Quincy Adams, to draft a formula for presidential etiquette. The Washington community reluctantly accepted this new protocol, which required White House entertainments to be more restricted.

The President's House had been newly reconstructed when Monroe was inaugurated in 1817. The scorch marks from the fire of 1814 were covered with white paint and afterwards, the President's House was called the White House.

Much was accomplished during Monroe's presidency, with the assistance of Secretary of State John Quincy Adams, and through Henry Clay's leadership in the House of Representatives. Congress passed the Missouri Compromise, masterminded by Clay, during Monroe's first administration. Florida was transferred from Spain to the United States through Adams' diplomatic efforts. In his seventh annual address to Congress, President Monroe reiterated Adams' foreign policy statement. Adams strongly opposed European intrusions into the Western Hemisphere where European countries were dominating and suppressing colonies in South America. Although Adams drafted this policy, it was called the Monroe Doctrine.

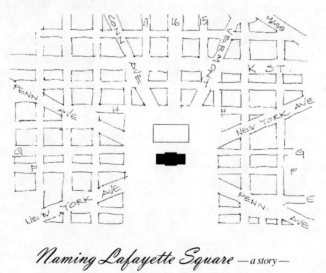

Naming Lafayette Square — a story —

In 1824, one of the greatest events of Monroe's presidency occurred. The Marquis de Lafayette came to Washington for a two-week visit as part of his grand, historic tour of the United States. In anticipation of the festivities, Congress turned its attention to the President's Park for the first time. The ground was leveled, walkways were installed, new trees and shrubs were planted, and a wooden fence was erected to keep out the local residents' cows, pigs, and sheep. Hundreds of cartloads of dirt were brought in to fill the gullies and mud holes. Charles Bulfinch, the third architect of the Capitol, was asked for advice on improving the commons. His plans have since been lost, but it is assumed that Bullfinch inspired some of the landscape improvements.

The celebration for the Marquis de Lafayette began on October 12, 1824, when "he was escorted to a barouche, which was decorated with the French colors and drawn by four gray horses. . . . A procession composed of military companies and civic societies, and which was two miles in length marched over the city with the honored guest. . . . At a certain point the hero was met by a chariot containing twenty-five maidens dressed in white muslin and blue scarfs, and with wreaths of red flowers on their heads, intended to represent the twenty-four states and the District of Columbia."[16] Henry Clay greeted Lafayette at the Capitol. Arches with banners, mottoes, and floral designs were displayed throughout the city. Atop the largest arch was a young, live eagle, which was said to have bent its head and flapped its wings when Lafayette passed beneath.

President Monroe greeted Lafayette at the White House while crowds filled the President's Park to pay their respects to the aged hero of the Revolutionary War. Lafayette was impressed with this new Capital City that he was seeing for the first time. With a sense of the future, he proclaimed Washington to be "the central star of the constellation, which enlightens the whole world."[17] General Andrew Jackson was also feted during Lafayette's visit due to his personal popularity won through his heroism during the War of 1812. After Lafayette's visit, the President's Park was popularly called Lafayette Park or Lafayette Square.

In 1819, five years before Lafayette's visit, the perimeters of the President's Park were determined for the first time. When Decatur erected his home, no streets were cut through the park. The city council immediately approved an appropriation of $150 "to open and gravel a carriage way 40-feet wide" from Pennsylvania Avenue to H Street, directly in front of Decatur's house, on the condition that Decatur advance the funds to be reimbursed later. The city council approved the same appropriation for Richard Cutts when he built his house on the other side of the President's Park. Thus, by 1820, the park was defined with two new boundaries called 16½ Street (Jackson Place) in front of Decatur's House and 15½ Street (Madison Place) in front of Cutts' House. Two previously existing streets bounded the north and south: H Street and Executive Way (Pennsylvania Avenue). Although the homes on Lafayette Square were eventually given numbers (and in the 1930s, re-numbered), the homes were more often referred to by the name of one of the well-known occupants.

In 1833, after the Treasury Department building burned, Robert Mills, architect of the Treasury, offered the suggestion to replace all of the government departmental office buildings with one monumental structure. The most convenient place for this new building would be across the street from the

White House, on Lafayette Park. President Jackson apparently did not like this idea, so the Treasury Department was redesigned and rebuilt on a much grander scale on its original site to the east of the Executive Mansion. The story, which is often told, of Jackson choosing this site to block the view from the White House to the Capitol cannot be justified because the view was already obstructed by trees that Thomas Jefferson had planted. In fact, the site allowed Robert Mills to give Pennsylvania Avenue a much-needed western terminus with the Treasury's massive south portico.

In 1834, Congress made a small appropriation for repairing the wooden fence around the park. The name of Lafayette Park was used officially for the first time in the appropriation document and has been used ever since. It is probably not coincidental that 1834 was also the year the Marquis de Lafayette died in France.

Carbery House — the first story —

17th and C Streets, NW — northwest corner

Thomas Carbery built his house in 1818, on the northwest corner of 17th and C Streets, NW. The house was located a short distance from the newly constructed Van Ness House. A few years earlier, Carbery had established wharves at the end of 17th Street where it met the Potomac River shore. Building materials unloaded at the wharves were used in constructing the new government buildings and, for rebuilding the buildings recently burned by the British. When Tiber Creek was converted in the 1820s into the City Canal (which later became Constitution Avenue, NW) the wharves gained importance when the passenger steamers stopped there. Carbery carefully chose a location for his house close to his wharves. When compared to the Van Ness House, Carbery's house was small but elegant, built of brick, two stories high with a gabled attic, and raised basement. Like John Van Ness, Thomas Carbery was active in public affairs and served as the mayor of Washington in 1822. In the

1830s, Carbery suffered a terrible misfortune when his wife and all of his four children died within a short time of each other.

Two of Carbery's three sisters moved into the house when he built it, and they continued living there after Carbery's death in 1863. A third widowed sister, Mrs. Ann Carbery Mattingly, also moved into the house in the early 1820s when she became gravely ill. Doctors diagnosed her as having a fatal cancerous tumor. A strange story was told about her which made the house famous and converted Carbery into a devout Catholic and a noteworthy philanthropist. Desperately seeking help for his ill sister, Carbery had written to a faith healer, Prince Hohenlohe of Hamburg, Germany. The prince agreed to pray for Ann on March 10, 1823, at a specified time. Carbery's family, along with a Catholic priest and the family physician, gathered around the dying woman's bed at the appointed hour of the prayer. Though she had been bedridden for a long time, that night she stood up, and soon thereafter she completely recovered. All those who were present gave signed testimonies documenting Mrs. Mattingly's miraculous recovery before Chief Justice John Marshall. Thereafter the house was called the "Miracle House."

Dolley Madison House — *the first story* —
25 Madison Place   (formerly 25 Lafayette Square)

©EDWARD F FOGLE '97

In 1822, Richard and Anna Payne Cutts moved from their fashionable F Street Row House when their new home was built on the east side of the President's Park across from Decatur House. Anna was Dolley Madison's younger sister. The Cutts' new house was brick and stucco, federal in style with three stories and an attic, and a front door that opened onto the park.

Richard Cutts had first come to Washington in 1801 as a member of Congress from the Maine District (which was, at that time, part of the

Massachusetts Commonwealth). By 1817, Cutts was employed as the second comptroller of the Treasury. Unfortunately, Cutts' financial obligations overwhelmed him and he mortgaged his new house on the President's Park in order to help pay his debts. For a short period he was even confined in debtors prison and arrangements were made to sell the house. James and Dolley Madison, who were living in retirement at Madison's Virginia estate, Montpellier, agreed to purchase the house and adjoining lots so that Dolley's sister, Anna, and her children would have a place to live. Many years later Dolley Madison would return to live in this house on Lafayette Square, where she reigned over Washington society until 1849. The house became known as the Dolley Madison House.

Ewell House — the first story —

722 Jackson Place, NW (formerly 14 Lafayette Square)

A short distance south of Decatur House, facing the President's Park, the Ewell House was built about the same time as the Dolley Madison House. In 1820, Dr. Thomas Ewell acquired two of the mid-block lots on 16½ Street (Jackson Place). Ewell had served as Naval Surgeon since 1808. His wife, Elizabeth, was the daughter of Secretary of the Navy Benjamin Stoddert. For many years, the Ewells had resided with Stoddert in his home, called the Halcyon House, in Georgetown on Prospect Street.

The Ewells were excited to have their own home in the president's neighborhood, and they moved into it in late 1820 before it was completed. Thomas Ewell was the author of a number of medical publications and was also known as an inventor. With his father-in-law, Ewell operated a small gunpowder mill near Bladensburg, Maryland, making gunpowder by a roller method he invented which lessened the risk of explosion. The Ewells enjoyed entertaining in their dignified new home for only a few years.

In the mid-1820s, two former secretaries of the navy leased the Ewell House. Monroe's former secretary of the navy, Smith Thompson, leased the house while serving as an associate justice of the U.S. Supreme Court. He was considered one of the most distinguished officials of the time. Next, Samuel L. Southard leased the Ewell House. Southard, a former senator from New Jersey, also had served as secretary of the navy under both President Monroe and President John Quincy Adams. Southard later served as secretary of the treasury and he briefly served as secretary of war.

By 1829, Major General John McPherson Berrien lived in the Ewell House. He was the son of a Continental Army officer and nephew (on his mother's side) of John McPherson, Lafayette's aide-de-camp. Berrien had been elected to the Senate in 1824, but soon abandoned his Senate position to become Jackson's attorney general. With the rest of Jackson's cabinet, Berrien was pressured to resign in 1831. Jackson offered him the post of minister to Great Britain, but he refused it and returned to his home in Georgia. In the 1840s, Berrien was twice re-elected to serve in the U.S. Senate, and he later was appointed as a member of the Board of Regents of the Smithsonian Institution.

In 1831, the Ewell House was again occupied by a secretary of the navy, Levi Woodbury, who stayed for ten years. He also served as secretary of the treasury and had the honor to lay the cornerstone of the new Treasury building in 1833. Initially, Woodbury had been a part of President Jackson's unofficial team of advisors, known as the "Kitchen Cabinet," along with his neighbor, Francis Preston Blair. When Jackson's first cabinet retired in 1831, Woodbury was appointed secretary of the navy. (Jackson's new cabinet also included Edward Livingston as secretary of state, Lewis Cass as secretary of war, and Louis McLane as secretary of the treasury.)

Woodbury was described as alert and self-confident. He had earned the title of "the rock of the New England Democracy" when he served as senator from New Hampshire. During Jackson's second administration, Roger Taney was appointed secretary of the treasury, but Congress rejected him. When Woodbury was appointed to replace Taney, however, Congress approved. Woodbery was retained as secretary of the treasury during Van Buren's administration. President Tyler appointed Woodbury as associate justice of the Supreme Court in 1845, and he served until 1851. Woodbury's daughter, Mary Elizabeth, married Montgomery Blair, son of their neighbor Francis P. Blair.

Blair House — the first story —

1651 Pennsylvania Avenue, NW

Surgeon General Joseph Lovell built his house near Lafayette Square in the early 1820s. His federal-style house was originally two stories tall with a simple portico and a fanlight window over the door. The house was later enlarged. Lovell served in the War of 1812 and was appointed surgeon general in 1818.

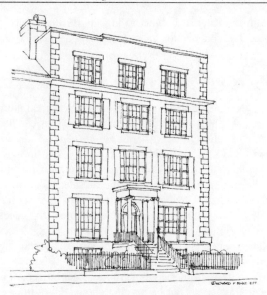

In the 1830s Dr. Lovell established a small medical library in Washington. He encouraged other physicians in various parts of the country to donate their personal books and pamphlets to this medical library. Fifty years later, more than 67,000 items were in the collection. In the 1880s, the Medical Library was housed on the second floor of the refurbished, old Ford's Theater on 10th Street, which had been purchased by the government and refitted for office use two months after Lincoln was shot there in 1865.

Tragically, both Dr. Lovell and his wife died unexpectedly within weeks of each other in 1836. Their eleven children were sent to live with relatives. The lovely home was advertised for sale in the *Globe* newspaper, as "a spacious, 2-story brick dwelling, with basement . . .[with] every convenience for a family . . . a well of excellent water, brick stable and carriage house, flower and fruit garden tastefully laid out and highly cultivated."[18] The grounds were enclosed by a high board fence which ran along Pennsylvania Avenue to 17th Street and north on 17th Street to H Street. The advertisement ran daily for several months until March 1837 when Francis Preston Blair, editor of the *Globe*, purchased the house for $6,500. The house has been known as Blair House ever since.

Francis P. Blair came to Washington from Kentucky in 1831 to establish his newspaper, in the political interest of Andrew Jackson. Blair and his partner, John Rives, also published *The Congressional Globe*, which reported the proceedings of both houses of Congress. This publication continued until 1873 when the federally published *Congressional Record* replaced it.

In his new home, Blair often hosted Jackson's intimate group of unofficial advisors, called the "Kitchen Cabinet." Duff Green had been a member of this unofficial cabinet when his paper, the *U.S. Telegraph*, was used to champion Jackson's politics. However, when John Calhoun resigned as Jackson's vice president in 1832, Green pledged his paper's devotion to Calhoun. Jackson gave

Green's place in the Kitchen Cabinet to Francis P. Blair, a clever writer who stoutly defended Jackson's actions and waged war against those who opposed him.

John Quincy Adams, the 6th President, 1824-1829

John Quincy Adams' presidential victory created great animosity among the politicians in Washington. In the 1824 election, four candidates had vied for the presidency: John Quincy Adams, Henry Clay, Andrew Jackson, and William Crawford. The votes were split four-ways, causing great confusion. Because no candidate had a majority of the votes, the Constitution required the House of Representatives to choose the president, but only from among three candidates. Henry Clay was eliminated because he had the fewest number of votes. Clay wielded his power in Congress to successfully gather support for Adams. Later, when Clay received the enviable appointment of secretary of state, he was accused of unfairly collaborating with Adams. Jackson bitterly called Clay the "Judas of the West." Clay replied that "if [he were] at liberty to draw from the whole mass of our citizens for a president," John Quincy Adams would not be his first choice. He further explained that he had refused to support Andrew Jackson, however, because, "I cannot believe that the killing of 2,500 Englishmen at New Orleans qualifies one for the various, difficult, complicated duties of the chief Magistracy."[19]

John Quincy Adams was highly educated, well traveled, and a fearless statesman. However, by his own admission, he was not very well liked. The years had proven that Adams was a great diplomat. He negotiated the Treaty of Ghent in 1814 and the transfer of Florida from Spain to the United States in 1818. He was against slavery and for Indian rights. He advocated internal improvements in the country through highway and canal construction. In 1828, Adams broke the ground for the Chesapeake and Ohio Canal in Georgetown. He sought funding for a national university, a national observatory, and scientific expeditions. Benjamin Tayloe noted that "Mr. John Quincy Adams' abilities and statesmanlike qualities were beyond dispute. . . . Although of a cold and unprepossessing exterior, and only appearing well in conversation when excited to it by others, he was a stickler for the forms of etiquette."[20] Benjamin Pearly Poore wrote "President Adams, although at heart instigated by a Puritan intolerance of those who failed to conform with himself, was a true patriot, and as a public man, was moved by the highest moral motives."[21] Nevertheless, he just was not popular.

Adams' wife, Louisa Catherine Adams, was the only first lady born outside the United States. Her father was American and her mother was English. Louisa's first glimpse of America was at the age of twenty-six, a few years after she and Adams married in London. She was said to be the best traveled lady of her time because she accompanied her husband on his many diplomatic missions. She was an accomplished musician and gained a reputation as a popular hostess while her husband served as Monroe's secretary of state. The bitter feelings from the election of 1824, however, made entertaining in the White House difficult. By the end of Adams' term in office, Louisa was anxious to leave Washington. However, in 1831, she returned when her husband was elected to the House of Representatives, where he served for seventeen years until his death in 1848. One year before he died, John Quincy and Louisa Adams had celebrated their fiftieth wedding anniversary.

Corcoran House — the first story —
1611 H Street, NW

While Adams was still president, in 1828, an important house was erected on H Street, facing Lafayette Square. Thomas Swann built a handsome, three-and-a-half-story brick house, between 16th Street and Connecticut Avenue, on the north side of H Street, NW. Swann was living in Alexandria, Virginia, in 1820, when he was appointed district attorney of Washington. Although, he held this position for twelve years, he rarely lived in his new home.

After Andrew Jackson became president, the Russian Baron Krudener leased Swann's house and stayed until 1832. His British counterpart, Sir Charles Vaughan, was living nearby in a house on I Street at the same time and the two diplomats entertained constantly. Baron Krudener gave a well-documented, lavish dinner party, attended by 500 guests, in honor of Secretary of State Martin Van Buren. The house quickly became known the most hospitable mansion in Washington because the extravagant entertaining offered by nearly all of its successive occupants.

The house gained prominence when friends of Daniel Webster purchased it and gave it to him while he was serving as secretary of state in 1841. A few years later, William Wilson Corcoran purchased the house and greatly enlarged it in the Victorian-style. Thereafter, it was called the Corcoran House.

Tayloe House — the first story —
21 Madison Place, NW (formerly 21 Lafayette Square)

In 1828, Benjamin Ogle Tayloe also built a fine, brick residence to the south of the Dolley Madison House, facing Lafayette Park. The house was three stories tall with an attic. Benjamin Tayloe was well educated and independently wealthy. Like his father, John Tayloe (of Octagon House), he loved racehorses and bred them at his country estate in Virginia. At the age of twenty-eight, Tayloe married Julia Maria Dickinson, daughter of a former member of congress from New York. Julia Maria wanted to be involved in society and wished for a home in the city. Tayloe purchased several lots on Lafayette Square in 1824 and, four years later his house was completed. The Tayloes decided not to move in immediately. Instead, they first leased their new home to Thomas Swann who was building his house on the north side of the park.

Henry Clay and Tayloe were great friends and their political views were similar. Tayloe was considered an important member of the Whig Party, supporting Clay in his several bids for the presidency. When the Democratic president, Andrew Jackson, moved into the White House in March 1829, Tayloe did not look forward to being his neighbor across Lafayette Square. In the last months of 1829, however, Tayloe and his wife finally moved into their new home. For forty years, Tayloe befriended, entertained, observed, and noted his opinions in his journal, about the most important persons of the day.

© EDWARD F POGUE EFF

The Tayloes were collectors of antiques and fine art. They purchased furniture that had belonged to George Washington, John Adams, Alexander Hamilton, and Henry Clay. They traveled extensively, collecting precious items that had once belonged to European rulers. Julia Maria Tayloe also collected autographs from their numerous acquaintances and visitors, which she kept in an autograph album. Among the many signers of this unique and priceless book (some of whom also added personal and original verses) were the Marquis de Lafayette, John Quincy Adams, Daniel Webster, John C. Calhoun, John Marshall, Martin Van Buren, William Henry Harrison, Zachary Taylor, and Millard Fillmore. The Tayloe House served as one of the chief centers of hospitality and social life in Washington.

Gunnell House — the first story —
Pennsylvania Avenue and Madison Place, NW

In December 1829, an article in the *National Intelligencer* newspaper mentioned "the corner house between the U.S. Bank and the President's House." This reference was to the Gunnell House that recently had been erected on the northeast corner of Pennsylvania Avenue and 15½ Street (Madison Place). Next door on Lafayette Square, the Rodgers House was being constructed at the same time. The Gunnell House fronted on Pennsylvania Avenue, with its long side porch overlooking Lafayette Square. Dr. James S. Gunnell, for whom this elaborate house was named, had the reputation of being one of the best dentists of the day. He was born in Loudoun County, Virginia, educated in Leesburg, Virginia, and during the War of 1812, he served as a lieutenant. In 1820, he graduated from the University of Pennsylvania with a degree in medicine and moved to Washington to practice dentistry.

When Dr. Gunnell moved into his grand home on Lafayette Square, he was married and had six children. The newspaper article also described the beautiful gardens with roses and flowering vines behind the house. In the spring of 1839, just after President Van Buren had moved into the White House, Gunnell received an urgent call from the president. He packed his dental tools and hurried to assist Van Buren; however, there was no dental emergency. Van Buren asked Gunnell to accept the position of postmaster general, which he held for two years before he returned to his practice of dentistry. Gunnell continued to reside in the house until 1852 when he died.

Rodgers House — the first story —

17 Madison Place, NW (formerly 17 Lafayette Square)

©EDWARD F FOGLE EFF

Between the Gunnell House and the Tayloe House, Commodore John Rodgers built his home on the property lots that Henry Clay traded him in 1827 for an Andalusian jackass. The Rodgers' House, completed in 1831, was a thirty-room mansion, three stories tall, and built of brick with a semidetached servants' house in the rear and stables nearby.

Commodore Rodgers, like his friend Commodore Decatur, enjoyed an illustrious naval career. He served with distinction in the undeclared French Naval War of 1798, in the Barbary War of 1805, and in the War of 1812. Commodore Rodgers became a hero in 1811, when his ship was attacked by a British warship. This incident was similar to an earlier attack on a frigate commanded by Commodore Barron. The British sloop *Little Belt* attacked Rodgers' frigate *President*. Commodore Rodgers, however, unlike Barron, successfully defeated the British in a brief battle. In August 1814, Commodore Rodgers was called from Philadelphia to defend Washington against the British when they burned the city, but he arrived too late to be of service. However, he sailed to Alexandria, Virginia, to halt the second advance of the British fleet and successfully forced their withdrawal. He then sailed to Baltimore to defend the harbor when the British tried to destroy Ft. McHenry. In 1815, Rodgers came to Washington to accept an appointment from President Madison to serve as chairman of the Board of Naval Commissioners, a position just below that of a cabinet member. Commodore Rodgers retired from naval service in 1827.

Rodgers and his family lived in a rural area of Washington called Greenleaf Point, prior to moving into their Lafayette Square home. Rodgers' son, John Rodgers, Jr., attained the rank of rear admiral and served as the superintendent of the Naval Observatory. John Rodgers, Jr. was responsible for selecting the location for the new observatory on upper Massachusetts Avenue. Rodgers' daughter, Louisa, married Brigadier General Montgomery C. Meigs of the Army Corps of Engineers. Meigs designed the Washington Aqueduct System and, years later, designated the Custis-Lee property in Arlington, Virginia, to be used as a Civil War military cemetery (Arlington Cemetery).

When his house on Lafayette Square was completed, Rodgers and his family were not quite ready to leave their country residence and move to the city. They leased their new house to a friend, Roger Taney, and his wife, who was the sister of Francis Scott Key. President Jackson asked Taney to serve as secretary of the treasury by recess appointment, after dismissing his previous Treasury secretary, William J. Duane. Jackson disliked Duane because he refused to remove government deposits from the Bank of the United States, which Jackson wanted to abolish. When Taney's cabinet appointment was later disapproved by the Senate, Taney retired to his home in Baltimore.

Taney was described by his associates as being considerate, dependable, generous, simple, direct, earnest, and effective. Unfortunately, he was always in dire financial need, although he was never in debt. He incurred heavy expenses caring for several invalid family members. In 1836, President Jackson appointed Taney as John Marshall's replacement on the Supreme Court. As chief justice, Taney wrote the decision for the Dred Scott vs. Sandford case, which stated that the Congress had no power to ban slavery from the territories. The Dred-Scott decision was later reinterpreted to mean, in essence, that freed slaves had no rights. Taney, who was raised in Maryland and inherited slaves, manumitted them and purchased others to enable them to work and buy their freedom. Though always in ill health, Taney continued to serve on the Supreme Court until 1864.

In 1835, the Rodgers family finally moved into their house on Lafayette Square. Two years later, Rodgers traveled to Europe seeking a cure for his ill health. Sadly, a few weeks after he returned to the United States, Rodgers was admitted to the naval hospital in Philadelphia where he died in 1838.

Bank of the United States — *the first story* —

Pennsylvania Avenue near 15th Street, NW — northwest corner

In 1791, while meeting in Philadelphia, Congress granted a twenty-year charter to the Bank of the United States. In 1800, the secretary of the treasury requested that a branch of the bank be established in Washington, because the bank served as the U.S. government's fiscal representative. The bank's first Washington location was near the northeast corner of 13th and F Streets, NW. However, the bank went out of existence in 1811 when its charter expired.

By 1816, proponents for the bank succeeded in its revival, and it was re-chartered for another twenty years as the Second Bank of the United States. This was the nation's largest private commercial bank and it wielded enormous financial power. Nicholas Biddle, who was a financier, editor, and diplomat, controlled the bank, which had twenty-five branches throughout the United States. In 1820, the bank's cashier, Richard Smith, purchased property for a new bank building in Washington. The site was across from the White House and the Treasury Department, facing on Pennsylvania Avenue between 15th Street and 15½ Street (Madison Place). A local architect, George Hadfield, was commissioned to design the neoclassical-style bank building and the cashier's house next door. Both were built of brick with stucco. In 1824, the bank moved to its new quarters near Lafayette Square.

State-chartered banks were growing in number and when Andrew Jackson became president in 1829. Jackson was obsessed with the idea of destroying the federally chartered bank and supporting the state banks. He ceased depositing federal funds in the Second Bank of the United States, dismissed his treasury secretary who disagreed with him, and vetoed the bill that would have re-chartered the bank in 1837. Jackson's actions "stopped the balance wheel which regulated the finances of the country . . . [and] in 1837 one of the most disastrous financial stringencies in American history occurred."[22]

Andrew Jackson, the 7th President, 1829-1837

In 1829, Andrew Jackson ushered in one of the most colorful eras in

American political history. He returned to Washington, however, amid an atmosphere of hatred and treachery. Jackson had wrongly blamed John Quincy Adams for slanders spoken against Jackson's recently deceased wife. He requested that Adams be out of the White House on the day of his inaugural. When he arrived in Washington, Jackson did not acknowledge Adams with either a personal call or a card. Adams was angry at having lost the election and perplexed at Jackson's lack of good manners. Even so, Adams was not yet ready to depart the city, so he leased the mansion that Commodore David D. Porter had built on Meridian Hill, above the White House.

Jackson was the first president elected as a Democrat, the first president from the West, and the first elected by the masses of common citizens. He was also the first president to be sworn into office at an outside ceremony on the Capitol's east portico. Tens of thousands of people poured into Washington to witness the pageantry of Jackson's inauguration. So many people swarmed on the east front Capitol lawn that Jackson had to enter the building by the west basement door. The mobs followed Jackson from the Capitol back to the White House, and once inside, the new president was nearly suffocated by the crowds. He escaped through a back door, leaving the mansion to be ruined by the riotous crowd which was enticed outside only when tubs of rum punch were put on the lawns surrounding the White House.

The following year, Jackson called for a celebration of Thomas Jefferson's birthday, because he felt that his new Democratic Party was directly descended from Jefferson's Democratic-Republican Party. At the birthday celebration, Vice President John Calhoun offered an offending speech, advocating secession for the Southern states. Jackson responded in a toast aimed to antagonize Calhoun, "Our Federal Union–it must be preserved!"[23] Calhoun continued to boldly defend Nullification (the action of a state attempting to prevent the execution of federal law within its territory). When South Carolina's legislature declared the high federal tariff on marketable goods was null and void in their state, Calhoun supported it. Congress reached a compromise on nullification, but the conflict between Jackson and Calhoun was never resolved. Calhoun resigned as vice president in 1832, just prior to the expiration of his term.

In the 1832 election, Jackson easily won the popular vote against his opponent, Henry Clay, who was a member of the newly formed Whig Party. During his second term, Jackson succeeded in dismantling the Second Bank of the United States in favor of an independent Treasury. This action eventually led the country into a severe economic depression, though not until Jackson was out of office. Jackson's last public reception was on George Washington's birthday in 1837. The citizens of New York sent a 1,400-pound cheese, which local citizens were invited to sample. The cheese party turned into another fiasco, much like Jackson's first inaugural reception. Historian George Bancroft observed the revelers in the White House to be: "apprentices, boys of all ages, men not civilized enough to walk about the room with their hats off -- starvelings, and fellows with dirty faces and dirty manners."[24]

Benjamin Ogle had much to say about Jackson: "A new era, far different from that of 'good feelings,' burst upon the country under the 'spoils system' of General Jackson. The 'hero' resembled the elder Adams in being influenced by his passions and by flattery. His political views were personal rather than the result of statesmanship and experience. The extent of his information was circumscribed. He saw things through the eyes of others, and was proud to take the responsibility in critical cases, as if based on his own judgement. He was, however, decided and unwavering, firm in friendship, and unforgiving in hatred. He required subservience from his friends. Through not Chesterfieldian in his manners, he was often dignified, affable, and kind."[25]

———————

During the first third of the 19th century, many dynamic leaders moved to the new Capital City. The first residents of the White House and their influential and powerful Lafayette Square neighbors set the pattern for the way the rest of Washington society lived, worked, and entertained. The revolutionary transformations the United States experienced during the first six presidential administrations in Washington, from Adams through Jackson, touched the lives of everyone in the country. The scientists and inventors who improved manufacturing and transportation brought their new ideas to Washington. Westward expansion was the promoted political policy of the day. The modern Industrial Age had begun. Andrew Jackson was living proof of these great changes when became the first president to leave Washington by railroad in 1837, when he was nearly seventy years old. The next thirty years would forever change the way the residents of Washington viewed the rest of the world and the way the world viewed Washington's power.

2

Holes in the Poles,

Rum Punches & Crushes

Neighbors to the Presidents :   Martin Van Buren - Andrew Johnson   (1837-1869)

By the 1840s, social life in Washington was becoming more sophisticated. The receptions and parties given by residents grew more and more competitive. The congressmen, cabinet officials, diplomats, and military officers, who came to Washington in the middle of the 19th century, had more money and self-confidence, allowing them to lease, buy, or build their own homes. Ambitious wives, anxious to demonstrate their skills as hostesses, could now travel to Washington by railroad, with their husbands. New luxury hotels were built to cater to temporary residents and those who preferred to avoid home-ownership.

Washington was distinctly Southern in manner and temperament until the inauguration of Abraham Lincoln in 1861. As early as the late 1840s, however, the new Northerners were making their presence known in society. They were military officers from the Mexican War, determined politicians such as the Radical Republicans, and savvy lobbyists. Although the presidents and their wives were still regarded as the social leaders of the Washington community, who set the style of entertaining in the middle of the 19th century, many powerful individuals with well-honed social skills were now sharing the pageantry of giving parties with a purpose.

Martin Van Buren, the 8th President, 1837-1841

When Martin Van Buren won the 1836 presidential election, he had already spent nearly half his life in Washington. He had worked hard to attain his goal of the presidency. Sixteen years after he first entered national politics, President Jackson offered Van Buren the office of secretary of state. This was the kingpin position in the cabinet because of Jackson's policy "to the victor go the spoils." The secretary of state was the chief dispenser of political patronage, making Van Buren the most sought after person in Washington. Van Buren used the "spoils system" to assist in dismissing thousands of faithful public servants, replacing them with Jacksonian democrats to whom favors were owed. In 1832, Jackson rewarded Van Buren with the vice presidency, which became Van Buren's stepping-stone to the presidency.

President Van Buren was a widower. He brought his four sons to live with him in the White House. These five bachelors entertained thirty or more guests for dinner nearly every night and they offered popular receptions and weekly parties. Benjamin Tayloe wrote of Van Buren, "he was fond of show . . . his entertainments . . . were very handsome."[1] In 1838, Dolley Madison, who had just returned to live on Lafayette Square, introduced her well-connected cousin, Angelica Singleton, into Washington society. Mrs. Madison enjoyed playing the matchmaker and encouraged the relationship between Van Buren's oldest son, Abraham, and Angelica. The following November, Angelica and Abraham were married. Angelica eagerly accepted the role of first lady, with Dolley Madison as her mentor. (Dolley also matched in marriage her grandniece, Adelle Cutts, to the Honorable Stephen A. Douglas.)

In 1839, Angelica and Abraham spent the summer in Europe, where Angelica acquired a few new ideas for receiving guests at White House receptions. She had a raised platform built in the East Room of the White House, where she would sit like a princess, wearing a long white gown and fresh flowers in her hair, often surrounded by her "ladies-in-waiting." This "living tableau" drew harsh criticism from the press and Van Buren's political opponents, who began to complain of his lavish, "Kingly ways."

Overburdened with work, Van Buren was the first president to stay in Washington year-round. He took refuge from the summer heat in a home called Woodley, located on a hill high above Georgetown. Every day he commuted to the White House. His first year in office was consumed with trying to resolve the financial panic of 1837, the worst the country had ever experienced. The panic resulted from his predecessor's poor fiscal policy, which had abolished the Bank of the United States without providing proper substitutes or controls for reinvesting government funds. The government money was divided among small "pet" state banks, which doled it out into unsecured loans, and lost it. When banks and businesses failed, Van Buren was blamed. Van Buren worked vigorously to establish an independent federal Treasury system, which was later opposed by President Tyler.

Van Buren's sense of humor and impartiality afforded him many friends. His few actual enemies criticized him more for his lavish lifestyle than rather his politics. He preferred action to talk. Although Van Buren was variously described as evasive and deceptive, clever and masterful, "the fox," "the little magician," a manipulator, and a strategist, there was never a malicious tone to the criticisms and never a doubt that he was personally well liked.

Dolley Madison House — *the continuing story—*

1520 H Street, NW

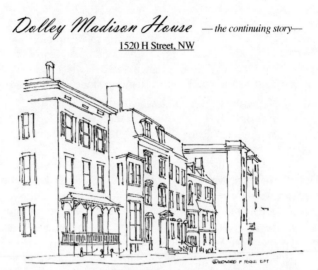

Much to the delight of Washington society, Dolley Madison moved back to Lafayette Square in 1837. She inherited the little house across from St. John's Church, which had once belonged to her now-deceased sister, Mrs. Cutts. After the death of her husband, Dolley yearned to return to the social life of Washington. She was seventy years old, but her youthful outlook made her the most popular lady on Lafayette Square and visitors flocked to her home. Every year on New Year's Day the White House reception would be held at noon, and afterwards guests invariably strolled across the Square to pay a visit to Mrs. Madison.

Financial difficulties plagued Dolley Madison, through no fault of her own. Her distress could be directly attributed to her son by her first marriage, Todd Payne, who involved his mother in his serious mishandling of money. Much of her inherited wealth had gone to pay his gambling debts. Though she and Todd were genuinely fond of each other, his debts became her tribulations. There was also the formidable financial burden involved with maintaining Montpellier, James Madison's Virginia estate. In 1837, President Jackson pressured Congress to approve an appropriation of $30,000 for the purchase of Madison's diaries recording the debates and events surrounding the framing of the Federal Constitution. Dolley Madison was then able to put a little of the money into the repair and refurbishing of her Lafayette Square house, though most of that money went to pay off Todd's debts and little was left over for Montpellier. Dolley's financial situation became so desperate that she had to return to Montpellier in 1840, where she was forced to sell parcels of the Virginia estate. Eventually the entire estate would have to be sold.

During Dolley's absence from Washington, between 1840 and 1844, she leased her Lafayette Square house. The first tenant was Senator William C. Preston of South Carolina, grandnephew of Patrick Henry. Years before, when James Madison was secretary of state, Preston had been invited to a party the Madisons hosted. He was a shy, awkward young man, and Dolley, observing his embarrassment in an unfamiliar social situation, put him at ease. She was reported to have said to him, "Are you William Campbell Preston, the son of my friend and kinswoman Sally Campbell? Sit down my son, for you are my son, and I am the first person who ever saw you in this world."[2]

Twenty years later, Preston had earned a reputation in the Senate as being one of the finest orators of the South, along with Henry Clay. When Clay delivered his nostalgic farewell address in 1842, he concluded by telling his colleagues: "And when you shall retire to the bosom of your constituents, may you meet with that most cheering and gratifying of all human rewards, a cordial 'Well done, good and faithful servant.' And now . . . I bid you a long, a last, and friendly farewell."[3] A solemn silence fell over the chamber as Clay's successor, John J. Crittenden, was sworn into office. Emotions overwhelmed Clay's senatorial peers; only Preston had the fortitude to respond. He declared, "What has just taken place is an epoch in legislative history."[4]

John Jordan Crittenden was the next tenant of Dolley Madison's house. He lived there from 1841 until 1843. President William H. Harrison appointed Crittenden as attorney general, but he resigned when Tyler became president. He then accepted the appointment to fill Henry Clay's vacated Senate seat. Crittenden was considered the Senate's ablest debater, as well as Kentucky's best-loved son, after Clay. In 1850, President Fillmore appointed Crittenden to serve again as attorney general. Crittenden was praised for his "intellectual vigor, integrity of character, and legal ability."[5] In 1854, he was reelected to Congress, and served for another nine years, until his death in 1863.

In 1844, Dolley returned to live on Lafayette Square. Although she was living in near poverty, with the help of her friends, she stayed on until her death in 1849. Both Mrs. Tyler and Mrs. Polk deferred to Dolley's judgment in matters concerning their roles as first ladies. Daniel Webster, Dolley's neighbor across the Square, generously and tactfully assisted her financially, without damaging her self-esteem. W. W. Corcoran came to her aid with loans, and other friends helped in unobtrusive ways. Both Daniel Webster and President Van Buren worked with Congress in 1848, for an appropriation of $25,000 to purchase of James Madison's unpublished papers. Just before the papers were to be delivered, Dolley's house caught fire. Dolley allowed herself to be rescued only after her husband's papers were safely removed from the third floor of the burning house.

On the Fourth of July 1848, Dolley Madison made one of her last public appearances at the ceremony for the laying of the cornerstone of the Washington Monument. She died a year later on July 12, 1849. The pallbearers at her funeral were Washington's most prominent members of society. An immense crowd gathered spontaneously on Lafayette Square in front of St. John's Church to follow the funeral procession to Congressional Cemetery, where Dolley's body was temporarily interred.

The 19th century writer Mary Clemmer Ames wrote about Mrs. Madison: "She was the only woman of absolute social genius, who ever presided in [the White House] . . . she instinctively made each individual, who entered her presence, feel that he or she was an object of especial interest."[6] Her constant companions were noble women, men of letters, and military heroes. "No eminent man retired from service of the state ever had more public recognition and honor bestowed upon him by the Government he had served than did this popular and ever-beloved woman."[7]

Captain Charles Wilkes purchased the Dolley Madison House in 1850. Wilkes was a man of imagination, action, and foresight. He completely modernized and dramatically changed the look of the house. Wilkes moved the house's front entrance from Lafayette Square to H Street. He then placed a long, wrought iron porch across the first-floor west side. Opening onto the new porch were floor-to-ceiling windows, which replaced the smaller, federal-style ones and the old front door. The interior floor plan was altered, the roof was raised, a bay added to the south, and a building was added to the rear.

Captain Wilkes (later Admiral) led the first naval expedition to Antarctica. His four-year voyage began in 1838 and it covered 87,000 miles while he circumnavigated the globe. With six ships, Wilkes explored the South Sea Islands, mapped the Oregon coast, documented Indian languages, measured volcanic action in the Hawaiian Islands, and returned with 4,000 zoological specimens (including 2,000 new ones), 50,000 plants, and 2,500 artifacts. Congress funded the voyage at the urging of James Cleves Symmes, Jr. from Ohio, who was convinced that the world was hollow with an entrance at the South Pole. The "holes in the poles" theory was embraced by New England whalers, who were interested in looking for new whaling grounds. Symmes and the whalers lobbied Congress to fund an exploratory expedition.

Two years into the voyage, Wilkes was not ready to quit though many of his sailors were. Although their two-year enlistment was up, those who tried to leave when the ships were in Hawaii were flogged until they reenlisted. This led to a court-marshal for Wilkes upon his return and a lukewarm reception for his incredible feats. His mountain of artifacts took fifteen years to process, resulting in twenty-three volumes of scientific data. These items arrived in Washington about the same time as a half-million dollar bequest from the eccentric British scientist, James Smithson, arrived. The bequest was to be used for a scientific research institution to be founded in Washington: "an establishment for the increase and diffusion of knowledge among men."[8] The Wilkes collection became part of the new Smithsonian Institution.

During the Civil War, Charles Wilkes was in command of the warship *San Jacinto* when it intercepted the British steamer *Trent*. Two Confederate commissioners, John Slidell and James J. Mason, were removed by Admiral Wilkes from the *Trent*. Their associate, George Eustis, was also taken. These men had been en route to England to enlist British aid for the Confederacy. Slidell was Wilkes' Lafayette Square neighbor. Mason was a former senator from Virginia who's home was located on Analostan Island (Roosevelt Island) in the Potomac River. Eustis was the son-in-law of Wilkes' neighbor, W. W. Corcoran. Wilkes immediately became a hero for this action on the high seas and received a gold medal from the House of Representatives. The British, however, protested vehemently. Lincoln, wishing to avoid another war involving Great Britain, asked Secretary of State William Seward to draft a proper apology. The Confederate commissioners were then released and allowed to go back to Europe. Wilkes was unofficially reprimanded and his act of heroism quietly denounced.

When Wilkes returned to his command, he leased his Lafayette Square home to the government as a residence for the commanding general of the City of Washington. General George B. McClellan was the first occupant, when he served as the city's commanding general. McClellan had moved into the house in August 1861, following the first Battle of Bull Run. A few months later, McClellan moved to a home a block away, on the corner of 15th and H Streets, NW, which had once belonged to Samuel Harrison Smith, the former editor of the *National Intelligencer*. After the Civil War, Wilkes and his family returned to the Lafayette Square house and stayed there until Wilkes' death in 1877.

Slidell House — the first story —
1607 H Street, NW

Construction of the Slidell House is believed to have been started in 1845 by Thomas Corcoran, the brother of W. W. Corcoran (who later purchased and remodeled the house next door). Thomas Corcoran served as assistant postmaster general until President Van Buren appointed Corcoran's Lafayette Square neighbor, Dr. James Gunnell, to that position. Gunnell's appointment was offered on the condition that his influential brother-in-law, B. F. Mackall of Georgetown, would serve as the assistant postmaster general. Thomas Corcoran died before his home could be completed, so W. W. Corcoran finished it.

The first resident of the house was Thomas Ritchie who purchased it from Corcoran in 1846. President Polk brought Ritchie to Washington to be the editor of the *Union,* a pro-administration newspaper. He was called "Father Ritchie" because he had been in the newspaper business for nearly fifty years (and also because he had nine children). Ritchie's first newspaper job was with the *Richmond Enquirer* in 1804. He continued to work with the *Enquirer* for forty-one years, wielding great power in Virginia political circles.

Thomas Ritchie was sixty-seven years old when he arrived in Washington. He had a remarkable capacity for work, taking no time to relax, except to read his favorite books of Virgil or his Bible. Ritchie was described as "a tall, lean, quick moving man, with brilliant eyes and striking profile . . . a toastmaster at dinners, leader of the dances, welcomer of distinguished guests."[9] In 1854 when Ritchie died, he was seventy-six years old. His funeral was held at St. John's Church on Lafayette Square. Corcoran was one of the pallbearers. Ritchie's house, later known as the Slidell House, was mentioned in his will: "There is no position in Washington that is more desirable for its beauty and its neighborhood. It has risen much in its value, since I purchased it from my friend Corcoran several years ago."[10] The Ritchie family leased the house to several famous residents until 1869, when it was sold back to W. W. Corcoran.

John Slidell was the first tenant to lease the home after Ritchie's death in 1854. For the next seventy years, Slidell's name would be associated with the house. Slidell was from New York, but following a scandalous business failure, he migrated to New Orleans and practiced law. He tried, unsuccessfully, to be elected to Congress from Louisiana. In 1853, however, he was appointed to fill the Senate seat of Pierre Soule, after Soule resigned. Slidell was reelected when Soule's term expired and he lived in the Lafayette Square house until 1861.

Slidell had been a moderate Union man until Abraham Lincoln became president. When the Civil War began, Slidell promptly resigned from the Senate and was appointed minister to France by the Confederacy. En route to Europe, Slidell's ship was intercepted by Admiral Wilkes. Slidell was removed from the ship, but later set free. He returned to France and was successful in convincing France to build two ironclad ships and four corvettes for the Confederate Navy. However, the U.S. legation to France discovered Slidell's clandestine plan and the U.S. minister protested to the French government. The French ships were sold to other countries. Slidell never returned to the United States and never asked for pardon, although he once made an appeal to President Johnson to be allowed to visit New Orleans. Slidell's request was never answered. He died as "a man without a country" in Great Britain in 1871.

Gideon Wells took up residence in the Slidell House during the Civil War. As a young man, Wells served as editor of the *Hartford Times* in Connecticut. While working for the newspaper, he became involved in state politics. Wells tried, unsuccessfully, to be elected to Congress. He traveled frequently to Washington, however, and with the help of his influential friends in 1846, he became the chief of the Bureau of Provisions and Clothing for the navy. Wells had been a member of the Democratic Party, but he left the party over the issue of slavery and helped organize the Republican Party. For his efforts, Lincoln appointed Wells secretary of the navy, a position he held until 1869.

The Civil War began a few weeks after Wells' appointment and he had to create a navy from almost nothing. He accurately predicted the war would be a long one. Wells was an early promoter of the use of ironclad ships, for which he was ridiculed until the May 1862 battle between the Union ironclad, *Monitor,* and the Confederate ironclad, *Virginia*, which was built (and renamed) from the raised hull of the burned Union ship *Merrimack*. The battle was a draw but it proved the superiority of the steam-powered, propeller-driven armored warships over conventional wooden ships. The ironclads forever changed naval warfare.

After the war, Wells was adamant in his policy of moderation during reconstruction and he strongly defended the Southerners against the Radical Republicans. He changed his political party affiliation several times saying it was not he, but the parties that changed. Wells was remembered for possessing the admirable traits of honesty, faithfulness, and a sense of duty.

Corcoran House — *the continuing story* —

1611 H Street, NW

The neighboring house to the west of the Slidell House became known as the Corcoran House after W. W. Corcoran purchased it in 1849. Before Corcoran owned it, Aaron Vail occupied the house from 1836 until 1840, while he served as chief clerk of the State Department. Vail also served as the acting head of the department during an absence of the secretary of state. Five years earlier, in 1831, Vail had been sent to England as Martin Van Buren's legation secretary. When Van Buren was recalled from England because the Senate did not approve his appointment, Vail stayed in London as acting minister and chargé d'affaires. Vail left Washington in 1840 to become minister to Spain.

Daniel Webster was the next owner of the house. Webster was raised on a farm in New Hampshire. As a teenager, he was so awkward and shy that he decided to leave school and was tutored at home by Reverend Samuel Wood. He proved to be a good student and was accepted to Dartmouth College where he developed a sense of determination and self-confidence. He also gained a reputation as a compelling speaker. After graduating near the top of his class, Webster studied and practiced law in Massachusetts, although his real interest was in politics. An eloquent anti-war speech that he presented against the War of 1812 precipitated his first election to Congress. After serving two terms he withdrew from Congress, but he often returned to Washington to argue cases before the Supreme Court. In 1824, Massachusetts' voters reelected Webster to the House of Representatives. In 1826 he was elected to the Senate.

A congressional debate, known as the "battle of the giants," occurred in 1830 over the issue of states' rights. The States' Rights men of South Carolina, led by John Calhoun, gathered information insinuating that it had been the intention of Mr. Webster to have New England secede from the Union during the War of 1812. The brutal, merciless attack became very personal against both Webster and the state of Massachusetts. General Robert Y. Hayne, senator from South Carolina, led the assault on Webster. He was a powerful speaker and relentlessly challenged the Constitution, hoping to establish the rights of Southern states to rule their own destiny. Webster was not an extemporaneous speaker, but he had spent the summer studying the great constitutional question of states' rights. Though he was in the midst of preparing a case to be brought before the Supreme Court, he quickly and skillfully composed his masterful retort. He ended his rebuttal against Hayne with heartfelt emotion, proclaiming: "Liberty and union– now and forever–one and inseparable!"[11]

There was little support for Webster's nomination by the Whig Party for the presidency in 1836. He considered leaving politics in order to pay his debts because "in financial matters, Webster did not possess qualities that gave him success as a statesman."[12] His friends in Massachusetts, however, reelected him to Congress. Webster campaigned for President Harrison in 1840, who, in turn, rewarded him with the appointment of secretary of state. When Webster returned to Washington, his friends bought him the Lafayette Square house that was nicknamed "the Gift House" and later, known as the Corcoran House.

During his residency, the house was always filled with guests and was the scene of extravagant dinners. He was said to have "made money with ease and spent it without reflection,"[13] and consequently, was constantly in debt to his wealthy friends. Webster, however, never forgot his humble beginnings. He was always early to bed and early to rise and, he kept a cow and chickens in the backyard.

Webster regarded his work as secretary of state as the greatest of his life. When Harrison died after only one month in office and Tyler became president, all of the Harrison's cabinet members resigned, except Webster. Though there was strong opposition to his remaining in office, Webster felt he had a duty to the public to carry to completion the negotiations he had begun with Great Britain. In 1842, the Webster-Ashburton Treaty finally settled the exasperating controversy over the adjustment of the northeastern Maine-New Brunswick boundary and the control of fisheries on the North Atlantic coast. Webster resigned from his cabinet position in 1843 and returned to his law practice. In 1844, he was again elected to Congress. Webster was outspokenly opposed to the War with Mexico in which his son, Major Edward Webster, would later lose his life. In 1850, President Fillmore appointed him, again, to serve as secretary of state. Two years later, oppressive debts and political disappointments lead to his final illness, cirrhosis of the liver. Webster died in October of 1852.

Webster moved from the house in 1844. He leased it to British Minister Sir Richard Parkenham, who had recently served in the British legation in Mexico. While serving as foreign minister in Washington, Parkenham signed the treaty that ended the British-American dispute over the Oregon-Canadian border in 1846. Parkenham also represented the controversial opinion adhered to in Great Britain that Texas should be an independent, nonslave-holding state. The British preferred not to rely on Southern slave states for their cotton trade.

In 1849, William Wilson Corcoran, Washington's greatest 19th century philanthropist, bought the Lafayette Square house from Daniel Webster. The house stayed in Corcoran's family until it was razed in the 20th century. Corcoran's wife was Louise Morris, the daughter of Commodore Morris. After five years of marriage, she died of tuberculosis at the age of twenty-one. Corcoran, who was twenty years her senior, never remarried. They had three children, though only one daughter, Louise, survived infancy. In the 1830s, Corcoran had started a brokerage firm in Washington, located in the Rhodes Tavern building. The brokerage firm evolved into a private bank that prospered and grew with the financial backing of Corcoran's partner, George Washington Riggs. After the dissolution of the Bank of the United States, deposits from the bank's Washington branch office were transferred to Corcoran's bank.

The Corcoran and Riggs Bank handled the sale of the government war bonds during the Mexican War. The war bond sale was intended to raise much needed money for the war effort. Purchasing war bonds was unpopular in the United States because Americans generally did not support the Mexican War. Corcoran decided to try and sell the U.S. government war bonds in England. He convinced London's largest banking concerns to purchase $5 million worth of bonds, which was the first recorded sale of American securities in Europe. Corcoran's sale of the war bonds helped establish U.S. credit abroad. After he returned from his successful trip to Europe, Corcoran collected a significant commission from the war bond sale.

Corcoran was a colorful, remarkably successful, powerful man and an optimist who believed in "Manifest Destiny." He was born in Georgetown in 1798. His first business venture was with his brothers in Georgetown. Unfortunately, it failed in the economic depression of 1823. After earning commissions from war bond sales, Corcoran felt his first responsibility was to locate his creditors (or their heirs) from his failed business of twenty-five years earlier and pay them back what he owed, with interest. It was a generous, unselfish, honorable gesture. Next, he purchased the house on Lafayette Square and proceeded to significantly enlarge and modernize it, utilizing the talents of James Renwick, the architect of the Smithsonian Institution's Castle. Renwick added a story to the house, two new wings east and west, and outbuildings behind. Andrew Jackson Downing, the famous landscape architect, was hired to design the beautiful gardens and grounds.

At the age of fifty-six, in 1854, Corcoran retired from banking and devoted his time to his art collection, real estate investments, philanthropic efforts, and friends. All the great leaders of the North and South came together in his home and it was called "the center of the most fashionable and distinguished society of the capital and his entertainments were of the most elegant and costly character."[14] Corcoran's home was also considered the "chief rendezvous for distinguished men . . . [and Corcoran] used to give weekly stag dinners."[15] Benjamin Tayloe wrote that "Mr. Corcoran . . . greatly improved the house and grounds, making it altogether the most splendid town establishment in the country . . . his magnificent entertainments threw all others in the shade. In General Pierce's time, Mr. Corcoran wielded a great influence in Washington. His splendid dinners are well remembered; the most grand, with a file of Senators on each side of the table, or intermixed with the foreign and Cabinet ministers; but the most beautiful when he occasionally assembled pretty women, for Mr. Corcoran had an eye to beauty. His taste in all respects is excellent."[16]

The most acclaimed sculptural masterpiece of the day was Hiram Powers' statue of the *Greek Slave*. Corcoran purchased the sculpture and had it installed in the bay of the new west wing of his home. Over the years Corcoran's expanded art collection outgrew the space in his house. In 1874, Corcoran transferred his collection from his home to a gallery building that was specially designed by James Renwick to display the sculpture, paintings, and other pieces of art. The new gallery was built next door to the Blair House and named the Corcoran Gallery of Art (the Renwick Gallery).

The Civil War forced Corcoran to leave the country because he had friends in both the North and the South. Corcoran felt he could not swear allegiance to the Union when his only daughter was married to George Eustis, secretary to the Confederate legation in France. Corcoran's home was nearly confiscated by the U.S. government during the early months of the war, when all of the city's large homes, schools, and churches were being seized and adapted for use as hospital space and military offices. In his diary, Gideon Wells noted, "private dwellings are taken to be thus used, among others my next door neighbor Corcoran's fine house and grounds. There is malice in this . . . it was vandalism."[17] According to an account given by Benjamin Tayloe, "By some magic, the French Minister, Mons. Mercier, telegraphed from New York that the house was his. Afterwards, on his going to the State Department, Governor Seward asked the Minister 'if the French flag was broad enough to cover Mr. Corcoran's house?' 'If it is not,' Mons. Mercier replied, 'we will make it so.'"[18]

Numerous, magnificent social events were given by the French minister, the Marquis de Montholon, while he resided at the Corcoran House during the Civil War years. Near the end of the war, a fabulous ball was held for General Grant by order of Louis Napoleon. This was the crowning entertainment of the season. A French warship was commanded to come from its dock in Annapolis to Washington so that its officers, in full dress uniform, might honor General Grant. The French minister wore the elegant, embroidered, Parisian court-dress. The British minister, also in formal attire, led the dances. Two new brides were the belles of the ball: Salmon Chase's strikingly beautiful, young daughter, Kate Chase Sprague; and Dolly Madison's charming, older grandniece, Adelle Cutts Douglas Williams (who had been widowed for some time, after the death of her first husband, Stephen A. Douglas).

Ashburton House — the first story —
1525 H Street, NW

@EONARD F FOGLE EFF

In 1836, Matthew St. Clair Clark built a handsome, square, double-sized mansion next to St. John's Church facing Lafayette Square. The mansion was the largest house in the city at the time. "Its lofty ceilings, spacious rooms, magnificent mahogany doors, and elegant woodwork speak eloquently of the solid thrift of a long past generation which built for comfort and for posterity."[19] St. Clair Clark was the clerk of the House of Representatives. Unfortunately, soon after he began building his house, he lost $200,000 in speculation and never moved into his grand new home. Instead, Joseph Gales, the editor of the *National Intelligencer*, leased the house. He and his wife gave weekly entertainments that became so popular they were called "crushes." For several social seasons Mrs. Gales' parties were said to be the models of elegance.

The British legation moved into the mansion in 1842 when the Gales moved out. Alexander Baring, Lord Ashburton, was the British minister at the time, for whom the house was named. Baring had visited Philadelphia in 1798 as a young man representing his father's London banking house. There he met and married the daughter of Senator William Bingham of Pennsylvania. Her family fortune allowed Baring to become a partner in the House of Baring Brothers. In 1835, Baring was made a baron, with the title of Lord Ashburton. In 1839, Daniel Webster met Lord Ashburton in London. This meeting was the beginning of a close and sincere friendship between the two men.

In 1841, Lord Ashburton was sent to Washington on a special mission concerning the northeastern boundary dispute between Canada and the U.S. Prior to his departure, Ashburton wrote to Webster to inquire about leasing a house. Webster secured the St. Clair Clark house for ten months, at a cost of $14,000. As a way of smoothing over the difficulties of the boundary dispute arbitration, the preliminary negotiations were carried out amidst fabulous entertainments. Because Webster and Ashburton vied to outshine one another in a friendly social competition, the social season was said to be unparalleled in all the early years of Washington's history. Grand receptions, dinners, parties, and balls followed one after the other. Lord Ashburton's French chef offered "the most perfect concoctions of culinary art. He had the rarest of wines and the most seductive French desserts."[20] Webster offered American delicacies: among them, Maine salmon, Massachusetts mackerel, New Jersey oysters, Maryland crabs, Virginia terrapin, and Delaware canvasback ducks. Webster's punch was also said to have played an important role in the negotiations. The ingredients included: "Medford rum, brandy, champagne, arrack, maraschino, strong green tea, lemon juice, and sugar,"[21] but the exact recipe is not known.

Webster and Ashburton reached an amicable agreement in August 1842 with the signing of the Webster-Ashburton treaty. By this treaty, the United States received most of the boundary territory in dispute along with navigation rights on the St. John River. The United States was also granted territory where rich iron deposits were later discovered. Webster, however, was left nearly bankrupt, in part, because he spent his own financial resources for the lavish entertaining during the negotiations.

After Lord Ashburton's departure, the house was leased temporarily by President Tyler's attorney general, John Nelson, and his wife who was the daughter of the Marine commandant. Society flocked to their dinners and dances, but the Nelsons' stay was brief. The British legation returned to the home. In 1844, British Minister Sir Henry Bulwer came to Washington with his young, handsome nephew, Robert Edward Bulwer Lytton, first Earl of Lytton. The Earl was described as having "very blue eyes and curling hair. . . . He at once became highly popular with the society girls and equally unpopular with their brothers because of his showy and somewhat eccentric style of dress."[22] He was charming and witty. Years later he became a well-known poet, using the nom de plume of Owen Meredith. He wrote that he found Washington to be an odd place, "a place where women have everything their own way and the cleverest man is only known as the husband of the charming Mrs. So and So."[23]

The Ashburton House was sold in 1853 to Miss Sarah Coleman and her sister and brother-in-law, Colonel and Mrs. William Grigsby Freeman (who later became the full owners). The Freemans, and their daughters who inherited the house, lived and entertained there for nearly a century. For many years, the Ashburton House was also known as the Freeman House.

William Henry Harrison, the 9th President, 1841

William Henry Harrison gained fame in the early 19th century as an Indian fighter. In 1811, Harrison led the militia near Tippecanoe Creek against the confederacy of Indians, led by Tecumseh. The battle was inconclusive, but the nickname of "Tippecanoe" stayed with Harrison the rest of his life. After the battle at Tippecanoe, Tecumseh and his Indian confederacy formed an alliance with the British. During the War of 1812, Tecumseh was killed when he and Harrison met in battle for a second time at the Thames River in Ontario.

Following his successful military career, Harrison became involved in politics. He was elected to the House of Representatives and later, to the Senate. He also served briefly as President Jackson's minister to Colombia before returning to his Ohio farm. Harrison drew national attention to himself in 1836, when he decided to campaign for the presidency. He won enough support from the Whig Party that, in 1840, he was nominated as their candidate. Harrison campaigned as a war hero from the West and the champion of the common man. He claimed he was raised in a log cabin and preferred drinking hard cider rather than wine. Slogans, songs, stump speeches, and parades overpowered any political issues. Martin Van Buren, who was Harrison's opponent in the 1840 election, was haughtily criticized as the rich man's candidate. William Henry Harrison, the candidate for the common man, won easily.

On inauguration day, Harrison, who was sixty-eight years old, rode through Washington on horseback. Standing outside in a cold, driving rain he delivered his inaugural speech of 8,000 words that lasted one hour and forty-five minutes. Harrison was fond of reading the classics and often quoted from them in his speeches. He did so during his long inaugural speech, which included this reference: "It was the remark of a Roman consul, in the early part of that celebrated republic, that a most striking contrast was observable in the conduct of candidates for offices of power and trust, before and after obtaining them, -- they seldom carrying out, in the latter case, the pledges and promises made in the former."[24] Exactly a month later Harrison died of pneumonia.

Because Harrison was the first president to die in office, the citizens of Washington were inexperienced in preparing for a president's funeral. The White House and the houses on Lafayette Square were heavily draped in black bunting. At sunrise on April 9, 1841, the artillery fired a salute from Lafayette Square. Thousands of people attended the funeral, many of whom came from out of town. A newspaper account of the day reported that "The coffin rested on a temporary catafalque in the centre of the East Room. It was covered with black velvet, trimmed with gold lace and over it was thrown a velvet pall with a deep golden fringe. On this lay the sword of Justice and the sword of State, surmounted by the scroll of the Constitution, bound together by a funeral wreath of yew and cypress. . . . After the services the coffin was carried to a large funeral car drawn by six white horses, each having at its head a black groom dressed in white, with white turban and sash. Outside of the grooms walked the pall-bearers dressed in black, with black scarves."[25]

Services were held at St. John's Church on Lafayette Square, and the funeral procession of officials, dignitaries, military men, and citizens followed from the White House to Congressional Cemetery, where the president's body was temporarily entombed. The procession was two miles in length. Meanwhile, Vice President Tyler, who had been at home in Virginia when Harrison died, reached Washington just in time for the funeral. He took the oath of office and then gave an inaugural address proclaiming that he was "not Acting President, but President!"

John Tyler, the 10th President, 1841-1845

Benjamin Tayloe gave a cutting description of President Tyler: "By virtue of his office, but for no other virtue or qualification, Vice President Tyler succeeded to the Presidency. . . . False once to the Democracy, he was also false to the Whigs. He was intoxicated by vanity, success, and power. In needy circumstances, with a large family, and poor prospect before him, Tyler sought office, if only for its emoluments. He was not sordid or dishonest in pecuniary affairs, but a man of generous impulses. With great confidence in himself, and great loquacity, he wanted refinement."[26]

The Whig Party that elected Tyler held no influence over him. When Tyler adopted his own policies, which opposed everything the Whigs supported, they excommunicated him. Articles of impeachment were even drawn up against him, but the members of the House of Representatives were not inclined to vote for them. The number of Tyler's supporters dwindled as he replaced all the members of his predecessor's cabinet, except for the secretary of state, Daniel Webster, who stubbornly remained to negotiate the Webster-Ashburton Treaty.

Social life in the White House was not dull, even though Tyler's wife, Letitia, could not entertain because she was physically handicapped by the time she arrived at the White House. Letitia, who kept quietly to herself, was described as still beautiful, though she was in her declining years. In 1842 she died. Seven of her eight children survived her. Tyler's oldest son's wife, Priscilla Cooper Tyler, served as first lady until mid-year 1844. She was pretty, intelligent, witty, and tactful and, as the daughter of a popular actor, she had also performed on stage. Poised and respectful, she charmed the president's guests. Dolley Madison was also on hand to advise Priscilla.

During the winter social season of 1842-43, a minor scandal ensued when sixty-four-year-old President Tyler became infatuated with a young debutante named Julia Gardiner. Julia's father, David Gardiner, was a wealthy, former senator from New York. Young, beautiful, and rich, Julia became the darling of Washington society. Within a year, President Tyler proposed marriage to Julia, but she refused him. However, a tragic event caused Julia to reconsider and accept the president's offer of marriage.

On the last day of February 1844, Julia, her sister, and father, were invited to attend an affair on the *Princeton*, which was the first screw-propeller driven, steam-powered warship, docked in Alexandria. The event had so captured the imagination of society that, the evening before the ship sailed, W. W. Corcoran had held a party in honor of those who were invited to sail on the *Princeton*. The president, his cabinet, congressional leaders, former President John Quincy Adams, and Julia Gardiner were among the many important guests who attended Corcoran's party and then boarded the *Princeton* the next day.

Captain Robert F. Stockton had planned a demonstration onboard the ship, of the newest, most formidable naval weapon, which was a cannon called "The Peacemaker." It carried a cannon ball weighing 225 pounds. The ship left Alexandria, while several hundred guests on board enjoyed the plentiful food and music. The *Princeton* fired "The Peacemaker" cannon in an impressive display when the ship passed Fort Washington. As the *Princeton* returned up the river, Captain Stockton consented to fire another shot. A number of people gathered on deck to watch. Tragically, the gun burst upon firing. Julia's father, David Gardiner, was killed, along with Secretary of State Abel P. Upshur, Secretary of the Navy Thomas Gilmer, Commander Beverly Kennon, Maryland Congressman Mason (the former foreign minister to the Hague), and two others. In addition, seventeen seamen were injured. The bodies of those killed were placed in coffins and brought to the East Room of the White House.

President Tyler had first proposed marriage to Julia Gardiner on George Washington's birthday, just a week before the *Princeton* tragedy. Following the death of Julia's father, Tyler again proposed that Julia should marry him, and she accepted. Both families, at first, were against the marriage. She was twenty-four years old; he was thirty years her senior. Nonetheless, the president and Julia were married the following June in New York. Because Julia was so young when she became first lady, most people forgave her childish ideas of receiving the White House guests, while sitting on a raised platform surrounded by twelve ladies-in-waiting (just as one of her predecessors, Angelica Singleton Van Buren, had done). Julia Tyler gave birth to seven children, making Tyler's total number of offspring fifteen, which was more than any other president had.

During Tyler's last year as president, three important events occurred. First, on May 24, 1844, Samuel F. B. Morse sent and received (between Washington and Baltimore) his first telegraph message: "What hath God wrought?"[27] Next, Congress approved the annexation treaty of Texas by a simple majority. In order to do this, Congress passed a joint resolution, at Tyler's suggestion, which ignored the constitutional provision requiring two-thirds vote by the Senate for the approval of treaties. Third, Tyler appointed Levi Woodbury to the Supreme Court. This was Tyler's third Supreme Court justice appointment.

Decatur House — the continuing story—

748 Jackson Place, NW

John Gadsby intruded on Washington society when he purchased Decatur House in 1836. Gadsby was not a war hero, a diplomat, or a politician. He was a wealthy, well-known, but not universally well-liked, hotelier. After the Revolutionary War, Gadsby had come from London to Alexandria, Virginia, where he became the proprietor of the City Tavern (Gadsby's Tavern). This was one of the best known hotels of the time. Possessing an excellent business sense, Gadsby established a stagecoach line to Philadelphia with the terminus at his hotel, thereby being assured of a steady stream of travelers.

Gadsby decided to move his business from Alexandria to Washington after the new federal city was established, because a city's social life was centered on the hotels with taverns. With John Eaton's encouragement, Gadsby purchased the Franklin House on Pennsylvania Avenue in the 1820s from Eaton's father-in-law. He entertained the Marquis de Lafayette at the Franklin House in 1824. Three years later, Gadsby constructed the National Hotel, near to the Capitol, at

6th Street and Pennsylvania Avenue, NW. When Gadsby purchased Decatur House, he was one of the wealthiest men in Washington. As a premier hotelier, he had perfected the art of entertaining and his personal parties were peerless.

Gadsby's hospitality at the National Hotel was widely praised. One patron declared, "who can forget his urbane manner, his careful attention to his guests, his well-ordered house, his fine old wines?"[28] However, some members of society were critical of his parties at Decatur House. The French minister, Chevalier de Bacourt, wrote, "He is an old wretch who has made a fortune in the slave trade, which does not prevent Washington society from rushing to his house."[29] Another equally unimpressed diplomat wrote of Gadsby's Decatur House parties, *"Je sais que c'est un cochon, mais j'y vais quand même."* [30] ("I know it is a pigsty, but I go there anyway.") After Gadsby died in 1844, his wife leased Decatur House to a number of tenants.

George Mifflin Dallas, President Polk's vice president, was the first person to lease Decatur House from Gadsby's widow. Dallas was from Philadelphia where he became involved in state politics and he served as Philadelphia's mayor. In the 1830s, he was appointed to fill a vacancy in the U.S. Senate and later, President Van Buren appointed him minister to Russia. His diplomatic skills were put to use in 1845. As Polk's vice president, Dallas was also president of the Senate during the time when Mexico was threatening war over the recent annexation of Texas. Dallas judiciously handled the admission of Texas into the Union, and for his efforts, the city of Dallas, Texas, named in his honor. However, politicians from Dallas' home state of Pennsylvania denounced him for another action in the Senate. He voted against his conscience when he supported a Southern-sponsored, low tariff bill. Dallas believed that he should be loyal to President Polk's policies. He was so bitterly attacked for this action that he feared for the safety of his wife and children who were living in Philadelphia. He moved his family to Washington and, once they were in residence, Dallas and his wife entertained frequently and Decatur House again became a center of society.

The next resident of Decatur House was Joseph Gales, who lived there for a brief time during the administration of President Taylor. Gales was a newspaperman, whose career began in 1810 when he purchased the *National Intelligencer*. This became Washington's official "Court Paper," reporting on the early congressional sessions. For years, Gales was the only congressional reporter and he was given a seat next to the president of the Senate. When he moved to Decatur House, Gales was a respected, wealthy, prominent figure in Washington. He and his wife entertained many distinguished acquaintances during their stay at the Decatur House, just as they had done years earlier, when they lived in the Ashburton House, across Lafayette Square.

John Alsop King and James Gore King were two brothers who next leased Decatur House. They served together in Congress in the 1850s. John, the older brother, represented New York, while James represented New Jersey. John later became governor of New York, and James later became president of the New York and Erie Railroad. When the King brothers left Washington, William Appleton, a member of Congress from Boston, moved into Decatur House. Benjamin Ogle Tayloe, who always kept a close watch over his neighbors, described Appleton as "a benevolent man, so much so that on a complaint by his steward, during a very cold spell of winter, that his wood, which had been left on the sidewalk by his order, was fast diminishing, he replied, 'I think it had better not be put away while the weather remains so cold.'"[31]

Southern sympathies were strong in Washington in the 1850s. The rector of St. John's Church was known to offer public prayers for the success of the Confederacy. Decatur House was occupied from 1857 until the beginning of the Civil War by two men who later would give their allegiance to the Confederate flag. The first was Howell Cobb, whom President Buchanan appointed as secretary of the treasury. Cobb was a member of the plantation aristocracy of Georgia. His family had always been active in politics and Cobb was descended from men who served in the Constitutional Convention. Politically, he was a moderate until he had to make a final choice at the outbreak of the Civil War. In 1861, he became chairman of the Secession Convention that created the Confederate States of America.

The next resident of Decatur House was a colorful character from Louisiana. Judah P. Benjamin, who was born in the West Indies, had Portuguese Jewish ancestry, was raised in South Carolina, and became a lawyer in Louisiana. He married a young woman named Natalie, from a New Orleans French Catholic family. Although Natalie eventually left him and moved to Paris, for many years Judah Benjamin continued to live with Natalie's parents, hoping for her return. He made a fortune, but soon lost it. He became involved in local politics and, in 1852, was elected to the U.S. Senate as a Whig. In 1856 he was elected again, as a Democrat, promoting secession.

Senator Benjamin leased Decatur House in 1859 in an attempt to lure his wife back from Paris. He decorated the house with the most expensive and extravagant furnishings money could buy. Natalie did return and it caused a social sensation. The congressional wives could not agree on whether or not to call on her socially. Henry Clay, the Great Compromiser, suggested to his wife that, "By all means, call. You have nothing to do with the lady's private life, and, as a mark of esteem to a statesman of her husband's prominence it will be better to call."[32] The society ladies decided to visit, en masse. However, Natalie never returned the call and she extended no dinner invitations to the Washington society ladies. She did, however, entertain the diplomatic corps, especially those from the French legation. Then, just as quickly as she had appeared, Natalie disappeared, returning to Paris. Judah Benjamin left Washington in February 1861. Jefferson Davis appointed him secretary of war and later, secretary of state, for the Confederacy. When the war ended, Judah Benjamin's allegiance was still with the South. He escaped to England to start life over, eventually becoming so successful that he was called the "American Disraeli" (likening him to Benjamin Disraeli, the British politician and author).

The government took possession of Decatur House after Senator Benjamin left. Other houses also annexed many including the Dolley Madison House, the Gunnell House, and the Corcoran Art Gallery building. Throughout the Civil War, these homes served as military headquarters.

Tayloe House — *the continuing story* —
21 Madison Place, NW

The Tayloe House became the center of society on Lafayette Square because Benjamin and Julia Maria Tayloe had so many personal friends and distinguished acquaintances. Countless parties were hosted by the Tayloes in their home. In 1837, the Tayloes left Washington for more than a year to travel to Europe, and were lavishly entertained throughout their journey. While in Paris, they visited, Baron Hyde de Neuville and his wife, who had lived briefly in Decatur House fifteen years before. They also traveled to Switzerland, Germany, Belgium, and England before returning home.

In April 1841, the newly inaugurated president, William Henry Harrison, visited the Tayloes at their home. Benjamin Tayloe recorded the event: "Our estimable President, Harrison, scarce seated in the chair of state one short month, was then dead. Mine was the last house he visited. The evening of the day of his visit to me, for a friendly object, he was taken ill, and in the course of a week the Rev. Dr. Hawley announced to Mr. Webster that 'he was *sorry* to inform him that President Harrison was in heaven.'"[33]

In 1846, on the Fourth of July, Tayloe's wife of twenty-two years, Julia Maria, died suddenly. Benjamin Tayloe found it difficult to properly care for his two sons and three daughters without his beloved wife. Julia Maria's dearest friend, Phoebe Warren from Troy, New York, offered her assistance to Tayloe. Phoebe was close acquaintance of the family and knew the children well. Three years later, Benjamin and Phoebe were married.

For many years Tayloe experienced problems with some of the investment properties he had inherited from his father. Among the properties were seven two-and-a-half-story row houses built in 1813, on Pennsylvania Avenue at 14th Street, NW. Several of the buildings had been connected in 1816 and converted into a hotel. Finding and keeping a good hotel manager had proven to be difficult. Tayloe had hired five managers in thirty years. While Phoebe was vacationing on a Hudson River cruise, she met a young steamboat steward named Henry Willard. He was an innovative host with good business sense. Phoebe introduced Willard to her fiancé, Benjamin Tayloe, who offered him the opportunity of managing his City Hotel. Henry Willard quickly transformed the run-down property into the premier hotel in Washington.

Benjamin Tayloe became president of the board of trustees of the Washington Orphan Asylum in 1855, succeeding Mr. Corcoran. He helped form the Association of Oldest Inhabitants of Washington, founded in 1865 to preserve the memories of the city. Several times, Tayloe was offered the nomination for the position of mayor of Washington but he always turned it down. During the Civil War, he remained in his home and held strongly to his philosophy of strict neutrality. All the while, he was constantly writing his voluminous journals. After the war ended in 1867, Benjamin and Phoebe decided to travel to Europe. They visited England and Italy. While in Rome, Benjamin Tayloe developed a sudden illness and died at the age of seventy-one.

Willard Hotel — the first story —
14th Street and Pennsylvania Avenue, NW — northwest corner

Henry Willard moved to Washington from New York in 1847 and worked miracles with Tayloe's City Hotel. Within a year the hotel was called Willard's Hotel and, after the Civil War, Henry purchased the hotel from Tayloe. Henry brought his brother, Edwin Willard, to Washington to assist him. Two more brothers, Joseph and Caleb Willard, soon followed. Henry believed that the reputation of a good hotel depended on accommodating famous guests and providing them with lavish banquets and meals. Willard's first famous guest was General Pierce, just before he was elected president. Many other presidents stayed at Willard's Hotel, including Taylor, Fillmore, Buchanan, and Lincoln. Several vice presidents also resided there and, the first Japanese delegation ever sent abroad arrived in Washington in 1860 to stay at Willard's Hotel.

In the 1850s Henry Willard bought the Presbyterian Church on F Street located next door to the hotel. He converted the church into the Willard Hall, which became a popular gathering place for assemblies, musicals, celebrations, theatrical productions, political meetings, and concerts. One very famous concert was given at the Willard Hall by the singer who was called the Swedish Nightingale, Jenny Lind.

Many popular social events were hosted at the Willard Hotel and Willard Hall. One of the grandest balls ever given in the city was held at Willard's in 1859, honoring the departing British ambassador and his wife, Lord and Lady Napier. This was the last social occasion before the Civil War where the Northern and Southern congressmen met under friendly circumstances.

In February 1861, Willard Hall was the site of the Peace Conference. Former president Tyler served as the chairman. The conference delegates were appointed by the governors of those states that had not yet seceded from the Union. The objective of the Peace Conference was to reach an agreement on a workable plan for peace that would bring the Union back together and prevent a war. The delegates' proposals were submitted to Congress, but Congress never acted upon them.

Both Northern and Southern members of Congress had resided in the Willard Hotel before the Civil War, but they used separate entrances provided by the ever-tactful Henry Willard. Northerners entered on Pennsylvania Avenue and Southerners entered on F Street. During the war, the Willard Hotel became the place in Washington where newspapermen, congressmen, statesmen, and generals came to exchange the latest news of the war. The newspaper correspondents chose to gather at the Willard because it was located across from the telegraph office and "Newspaper Row" and, it had an excellent bar.

In 1861, at the beginning of the Civil War, Julia Ward Howe stayed in the Willard Hotel. She was invited to visit McClellan's army headquarters in nearby Virginia (Bailey's Crossroads), where she heard the infantry marching and singing a haunting song. When Julia returned to her hotel room, she was inspired to write new words to that melody. The song became known as the Battle Hymn of the Republic. Julia's brother, Sam Ward, spent so much of his time in the lobby of the Willard Hotel, gathering and sharing information and favors that he became known as the "King of the Lobby." General Grant was said to have coined a term to describe him; he called Sam Ward a "lobbyist."

At his own expense, Henry Willard often fed the Civil War troops who were marching through Washington. One of Henry's brothers, Edwin Willard, lost his life while serving with the Union Army during the war. Another brother, Joseph Willard, also served in the Union Army. He apprehended a Southern beauty named Antonia Ford who worked as a spy for the Confederacy. They fell in love. She was imprisoned for several months in the Old Capitol Prison (located where the Supreme Court now stands). In order for Antonia to be released, she was required to swear allegiance to the Union. She agreed and soon afterwards, she and Joseph were married. They had one son, Joe, Jr., who later inherited the Willard Hotel. Antonia and Joseph also had two daughters, one of whom married Theodore Roosevelt's son, Kermit.

Caleb Willard, Henry Willard's third brother, decided to go into business for himself toward the end of the Civil War. He purchased the Ebbitt Boarding House, located across the street from the Willard Hotel, and transformed it into a first class hotel. Henry Willard later became the manager of the Occidental Hotel, located next door to the Willard Hotel on Pennsylvania Avenue. Joseph Willard kept control of the original Willard Hotel and deeded it to his son. Nathaniel Hawthorne, who had stayed at the Willard during the War, wrote that "Willard's Hotel could more justly be called the center of Washington and the nation than either the Capitol or the White House or the State Department."[34]

Ebbitt House — the first story —

14th Street and F Street, NW — southeast corner

William Ebbitt established a boardinghouse in 1856 by combining two of the old, four-story, F Street Row Houses into one structure. Forty years earlier, these houses were considered to be Washington's premier residences. They were located across the street from where John Quincy Adams had once lived. In 1864, Caleb Willard purchased Ebbitt's Boarding House and converted it into a hotel. He also bought the two adjacent F Street properties from Bushrod Washington Reed and Richard Forrest. The Forrest and Reed properties were separated by an alley, which Caleb Willard filled with a series of bathrooms. Eight years later, in 1872, Caleb demolished the old houses and in their place he built a fabulous, Victorian-style hotel. The hotel was a handsome, six-story structure with a mansard roof, bulls-eye windows, and a main entrance on F Street.

The Ebbitt House became known as "Army-Navy Hotel" because the residents included Admirals Rodgers, Admiral Farragut, Admiral Porter, and Admiral Drayton as well as General Winfield Scott Hancock, General Custer, and General William T. Sherman. William Howard Taft stayed at the Ebbitt when he served as solicitor general. William McKinley stayed there when he was a member of Congress and, it was from the Ebbitt House that McKinley left to take the presidential oath of office. The elegance of the hotel had little effect on the shoddiness of the neighborhood nearby. Just south of the Ebbitt House was "Newspaper Row," a unique, vibrant area of rundown old homes, which had been converted into offices for the big city newspapers.

Newspaper Row — *the first story* —
14th Street and Pennsylvania Avenue, NW — northeast corner

In 1844, Western Union set up its telegraph office at the northeast corner of Pennsylvania Avenue and 14th Street, NW. Like a magnet, Western Union attracted newspaper correspondents who set up their offices in close proximity. Boys were hired to deliver the news that came by telegraph, at all hours of the day, to the local newspaper offices. A half a dozen or more small houses lined the east side of 14th Street, known as Newspaper Row. The houses remained standing throughout the 19th century. This location placed the correspondents not only close to the White House but also to government departments and main lines of city communication. Initially, Newspaper Row was comprised of eight newspaper offices from New York, as well as two from Philadelphia, two from Cincinnati, one from Savannah, one from Baltimore, two from Boston, one from Chicago, one from London, and the American Press Association.

In 1848, the Associated Press was organized as an independent press that changed the work of gathering the news. "News, not opinions" became the motto of the times. The old political newspapers that had served as the voice of the president, or the party in power, became a thing of the past. Special correspondents now struggled to get political gossip or important tidbits of information, for the exclusive use of their papers, in advance of the Associated Press. On September 18, 1867, first meeting of the Washington's Press Club was held and, soon afterward, its offices were established on Newspaper Row.

James K. Polk, the 11th President, 1845-1849

James K. Polk was nicknamed "The Napoleon of the Stump." He was a brilliant speaker and orator who came to Congress in 1825 as a representative from Andrew Jackson's former district in Tennessee. Polk quickly attained the powerful rank in congress of Chairman of the Ways and Means Committee. He became majority leader and then, in 1835, Speaker of the House for two terms. Polk dropped out of national politics for five years, until 1844, when he was chosen as the compromise candidate for the presidency. The votes for the Democratic candidate's nomination were split between Martin Van Buren and Lewis Cass, neither of whom could secure the necessary two-thirds majority. Polk, the Democratic compromise candidate, won the nomination and the presidency, defeating the Whig's candidate, Henry Clay.

Polk's wife, Sarah Childress Polk, while growing up in the early 19th century, had been given the rare advantage of a higher education. Her intelligence and social skills were put to great use when she served as first lady.

She was very religious, so dancing was never part of the sedate entertainment offered at the White House, and alcoholic beverages, of any kind, were served sparingly. However, Sarah's tact, beauty, and kindness more than made up for the sober atmosphere of the White House parties. Engaging in lively conversation was her favorite pastime, and friends enjoyed her company because she was sympathetic, responsive, and a good listener.

Polk appointed George Bancroft as secretary of the navy and William L. Marcy as secretary of war. Soon after Polk's inauguration, America became involved in a dispute with Mexico over the southern boundary of the newly annexed Texas territory. This led to war in 1846. Two years later, in 1848, the Peace Treaty of Guadalupe Hidalgo was signed. Under the treaty, the United States paid Mexico $15 million and, Mexico ceded 500,000 square miles of territory to the U.S., including the future states of Arizona, Nevada, New Mexico, Colorado, and California (where gold would soon be discovered).

President Polk's leadership was perhaps the strongest of any presidency between the terms of Jackson and Lincoln. With the help of Secretary of State James Buchanan, Polk accomplished the four goals he had set for himself as president. First, he resolved the Oregon-Canadian boundary dispute; second, he acquired California and the New Mexico territory; third, he lowered the tariff, in support of the Southern states; and last, he reorganized an independent Treasury, which Van Buren had previously established and Tyler abolished. In spite of Polk's strong leadership, Benjamin Tayloe, observing from across Lafayette Square, offered a less-than-flattering description of him. "Mr. Polk was a man of mediocrity in every respect, of ignoble appearance and manner, but civil. I knew but little of him personally. His wife was amiable and her manners were kind and cordial. No one felt unkindly toward her."[35] Polk honored his commitment to serve only one term as president. Unfortunately, just three months after leaving the White House in 1849, he died.

Marcy House — the first story —
736 Jackson Place, NW (formerly 22 Lafayette Square)

William Learned Marcy came to Washington as a senator from New York in 1831. However, he resigned his senate seat before his term was completed. He returned to New York to serve as governor from 1833 until 1839. Five years later, President Polk appointed Marcy to serve as his secretary of state. In 1845, Marcy returned to Washington and purchased a new house on Jackson Place, south of Decatur House. Marcy's new residence was a Victorian-style town house, three stories tall, with an attic and full basement. A broad sweeping staircase lead up to a grand doorway with a fancy, fanlight window above it.

Although Marcy had tried several times to be nominated as the Democratic candidate for the presidency, he was never able to secure the Party's majority vote. In 1852, Marcy had been a contender for the presidential nomination against Franklin Pierce. After Pierce won the nomination and the election, he appointed Marcy, again, to serve as secretary of state. From 1853 until 1857, Marcy lived in a larger house near Lafayette Square, on Vermont Avenue.

Marcy had a reputation as a card player. The British Minister Labouchere enjoyed telling a story about Marcy's card playing during their negotiations for a reciprocity treaty between Canada and the U.S. One night, during the beginning of the negotiations, the two men played whist, a British card game. Marcy became very upset when he realized that he lost the game. The next day, their negotiations went badly. The British minister explained that, after that evening, Marcy won the card games whenever they played. Though the stakes were small, Marcy flattered himself by beating the British at their own game. During the morning negotiations following these card games, Marcy was always in a good humor and was generous in his concessions toward Canada.

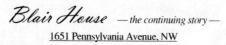

Blair House — the continuing story —

1651 Pennsylvania Avenue, NW

A thousand guests were invited to a spectacular wedding, in April 1843, that was celebrated in the gardens of the Blair House. Francis Preston Blair's daughter, Elizabeth, was the bride; she married Samuel Phillips Lee (known as Phillips). Lee was born at Sully Plantation in Virginia. He was thirty years old when he married "Lizzie." Phillips Lee was a cousin of Robert E. Lee and, he was related to the only two brothers who together signed the Declaration of Independence, Richard Henry Lee and Francis Lightfoote Lee. Phillips Lee joined the navy at the age of thirteen and already had a distinguished naval career by the time he was married. During the Mexican War, in 1846, he commanded the warship *Washington* in the Gulf of Mexico. During the Civil War, he had the distinction of commanding Admiral David Farragut's advance at Vicksburg. Phillips' allegiance, during the war, was with the Union, which forced him to serve against his cousin, Robert E. Lee.

In 1844, Francis Preston Blair strongly opposed the annexation of Texas, endorsing the views of his friend, President Van Buren. Blair spoke out against the Texas annexation in the *Globe* (Blair's newspaper that had long served as the voice of the Democrats). This earned him the animosity of the Southern senators, such as John Calhoun. South Carolina agreed to cast its vote for Polk as president, in 1844, on the condition that Blair be removed from the editorship of the *Globe*. As a consolation to Blair, Polk appointment him minister to Spain. Blair declined. He chose, instead, to retire to his 200-acre country estate in Maryland, called Silver Spring, where he lived for thirty more years.

Blair did not retire from active life in the Washington community when he moved to Silver Spring. He commuted from his country estate to the city, almost daily, to oversee his financial matters and, Blair's political associates always found their way to his home, at the end of the Seventh Street Pike (Georgia Avenue) across the Maryland state line. For many years, Blair shared the Silver Spring country estate with his daughter and son-in-law, Lizzie and Phillips Lee. Though the *Globe* ceased to exist after Blair moved from his Lafayette Square home, Blair's partner, John Rives, continued to publish the journal called the *Congressional Globe*, which served as the official record of the sessions of Congress. Thomas Ritchie's newspaper, the *Union*, became the officially recognized pro-administration paper under President Polk.

George Bancroft leased the Blair House in 1845, while he served as secretary of the navy under President Polk. Although he held the position for only a year, he accomplished a great deal. Bancroft worked to establish a Naval Academy at Annapolis, in October 1845. (Years later, Bancroft Hall, the huge midshipmen's dormitory on the campus, was named in his honor.) In January 1846, Bancroft issued the order for Zachary Taylor to cross the Rio Grande and invade Mexico, which started the Mexican War. Bancroft, who never sought the cabinet post that Polk had given him, was delighted a year later, when he was offered a position he preferred. Polk appointed Bancroft to serve as minister to Great Britain; a position he held for three years. Bancroft was later appointed as Minister Plenipotentiary to the court of Berlin (Prussia) by both Presidents Johnson and Grant. In 1874, Bancroft retired from diplomatic service and, when he returned to live in Washington a year later, he moved into a home on H Street across from Decatur House. He lived and entertained there for another sixteen years, until his death in 1891.

John Young Mason succeeded Bancroft as secretary of the navy and also as the occupant of the Blair House. Mason had served as Polk's first attorney general, and before that, as President Tyler's secretary of the navy.

Mason was pleased with these positions because his government salary helped him maintain his land in Virginia and assisted in educating his six daughters. In 1853, President Pierce appointed Mason as Minister to France.

Thomas Ewing was the next resident of the Blair House. President Taylor appointed him to the new cabinet position of secretary of the interior in 1849. Ewing had been a senator from Ohio in the 1830s. His friends described him as a great man, physically and intellectually, and a famed orator who "breathed his own spirit into vast audiences, and swayed them with resistless power."[36]

In May 1850, Blair House was again the scene of a fabulous wedding. Thomas Ewing's daughter, Ellen, married William Tecumseh Sherman (who was called "Cump"). Sherman was Ewing's adopted son and, years earlier, Ewing had secured Sherman's appointment to West Point. The wedding was a grand affair, attended by many influential guests including President Zachary Taylor, Daniel Webster, and Henry Clay.

In 1850, Ewing was appointed to fill Ohio Senator Thomas Corwin's unexpired term in Congress. He left Blair House and he moved to Capitol Hill. Corwin had resigned from the senate when President Fillmore appointed him as secretary of the treasury. Corwin then moved into Blair House. He was strongly patriotic and, he was also a master of conversational wit. Corwin delighted in twisting the words of others: Decatur's famous 1816 quote, "Our country. . . may she always be right; but our country, right or wrong!" was reinterpreted by Corwin as: "Our country when right; when wrong, we must try to right her."[37] Attorney General John J. Crittenden of Kentucky, who formerly had lived in the Dolley Madison House, also resided briefly with the Corwins at Blair House.

The Blair family once again took possession of Blair House in 1852, when Montgomery Blair and his wife, Elizabeth, returned to Washington from St. Louis, Missouri. Montgomery Blair was Francis P. Blair's oldest son. He had practiced law and successfully invested in real estate, while living in St. Louis. His wife, the former Elizabeth Woodbury, was the daughter of Blair's Lafayette Square neighbor, Levi Woodbury.

After Montgomery Blair returned to Washington, he continued practicing law. He was the plaintiff's representative in the famous 1857 Supreme Court case, Dred Scott vs. Sanford. In this case, the Supreme Court ruled that slaves were not citizens so, Dred Scott, a slave, could not sue for his freedom, even though he had been taken by his master to live in the free state of Illinois. The Blairs had been Southern Democrats, but the outcome of the Dred Scott case caused them to become supporters of the Republican Party. Two years later, Montgomery Blair furnished the legal defense for John Brown, after his raid on

Harper's Ferry. Blair endorsed Lincoln for president in 1860, and became one of Lincoln's most trusted confidants. While serving as Lincoln's postmaster general, Montgomery Blair advocated free postal delivery in all cities with a population of 50,000 or more. At the end Civil War in 1865, Blair's proposal for free postal delivery was approved and implemented.

Francis Preston Blair built a townhouse next door to Blair House, in 1858, for his daughter, Elizabeth, and her husband, Samuel Phillips Lee. The Lee house was three stories tall and built similar in style to the, then, thirty-year-old Blair House. Montgomery Blair, who now lived in the Blair House, enlarged it by adding a fourth floor and a parapet (his father had added a third floor in the 1830s). Francis P. Blair and his wife, Eliza Gist Blair, spent their winters in Washington, visiting their son and daughter in the two Lafayette Square homes. In the summer months, they enjoyed their country estate, Silver Spring.

Because of the Blair family's relationship to Robert E. Lee, President Lincoln asked Francis Preston Blair to speak with Lee concerning his allegiance to the Union. Years later in a letter to the editor of the *New York Evening Post*, Montgomery Blair described the event: "Gen. Lee said to my father, when he was sounded by him, at the request of President Lincoln, about taking the command of our army against the rebellion, then hanging upon the decision of the Virginia convention, 'Mr. Blair, I look upon secession as anarchy. If I owned the four million of slaves in the south, I would sacrifice them all for the Union; but how can I draw my sword upon Virginia, my native State?'"[38] Blair House has been called the "House of Hard Decisions."

Zachary Taylor, the 12th President, 1849-1850

Zachary Taylor, who was born in Virginia and raised in Louisville, Kentucky, chose to be career soldier. From the age of twenty-three, he fought in many victorious battles and earned a reputation as a hero. He fought in the Indian campaigns of the Ohio Valley, on the western frontier, and in Florida. During the Mexican War, President Polk feared Taylor's popularity, realizing that such a hero was a prime candidate for the Whig Party in the next presidential election. Polk deliberately sent Taylor to fight in Buena Vista. That battle was much less important than the glorious mission of capturing Mexico City, which Polk had assigned to General Winfield Scott. However, Taylor accomplished a great victory at Buena Vista and returned a hero. The Whig Party nominated Taylor as their candidate for the presidency and, he won the election, by a close vote, against the Democratic candidate, Lewis Cass.

Taylor was elected president, having no political experience, though he did have a well-defined agenda. He wanted government aid for agriculture, a transcontinental railroad, and statehood for California (where gold had been discovered, attracting thousands of settlers). Taylor was a slaveholder, but he was also a Union man. He believed the Union should be preserved at all costs.

Taylor was known as a man of few words, but when he spoke he went right to the point. He described his wife, Margaret, as being like "a soldier," perhaps because she accompanied him on his early frontier campaigns. Margaret possessed little social ambition and was not in good health when Taylor became president. So, their daughter, Elizabeth, agreed to accept the duties of the first lady. Taylor then asked Elizabeth's husband, William Bliss, to be his private secretary. Another daughter, Sarah Knox Taylor, had married Lt. Jefferson Davis, in gentle defiance of her parents. However, three months later, Sarah died of malaria. Years later, after Davis remarried, Taylor and Davis renewed their friendship. The Taylors' only son, Richard, became a Confederate general.

Taylor asked his most trusted advisor, John J. Crittenden, to be secretary of state. Crittenden reluctantly refused, knowing that accepting the appointment would cause tremendous friction between Taylor and Henry Clay. Crittenden had offended Clay by supporting Taylor, instead of Clay, for the Whig Party presidential nomination. Although Clay was seventy-four years old and in poor health, he was the dominant Whig Party leader and still wanted to be president.

When Taylor recommended that California become a state, Henry Clay became a catalyst in the Senate for a series of intensely exciting events. If California were admitted into the Union, it would be a free state, probably followed by Minnesota, Oregon, and other northwestern free states. The South could not hope to have an equal number of slave states admitted in such rapid order and, therefore, the South feared the possible imbalance of power among the representatives of free and slaveholding states in Congress. In January 1850, Henry Clay proposed a compromise that included several specific objectives. First, the organization of new territories in which slavery would be allowed. Second, the immediate admission of California into the Union. Third, the abolition of slave trade, but not slavery, in the District of Columbia. Clay's recommendations brought on a brilliant debate that lasted for months.

South Carolinian John Calhoun, who was deathly ill, requested that a friend read his remarks, pleading for equilibrium in the Union (meaning that the immediate admission of California would upset the free-state/slave-state balance). Daniel Webster, of Massachusetts, agreed with Calhoun, shocking everyone by denouncing the radical abolitionists and advocating Clay's compromise, even though it included more stringent fugitive slave laws. However, Webster still condemned secession. Senator Thomas Hart Benton of Missouri, along with two freshmen senators, Salmon P. Chase and William H. Seward, led the Northern opposition to a compromise that would support any form of slavery. Benton angered Senator Foote of Mississippi to such a degree that Foote pulled a revolver on him in the Senate Chamber. Benton shouted, as he approached Foote, "Let the cowardly assassin fire!"[39] Friends of each man quickly swarmed upon them and defused the situation.

Clay's propositions were divided up and initially defeated, but all were subsequently passed, after being rewritten as different measures. Calhoun's speech that was read by his friend, was the last that he would give in the Senate; he died four weeks later. Clay said of Calhoun, "I was his senior in years, but in nothing else. . . . I know that I shall linger here only a short time, and shall soon follow."[40] However, it was President Taylor who would soon follow. On the Fourth of July 1850, President Taylor attended the ceremonies at the

Washington Monument. Although he was exhausted, Taylor endured the long patriotic speeches and remained outside in the heat and bright sun, all day. Upon returning to the White House, Taylor consumed large quantities of iced milk and cherries. That night he suffered severe cramps and, within a few days, he was overcome with fever. On July 9, 1850, Zachary Taylor died.

Benjamin Tayloe had only kind things to say about President Taylor. He wrote, "General Taylor was as honest and straightforward as he was brave; a polite, modest and unassuming gentleman. My own relations with him were agreeable and somewhat intimate. . . . I believe the sterling integrity of General Taylor was never more suspected than that of General Washington and was above suspicion."[41]

Millard Fillmore, the 13th President, 1850-1853

When President Fillmore was sworn into office to complete Taylor's term, he was not well received, politically, by many prominent members of Congress. Fillmore immediately replaced Taylor's cabinet with his own. John J. Crittenden succeeded Reverdy Johnson as attorney general, Daniel Webster was appointed secretary of state, and Thomas Corwin was appointed secretary of the treasury. As president, Fillmore signed the bills that contained Clay and Webster's Compromise of 1850, which Taylor had been against. Southerners objected to the compromise because it allowed the federal government to make laws about slavery issues, rather than leaving slavery issues up to the states.

Several memorable events occurred during Fillmore's administration. On the Fourth of July 1851, President Fillmore was invited to lay the cornerstone for the new additions to the Capitol. Two new large wings were being constructed for the House and Senate, on the east and west of the old building. In 1852, Louis Kossuth, the exiled Hungarian revolutionary, was invited to address a joint assembly of Congress. The only other foreigner to previously receive such an honor was the Marquis de Lafayette. That same year, Henry Clay, the Great Compromiser, died in the National Hotel. Daniel Webster died just a few months after Clay. The freshman Senator from Massachusetts, Charles Sumner, was sworn into office to take Webster's place. Four years later, Sumner became famous for a caustic abolitionist speech he delivered in the Senate Chamber, which nearly cost him his life. Before Fillmore left office, he sent Matthew Perry on an expedition to open trade with Japan. Fillmore also secured funds for railroad construction and for modernizing the White House.

"Mr. Fillmore," wrote Benjamin Tayloe, "in the honest administration of the Government followed the example of the 'illustrious predecessor,' and with a natural dignity sustained that of the Presidential mansion as of yore. The era of good feeling was restored, and with it the restoration of the prosperity of the country under the able counsels of Clay and Webster. Fillmore was too upright and dignified to suit the vulgar, trading politicians who ruled his successors in a way that led to the present deplorable state of the country."[42]

Washington social life was animated and delightful during the three years of Taylor's term that Fillmore completed. Abigail Fillmore was a gracious hostess, who had formerly been a schoolteacher and was always a student. Though in poor health, she entertained elegantly. To the delight of society, there were also many grand, public amusements in Washington during Fillmore's administration. Jenny Lind, the Swedish nightingale, came to perform at Willard Hall in 1851. A story was told about Jenny Lind and the aging Daniel Webster, who attended her performance. As Lind sang her final song, "Hail Columbia," Webster stood up and joined in, with his deep, melodious voice, singing each chorus, while his wife tried in vain to make him stop. Jenny Lind was delighted. Webster ended with a grand, low bow to Ms. Lind, who returned the gesture with a slow, deep curtsey, while the audience applauded. Nine times he re-bowed and she re-curtsied, while a joyous audience riotously applauded.

Fillmore lost the Whig Party nomination for president, in 1852, to General Winfield Scott. However, Scott lost the election to the Democratic candidate, Franklin Pierce. The Whig Party dissolved shortly thereafter. Fillmore and his wife, Abigail, attended President Pierce's inauguration. During the ceremony, Abigail caught a cold and died three weeks later. Fillmore tried one more time, unsuccessfully, to be elected president, in 1856, by joining the "Know Nothing" Party. The Know Nothings were openly opposed to immigrants, especially Catholics, believing that they threatened the government and promoted radical ideologies. Fillmore retired from politics in 1857, moved to Buffalo, New York, and married a wealthy, young widow. In 1874 he died.

Andrew Jackson Statue — a story —
Center of Lafayette Square

The bronze statue of Andrew Jackson tipping his hat, seated on a rearing horse in the center of Lafayette Square, was the first of its kind in America. The statue stood alone for nearly fifty years. By the beginning of the 20th century, however, four statues of foreign-born, Revolutionary War heroes, including Lafayette, would be added to the park. Congress had authorized the Jackson statue in 1848. President Millard Fillmore chose the Lafayette Square site for the statue and presided at the dedication ceremony on January 8, 1853.

The dedication day commemorated the 29th anniversary of the battle of New Orleans, the greatest battle of the War of 1812. Andrew Jackson had led his troops in this battle that actually was fought two weeks after the Treaty of Ghent was signed (word of the war's end had not yet reached New Orleans). Many of Jackson's 4,500 men were expert marksmen. When the 7,500 British troops attacked the entrenched American soldiers, the causalities for the British were devastating. After two assaults, 2,036 British were killed or wounded. Only eight Americans were killed and thirteen wounded. After thirty minutes of fighting, the British were driven back and Jackson became a legendary hero.

Together, the Democratic Party and the Jackson Memorial Committee, headed by John Van Ness, raised $12,000 to pay for the estimated cost of the monument. The committee commissioned Clark Mills, who had both talent and connections, to sculpt and cast the Jackson statue that would be placed in the most important park in the city. Mills was trained as a plaster ornament maker and admitted that he had never seen Jackson, he had never seen an equestrian statue, and he had never worked in bronze. Fortunately, he had tremendous self-confidence and inventiveness. Mills had recently won a gold medal of merit for a bust that he carved of John Calhoun. He invented a new modeling technique that he used on the bust. First, he made a plaster mask directly from Calhoun's face and then, using the mask as a model, he carved the bust out of marble. Mills had also just received two other commissions for busts of Daniel Webster and John J. Crittenden.

For the equestrian statue, Mills' first task was to learn about horses. He bought a thoroughbred horse and spent a year training it to rear up on its hind legs, in perfect balance. Next, Mills obtained every available portrait of Andrew Jackson and interviewed his friends to find out more about him. Mills acquired Jackson's military uniform, his sword and equipment, and he even borrowed Jackson's horse's saddle and bridles, in order to study every detail for his work. After two years of dedicated labor, Mills sculpted his first plaster model. He then needed to build a foundry in order to cast the bronze statue from the model. The first foundry was set up below the Treasury Department building, but it was inadequate, so Mills built a larger foundry in Bladensburg, Maryland.

Six castings were made before Mills was satisfied with the statue. When the first attempt at casting failed (using the bronze from a cannon Jackson had captured at Pensacola, Florida), the navy supplied Mills with surplus brass and copper. The final casting was made in ten pieces, weighed fifteen tons, and measured 9-feet high and 12-feet wide. The statue was so popular that a second casting was made for the city of New Orleans and a third for the city of Nashville. Congress was so pleased with the result of Mills' work that they appropriated another $20,000 to give to him because the original $12,000 did not come close to covering his expenses. He next received a commission to create the equestrian statue of George Washington, which was placed eight blocks northwest from the White House in the center of Washington Circle. Mills was later commissioned to cast the statue of Freedom, designed by Thomas Crawford, which stands atop the Capitol dome.

Thousands of people flocked to Lafayette Square to witness the unveiling and dedication of the perfectly balanced horse and rider. Although the statue faces west, the eyes of both Jackson and his horse seem to be glancing back toward the White House. The quote on the granite pedestal, "The Federal Union, It Must Be Preserved," was part of Mills' original design for the base, but was not actually inscribed until 1909. While Jackson was proudly portrayed as a hero on a charging stallion by the Democrats, the Whigs satirically depicted him riding a jackass, during his presidential campaigns. Ironically, the donkey has been affectionately retained as a symbol of the Democratic Party.

Franklin Pierce, the 14th President, 1853-1857

Franklin Pierce's nomination and election to the presidency in 1852 was unexpected. Although he was a loyal Democrat who served in Congress in the 1830s, he had left Congress because his wife disliked life in Washington and wished to return to New Hampshire. Pierce stayed active in local state politics, but had refused any political appointments to serve in Washington. Like Polk, Pierce became a compromise candidate when none of the four major contenders, James Buchanan, William L. Marcy, Stephan A. Douglas, or Lewis Cass, could secure a majority vote for the Democratic nomination.

Pierce was a Northerner with Southern sympathies. In his inaugural address, he declared that slavery was constitutional. In 1854, he signed the Kansas-Nebraska Act, nullifying Henry Clay's earlier Compromise of 1820. The new 1854 Act gave citizens of the territory of Kansas the right to decide for themselves, whether to enter the Union as a slave state or free state, even though Kansas was north of Missouri's southern boundary. The disastrous result was that both pro-slavery Southerners and abolitionist Northerners tried to seize control of Kansas through "squatter sovereignty." The resulting deplorable fights between Northerners and Southerners gave the state its nickname, "Bleeding Kansas." Just before the Civil War began, on January 29, 1861, Kansas became the 34th state and was admitted to the Union as a free state.

Among the members of President Pierce's cabinet were William L. Marcy as secretary of state and Jefferson Davis as secretary of war. Davis and his second wife, Varina, entertained lavishly and continuously in their home, which was located on I Street, just a few blocks northwest of Lafayette Square. Although Varina was a brilliant hostess in the pre-war society, she was also a master of sarcasm and was known to have intimidated many people.

Jane Means Appleton Pierce was a popular and gracious first lady, despite her poor health, her disaffection for Washington, and the fact that she was in mourning for a young son who had been killed in a train accident just prior to her coming to the White House. (The Pierce's two other sons had also died young.) On weekdays the Pierces routinely invited six guests for dinner and, once a week at a state dinner, they would entertain thirty-six people. During the social season, the president and first lady received visitors every morning and evening. Jane Pierce's evening receptions brought hundreds of carriages to the White House, where guests would wait patiently to go through the receiving line in order to meet the president. Military leaders in full uniform and members of the Diplomatic Corps in official costume accompanied radiant ladies. Office-seekers came in quest of a job, along with office-holders, who hoped to retain their positions. Native American Indians added to the pageantry to the parties when they arrived in the full tribal dress.

When Franklin Pierce was first elected as president, he advocated tranquility at home and was one of the most popular men in the country. Within the first year of his term, however, his popularity dwindled. Not only did his opponents denounce him, but also his choice of political appointments displeased the leaders of his own party. When Franklin Pierce left the presidency in 1857, he abandoned politics altogether. Benjamin Tayloe observed that, "General Pierce was . . . elected over General Scott to be the tool of the Nullifiers, and the greatest credit he seems to deserve is his fidelity to his party. He was always well-dressed, and polite and courteous. . . . In my humble opinion, General Pierce, as President, did irreparable injury to the country by furnishing the ground of the civil war. . . . He united the Democracy but divided the Union. On the latter fell the Pandora's box burnished by Pierce, and filled to the brim by his successor, Buchanan."[43]

Gunnell House — the final story —
Pennsylvania Avenue and Madison Place, NW — northeast corner

After the death of Dr. James Gunnell in 1852, his handsome house, nearly a quarter of a century old, was purchased by Lafayette Maynard, an acquaintance of Benjamin Tayloe's. Maynard had been a lieutenant in the navy. He leased the Gunnell House to Fillmore's postmaster general, Samuel D. Hubbard, who was a former member of the House of Representatives from Connecticut. Benjamin Tayloe wrote of Mr. Hubbard, "his entertainments have left pleasant recollections. His wife was the reigning spirit, -- intelligent, industrious, spiritual, and ambitions."[44] With the advent of the Civil War, the house was taken for military use and became the headquarters for the Commanding General of the City of Washington, General Heintzelman, and his staff. The Gunnell House would never again be used as a home and in 1869, the house was razed.

Vermont Avenue Houses — the first story —
Vermont Avenue between H and I Streets, NW — west side

In the early 1850s, W. W. Corcoran commissioned James Renwick to design and build several town houses near Lafayette Square. Like John Tayloe a generation before him, Corcoran recognized the value of real estate in close proximity to the White House. In May 1853, Corcoran's friend, Thomas Ritchie wrote him, "I see by the papers that you are about to build up your suspended houses. Well, be it so; go on with your magnificent structures, but I beg you not to construct them of white marble. I wish to be the occupant of the only white house which graces our side of the Square . . ."[45] Corcoran built a dozen houses in the neighborhood, including three large, row houses on Vermont Avenue.

William L. Marcy occupied the middle house of the three Vermont Avenue Row Houses, while serving as President Pierce's secretary of state. In 1831, Marcy had come to Washington was a freshman senator from New York, but he did not finish his term. In 1845, he returned to Washington as President Polk's secretary of war and he moved to Lafayette Square. First, he leased a room in Mrs. Latimer's Boardinghouse (the Rodgers House). Soon afterwards, Marcy moved across the Square, into a grand, new row house on Jackson Place. In 1853, he moved to the even grander, new row house on Vermont Avenue.

Reverdy Johnson occupied the Vermont Avenue house to the north of Marcy's for many years. Johnson's interesting political career included one elected position and several political appointments. In 1845, he had been elected to serve in the Senate from Maryland. He resigned from the Senate in 1849, when President Taylor appointed him attorney general. Johnson then resigned as attorney general in 1850, when Fillmore became president and appointed John J. Crittenden to replace him. In 1861, Johnson was appointed to serve as a member of the Peace Conference, which met in the Willard Hall. In 1868, he was appointed to serve as minister to Great Britain by President Johnson, but was recalled a year later by President Grant. He died in Annapolis in 1876.

The Vermont Avenue house, to the south of Marcy's, was occupied by Lewis Cass of Michigan, while he served as President Buchanan's secretary of state. Twenty years earlier, in 1836, Cass had resigned as President Jackson's secretary of war and was appointed minister to France. In 1844, Lewis Cass and Martin Van Buren competed for the Democratic presidential nomination that was given, by compromise, to James K. Polk. In 1848, Cass was chosen as the Democratic candidate for president, but lost the election to Zachary Taylor.

James Buchanan, the 15th President, 1857-1861

James Buchanan's presidency was dominated by the tensions between the North and the South. His political views were moderate and he divided his cabinet appointments equally between Secessionists and Unionists. His policy of moderation was often interpreted by the North as taking a stand for the South, and vice versa. Buchanan considered slavery unjust but believed that the constitution allowed slave ownership in the Southern states. He was a Unionist but he enforced the Fugitive Slave Act and supported the Supreme Court's Dred Scott decision. When Buchanan recommended that Kansas be admitted to the union as a slave state, leaders of his own Democratic Party turned against him.

By the time Buchanan became president, he was an experienced politician and diplomat. He had served in Congress from 1821 until 1831, when President Jackson appointed him minister to Russia. He returned to serve in the Senate from 1834 until 1845, when President Polk appointed secretary of state. In 1853, President Pierce appointed him minister to Great Britain. He then worked with Minister to Spain Pierre Soulé and Minister to France John Y. Mason, in drawing up the Ostend Manifesto, justifying the U.S. Acquisition of Cuba.

When he was inaugurated, Buchanan was sixty-six years old. His good sense of humor and cordial manners made the White House a welcoming place. He was known as a methodical man and his rigid honesty caused him to leave the White House poorer than when he entered, because he insisted on not using government funds for any household expenses or entertainments.

Buchanan was the only bachelor president. He had been engaged to a young woman in 1819. However, they quarreled, separated and, before they could reconcile their differences, she died rather suddenly. He decided never to marry. After becoming president, he asked his niece, Harriet Lane, to serve as the White House hostess. Buchanan had become her guardian after she was orphaned at the age of eleven. She had traveled with Buchanan to Great Britain. Harriet was enamored with court life, which, in turn, influenced her enthusiasm for offering formal entertainments at White House. Washington society was delighted by the gaiety after the sober years of the Pierce administration.

Described as a brilliant host, Buchanan offered a dazzling White House reception for a visiting Japanese Delegation. This was the first reception of its kind, specifically planned to honor foreign diplomats. The Japanese came to Washington to negotiate the first commercial treaty between Japan and the U.S. Buchanan also presided over the farewell ball for British Lord and Lady Napier.

When the Prince of Wales, future king of England, came to Washington for a week's visit, he was royally entertained at the White House. A trip was planned for the prince to Mt. Vernon, in order that he might view the tomb of George Washington, after which, he would travel south to visit Richmond. Benjamin Tayloe suggested to President Buchanan that Commodore Shubrick should send a fine navy vessel from Norfolk to Washington for the purpose of properly transporting the prince. However, according to Tayloe, "Mr. Buchanan sent the Prince . . . to see Virginia under the most unfavorable circumstances, in a revenue cutter to Aquia, thence by railway through a poor country to Richmond . . . [and] chose to pursue his own programme, to the mortification of at least every Virginia gentleman, if not of others."[46]

Tayloe continued his commentary on Buchanan by adding, "Mr. Buchanan was . . . without intending it, our political Judas. He was ambitious for another term of the Presidency, and with that object in view was willing that diversions should exist in his party, in hope of its reunion for his benefit. . . . Mr. Buchanan had not the advantages of a liberal education; he had, however, the advantages of foreign travel, and was often agreeable and instructive in conversation. He was not deficient in talent or culture, but lacked judgement and firmness."[47]

Ewell House — *the continuing story* —

722 Jackson Place, NW

©EDWARD F FOGLE EFF

During President Tyler's administration, Senator William Cabell Rives from Virginia occupied the Ewell House in 1841. (Twenty years later, Rives would be one of five men appointed by President Buchanan to attend the Peace Conference prior to the outbreak of the Civil War.) Rives occupied the house for one year, then a friend of Dolley Madison's, John Canfield Spencer, moved in. Spencer had served as secretary of war under President Tyler and, in 1843, he was asked to serve as secretary of the treasury, a position that garnered him high praise, but which he held for only a year.

———————

Thomas Ewell's widow, Elizabeth, sold the Ewell House in 1850 to Francis Stockton, a purser in the navy. Stockton's wife, Anna, was one of Stephen Decatur's favorite nieces. Anna had been living at Decatur House when Decatur died in 1820. For eight years, the Stocktons enjoyed living and entertaining on Lafayette Square in the Ewell House. However, after Francis Stockton died in 1858, Anna Stockton decided to lease the house. Her first tenant was Daniel E. Sickles, a congressman from New York, who had been in Washington for only a year. Sickles and his beautiful young wife, Theresa, entertained elegantly and were immediately embraced by Washington society. Sickles' coaches were among the finest in Washington and his wife's dazzling jewelry was the talk of the town. Theresa was ravishingly attractive and her flirtations led to a tragic love affair with Philip Barton Key.

The Honorable Philip Barton Key was the U. S. District Attorney for the District of Columbia. He was also the son of Francis Scott Key and nephew of Supreme Court Justice Roger Taney. Key was a handsome widower with four children and a reputation of being far too charming and eligible. Peggy O'Neale Eaton was said to have nearly locked up her eighteen-year-old daughter, Virginia, when Virginia became infatuated with the virile, debonair lawyer.

Across Lafayette Square from the Ewell House was the Rodgers House that had been recently converted into the Washington Club, a fashionable and exclusive gentlemen's club. Both Philip Barton Key and Daniel Sickles were members. One evening, Dan Sickles invited Philip Barton Key to attend a dinner party at his new residence, the Ewell House. Key's charisma attracted the attention of Dan Sickles' wife, Theresa. Key and Theresa immediately fell in love. This infatuation between them quickly matured into an affair that nearly everyone in Washington knew about – except Dan Sickles. Key even rented a little house on 15th Street, NW, not far from Lafayette Square, where the lovers could secretly meet. They called the little house, their "nest."

When Sickles finally learned about his wife's affair with Key, he was irate. He confronted Theresa who confessed everything in exacting detail. At Sickles' insistence, she wrote a revealing, descriptive account of how the two lovers would signal each other with handkerchiefs (she from her window and Key from the Lafayette Square). Theresa's confession caused Sickles' anger to intensify to such a point that he remained awake all night planning his revenge.

The next morning, February 27, 1858, Sickles spied Key in the park pulling out his handkerchief and waving it toward the window of Sickles' house. Sickles, armed with a revolver and two single-shot Derringers, rushed out into Lafayette Square. Upon seeing Sickles (but not seeing the hidden weapons), Key extended his hand in greeting. Sickles refused to acknowledge the gesture. "You have dishonored my wife and my family," Sickles was said to have shouted before pulling a gun from his shirt and shooting Key at point-blank range. Key was seriously wounded and struggled to hide behind a tree, pulling a pair of opera glasses from his pocket that he hurled at Sickles. Sickles approached Key and shot him again. While Key was pleading for his life, Sickles shot him a third time and left him prostrate and dying on the ground. Sickles calmly turned and walked back across Lafayette Square to Judge Black's house and waited for police officers to arrest him. The mortally wounded Key was taken into the Washington Club. His friends from next door, the Tayloes, immediately came to his side and were with Key when he died a few hours later. The next day, the circuit court entered a written eulogy to Key in its records: "[Philip Barton Key] had fine talents and many noble manly, generous qualities, which endeared him to his friends . . . his generous manner and professional ability won our affection and respect."[48]

Sickles was arrested, held in jail, and charged with murder. Edwin M. Stanton, who would later become President Lincoln's secretary of war, was retained as Sickles' lawyer. Stanton turned the trial into an extraordinary event. Every intimate aspect of the affair was brought out in the trial and some of it even published in the papers. Stanton was extremely persuasive in his presentation that Sickles and every other man had the right to protect his home and family. Stanton offered a plea based on an "unwritten law" of temporary aberration of the mind, and Sickles was acquitted. Theresa Sickles' reputation was ruined and she moved to New York. Sickles eventually agreed to take Theresa back as his wife, perhaps out of love for their young daughter. Theresa was humiliated, but returned to Washington. Unfortunately, just a few years later, she died.

After finishing his term in Congress, Sickles served in the Civil War and earned the rank of major general. He fought in the battle of Gettysburg and was severely wounded, losing one leg, which he saved and gave to the Army Medical Museum, where it is still preserved. Stories are told of how Sickles would faithfully visit his severed leg each year on the anniversary of its loss.

Francis Stockton's widow, Anna, and her sister, Miss Mary McKnight, moved into the house when the Sickles moved out after the trial, and the two women remained there for several years. Towards the end of the Civil War, Anna leased the house to William Dennison, a close friend and advisor to President Lincoln. Dennison was appointed by Lincoln to replace Montgomery Blair in the office of postmaster general when Blair resigned in 1864.

Rodgers House — the continuing story —
17 Madison Place, NW

After the death of Commodore Rodgers in 1838, his house was leased to James K. Paulding of New York. President Van Buren had just appointed Paulding as secretary of the navy. Paulding and Rodgers had worked together in 1815 when they served on the Board of Navy Commissioners. While serving as secretary of the navy, Paulding was responsible for sending Admiral Wilkes on his four-year voyage as commander of the South Seas Exploring Expedition. When William Henry Harrison was inaugurated as president in 1841, Paulding returned to New York, where he concentrated on his poetic and journalistic pursuits.

In 1841, the Rodgers House was leased as a boardinghouse to Mrs. Latimer and later, to Mrs. Keller. They catered to members of Congress and cabinet officials. In contrast to many of the boardinghouses in Washington that were small row houses with cramped quarters, the Rodgers House was luxurious and roomy. In 1845, when President Polk was inaugurated, the White House was in need of paint and repairs. Mrs. Latimer's boardinghouse became a temporary presidential residence for the Polks who lived there for a month during the White House refurbishment. In 1850, Mrs. Keller took over the boardinghouse management. Listed among the many boardinghouse residents were Congressmen Hamilton Fish of New York, Senator William C. Preston of South Carolina, and Pierce's secretary of state, William L. Marcy.

The Washington Club leased and occupied the Rodgers House in late-1857. However, the negative publicity concerning two of its members in 1858 perhaps hastened its demise. The tragic event involving club members Philip Barton Key and Daniel Sickles (who killed Key) combined with the changes that were taking place in Washington due to the impending threat of a civil war, forced the Washington Club to close by 1860.

In March 1861, the Rodgers House was returned to its original function as a single family home. William Seward, who had just been appointed to serve as Abraham Lincoln's secretary of state, rented the house. New amenities were installed and the house was furnished by April, when Seward and his family arrived. Parties and receptions were given so frequently by Seward that he complained he was spending twice his annual salary for his living expenses in Washington. Seward was well known for his wit and his eccentricities and, also for his reputation as a great orator and philosopher who knew how to tell the truth without causing any disrespect. President Lincoln and Seward were close friends, through they regularly disagreed on official matters. Lincoln visited Seward so frequently at the Rodgers House that the house was referred to as the president's second White House.

Seward was at home on the ominous evening of Friday, April 14, 1865, which was the night President Lincoln was shot. Seward was recovering from a carriage accident a week earlier, in which his horses had broken loose, forcing him to jump out of the carriage. In doing so, he broke his arm and fractured his jaw. At ten o'clock that night, approximately the same time that John Wilkes Booth had entered Ford's Theater and shot President Lincoln several blocks away, Lewis Paine knocked boldly on the front door of Seward's home.

Paine was a part of John Wilkes Booth's conspiracy to assassinate four great men at the same time on the same night. Booth truly believed that if his plan worked, the country would be thrown into such a state of turmoil that the South "could rise again," and Booth would be a hero. Secretary of State Seward was one of the four men Booth had targeted to be killed. Booth himself had planned to assassinate both President Lincoln and General Ulysses S. Grant (who was to have accompanied Lincoln to Ford's Theater that night, but canceled earlier in the day, unbeknownst to Booth). A third conspirator, George Atzerodt, was assigned to assassinate Vice President Johnson, but he lost his nerve and failed to carry out the plan.

Lewis Paine claimed to be a messenger, that night, bringing a prescription for Seward from his physician, Dr. Verdi. Paine demanded to see Seward. The servant who answered the door was suspicious, and refused to let Paine enter. Paine insisted, forcing his way into the house. Seward's son, Frederick, tried to stop Paine, but Paine struck Frederick repeatedly on the head with a pistol until he was unconscious. Paine rushed into Seward's bedroom where he attacked Major Augustus Seward, another of Seward's sons. He then assaulted Mr. Hansell and the two male nurse attendants by Seward's bedside, and stabbed

Seward in the throat and face. Seward's fractured jaw was wired and his neck was in a brace, preventing Paine's knife from delivering fatal wounds, though Seward's face was severely slashed. Seward rolled off the side of the bed near the wall and Paine thought Seward was dead. As he made his escape from the house, Paine assaulted Seward's daughter, Fanny, and a guard.

Secretary of the Navy Gideon Wells, who lived across the Lafayette Square, was awakened by the commotion and rushed to Seward's House. Surgeon General Joseph Barnes was attending to Seward when a messenger arrived with the news that the president had been shot. Wells, Barnes, and others immediately rushed to Ford's Theater. Members of the Tayloe family, from next door, came to Seward's home and stayed with him through the night.

Seward's wounds healed and he resumed his duties as secretary of state three months after the attack. His wife, however, never recovered from the shock of the attack on her husband and died two months later. Seward's daughter Fanny died the next year.

On March 30,1867, Seward negotiated a treaty with Russia to purchase the Alaska territory for $7.2 million. The deal, at the time, was dubbed "Seward's Folly." Alaska had been offered for sale, for the first time, in 1859, but the advent of the Civil War delayed further negotiations. When the opportunity came to resume negotiations, Seward did not hesitate to act on it. To finalize the treaty, Seward worked through the night, with his Russian counterpart, Baron Stoeckl. At four o'clock in the morning, they reached agreement on the treaty.

Jackson Place Row Houses — the first story —

700 - 712 Jackson Place, NW   (formerly 2 - 8 Lafayette Square)

A princely row of spacious, Victorian-style houses was built near the southwest corner of Lafayette Square in the late 1850s, during Buchanan's administration. The corner house, at 700 Jackson Place, was built by Dr. Peter Parker who had served as the U.S. minister to China under Secretary of State William L. Marcy. Parker was called the "Father of the Medical Mission to China," and served as a Chinese interpreter to the American legation in the 1840s. Parker lived in the Jackson Place house he built, until his death in 1888. The house next door to Parker's house, at 704 Jackson Place, was built by General Townsend. He leased it to Franklin Dick who was Montgomery Blair's law partner. The third house from the corner, at 708 Jackson Place, was built by Mr. Trowbridge, a retired Army officer and friend of Benjamin Tayloe.

The fourth house from the corner, at 712 Jackson Place, was built in the early-1850s. By the 1860s, near the end of the Civil War, Major Henry Reed

Rathbone, leased the house. Major Rathbone became famous because of his association with Lincoln at Ford's Theater, on the night of the assassination.

On the evening of April 14, 1865, twenty-eight-year old Major Rathbone was invited by his fiancé, twenty-year-old Clara Harris, to accompany her, and the Lincolns, to a performance at Ford's Theater. Clara, and her father, Senator Ira Harris of New York, lived on H Street in a home next to the Dolley Madison House. General Grant and his wife originally were invited to go with the Lincolns to the theater that night, but suddenly canceled their plans. Julia Grant had expressed concern, to her husband, about accompanying the unpredictable Mrs. Lincoln. Earlier that year, at a public gathering, Julia had been mortified by one of Mrs. Lincoln's unprovoked, angry outbursts. When the Grants declined the invitation, the Lincolns asked Senator Harris to accompany them. Harris was unavailable, but he asked his daughter and her fiancé to go instead.

Rathbone was sitting near President Lincoln, in the presidential box at Ford's Theater, when John Wilkes Booth entered the box and fired the single, fatal shot at Lincoln's head. Rathbone immediately grabbed Booth's coattails to prevent him from jumping onto the stage, twelve feet below. Booth, however, pulled out a dagger and stabbed Rathbone, inflicting a deep wound to his arm which prevented Rathbone from further detaining Booth. Rathbone was always plagued by the regret that he had not been able to stop Booth from killing the president or to keep him from escaping. Many years after he and Clara were married, they were sent on a diplomatic mission to Germany, in 1894. He went totally mad, shot and killed Clara, and tried, unsuccessfully, to take his own life. Rathbone spent his final years in an insane asylum in Hanover, Germany.

Bank of the United States — the final story —
Riggs Bank — a first story —

Pennsylvania Avenue and 15th Street, NW — northwest corner

In 1837, when Andrew Jackson revoked the charter of the Bank of the United States, he ordered the removal of government deposits from the bank. Nearly all of the business of the Washington branch office of the Bank of the

United States was acquired by the Corcoran Bank, a local, commercial bank of deposit. Two years later, the bank became a partnership and was renamed, the Corcoran and Riggs Bank. Corcoran's new partner, George Washington Riggs, was the son of Elisha Riggs, Sr. Elisha Riggs was a successful Georgetown banker. Elisha Riggs also had ties to a banking concern in London, established by his old friend from Georgetown, George Peabody. As Corcoran's new partner, George W. Riggs brought abundant capital to the new bank because of his connections. Riggs, in turn, profited from Corcoran's association with President Jackson, as well as Corcoran's knowledge of government affairs.

In 1844, the Corcoran and Riggs Bank purchased the handsome, stuccoed, bank building at the northwest corner of Pennsylvania Avenue and 15th Street, NW. This bank building originally had been built for and used by the Bank of the United States. Between 1846 and 1848, the Corcoran and Riggs Bank earned huge profits due to Corcoran's skill in negotiating the sale of the U.S. Government War Bonds to European investors, to help finance the war with Mexico. George Peabody had assisted Corcoran with the bond sale in London. In 1848, George W. Riggs retired and his son, Elisha, managed the bank. When Corcoran retired in 1854, George W. Riggs came out of retirement and returned to work in the bank until his death in 1881.

Riggs House — *the first story* —

1617 I Street, NW

ⒸEONARD F FOGLE EFF

About the same time W. W. Corcoran was remodeling his house on Lafayette Square, George W. Riggs was building his home two blocks away, on I Street, between 16th and 17th Streets, NW. A Baltimore architect, R. Snowden Andrews, designed the palatial, thirty-room, Italianate-style mansion, which was built in 1856. The lot and gardens extended a full block north, to K Street. Beyond the gardens were only woods and commons, with no other residences. George W. Riggs entertained society with fabulous parties and receptions during the administrations of Presidents Buchanan, Lincoln, and Johnson.

The Riggs House was a Victorian masterpiece. The first floor contained a triple drawing room with an ornately carved interior, as well as the lavishly decorated library and dining room, which were located across a central hall from the drawing rooms. Ten or twelve marble fireplaces decorated various grand rooms. The house boasted a passenger elevator, silver vault, wine cellar, and bell system to summon servants, who lived in a separate house in the back.

George W. Riggs had several children, and two of his daughters continued to live in the Riggs House for many years after their father's death. The two daughters, Jane and Alice, were called "the beautiful Riggs girls" in their youth. They were among the select group of Washingtonians invited to all the exclusive social affairs. They, in turn, entertained the elite members of Washington society at the Riggs House. In 1860, they attended the ball given by President Buchanan in honor of the Prince of Wales (later Edward VII). Neither of the two sisters ever chose to marry and both lived to a very old age.

The Riggs House was considered "a mecca of the wealth, fashion, civic and intellectual leadership of the day."[49] In 1868, an important event was hosted at the Riggs House. Secretary of State William Seward and the Russian Baron von Stoeckl met with George W. Riggs in his library to sign the papers that transferred Alaska to the United States. Stoeckl signed the receipt accepting the U.S. Treasury draft for $7.2 million in exchange for the Alaska territory. The bank draft was handled through the Riggs Bank.

Abraham Lincoln, the 16th President, 1861-1865

Abraham Lincoln first came to Washington as a member of the House of Representatives in 1846. When he was elected, he promised the Illinois Whig Party leaders he would serve only one term. During his two years in Congress, he established a reputation as a storyteller and charmed small audiences with quaint anecdotes. When Lincoln returned to Washington as the president-elect on February 23, 1861, two weeks before his inaugural, he took up temporary residence at the Willard Hotel. Lincoln's first reception in Washington was held the following day at the Willard Hall, next door to the hotel, where Lincoln was introduced to the members of the Peace Convention. Later the same day, ladies crowded into the hotel lobby, along with members of Congress, newspaper correspondents, and local citizens who wanted to be introduced to the new president-elect, Abraham Lincoln.

Lincoln delivered his inaugural address March 4, 1861, believing every word that he spoke: "The Union of these States is perpetual," he said. "We are not enemies, but friends. . .Though passion may have strained, it must not break our bonds of affection."[50] However, seven states had already seceded by the time President Buchanan left office and, the remaining Confederate states were quick to follow. On April 17, 1861, Lincoln called for volunteers for the Union Army. Three months later, the first Battle of Bull Run was fought on the 21st of July. The war brought four years of criticism, destruction, devastation, heartbreak, and tragedy to the citizens of the country and to the president.

President Lincoln and his wife, Mary Todd, offered their first public reception on New Year's Day 1862. The weather was almost spring-like, and crowds of dignitaries, officials, military leaders, and members of Congress came to pay their respects. Generally, though, the members of Washington society were not pleased with the new administration, so Secretary of State Seward persuaded Lincoln to hold an evening reception, two months later. The invited guests included important military leaders and congressmen, who, if just for a few hours, seemed able, to lose themselves in the gaiety of the affair and in the company of the pretty ladies. Dinner was served at eleven o'clock. On the table were confectionery ornaments, including a replica of an armed steamship displaying a miniature U.S. flag. The party continued until three o'clock in the morning. Many who attended the reception that night would not live through the war to return. The abolitionists were unmerciful with their criticism of President Lincoln for spending money for a party that they felt should have been spent on the soldiers.

Mary Todd Lincoln was a controversial first lady and the target of continual criticism. She was subjected to a congressional investigation because her family had ties to the Confederacy. Her White House receptions were denounced as inappropriate while the country was at war. She was later criticized when she banned flowers and music from the White House for a year, after the death of her son, Willie. Twelve years earlier, she had lost another son, Edward, who died in 1850 at the age of four. Mary Todd was under constant pressure and she suffered from agonizing migraine headaches. Her emotional problems and bizarre behavior intensified while she lived in the White House. Her insecurity caused her to compulsively purchase clothing that she could not afford and she became paranoid, living in continuous fear of the creditors.

Following the death of eleven-year-old Willie Lincoln, in 1862, the mood in the White House could not have been sadder. The temperament outside was nearly as gloomy. Troops were mustered in Lafayette Square. The grand homes and some of the churches nearby were used for military hospitals or offices, but the makeshift hospitals and local graveyards were inadequate to accommodate the huge number of wounded and dead brought from the battlefields. Infantry soldiers marched constantly through the streets. The city filled with strangers looking for loved ones, work, favors, or a quick way to make money. As an escape from the dismal existence that permeated everyday life in Washington, citizens entertained at private dinner parties and, they flocked to the theater.

Lincoln's last public speech was given on the evening of April 13, 1865. Richmond had fallen, Jeff Davis had fled and, five days earlier, Lee had surrendered. Wild and joyous crowds filled Lafayette Square to hear what the president had to say. Lincoln spoke briefly and concluded his address by asking the band to play "Dixie!," a song that Lincoln felt now belonged, not just to the South, but to the whole nation. The very next evening, John Wilkes Booth shot and mortally wounded Lincoln at Ford's Theater. The unconscious president was carried from the theater to a bedroom in the Peterson boardinghouse, across the street. Lincoln never regained consciousness and he died the next morning.

Andrew Johnson, the 17ᵗʰ President, 1865-1869

Andrew Johnson's family was poor and he received no formal education. Amazingly, as a young man, he rose rapidly in the ranks of politicians. For eight years, beginning in 1835, Johnson served on the Tennessee state legislature. For the next ten years, he served in the House of Representatives. Johnson left Congress for four years, when he was elected governor of Tennessee. In 1857, he was elected to the U.S. Senate. Johnson surprised his fellow Southerners in Congress by remaining loyal to the Union. He stayed in Washington when all other Southerners left the city as their states seceded. Johnson was the only Southern senator serving in Congress during the Civil War. After Union forces captured Tennessee in 1862, President Lincoln sent Johnson to be the military governor of the state. Under Johnson's governorship, Tennessee became the only state to outlaw slavery before the Emancipation Proclamation was issued.

At the urging of Secretary of State Seward, Johnson was chosen as Lincoln's vice president in his second presidential campaign. A little more than a month after the election, Lincoln was assassinated and Johnson was sworn in as president. He was sympathetic toward the South and tried to implement Lincoln's policy of lenient Reconstruction. However, the Radical Republicans in Congress spitefully sought to punish the South. By 1867, the Radical Republicans held the majority in Congress and could easily override President Johnson's vetoes. Despite Johnson's veto, Congress passed the Tenure of Office Act, which prohibited a president from removing a cabinet official without Senate approval. Johnson and Secretary of War Edwin Stanton were in constant conflict over nearly every issue. Johnson defied the Tenure of Office Act and removed Stanton from the cabinet. The Radical Republicans saw this as their opportunity to get rid of Johnson and, they voted to impeach him. Chief Justice Salmon P. Chase presided over the trial, but in the end, the vote was one short of the two-thirds majority needed to remove Johnson from office. The decisive vote was cast by freshman Senator Edmund Ross, of Kansas.

Johnson married Eliza McCardle in 1827. She was teaching school when they met and Johnson was working as a tailor. Johnson was self-educated, so Eliza helped him learn how to write properly and, within two years of their marriage, Johnson began his career in politics. Eliza did not enjoy social life and spent her time managing their home and raising their five children. When Johnson became president, Eliza was an invalid who suffered from a form of tuberculosis. She made only two public appearances during the time she served as first lady. Her daughter, Martha, often acted as the White House hostess, though she took little pleasure in her role in public life.

The remainder of Johnson's term was filled with turmoil however, he stayed in politics after he left the presidency. Johnson tried, unsuccessfully, to be elected to the U.S. Senate in 1870 and to the House in 1872. Finally, in 1874, he was elected to the Senate. Once he was back in Congress, he resumed his old fight for lenient reconstruction, but he only lived five months into his term.

———————

After the Civil War ended, Washingtonians optimistically looked to the future. The tumultuous times of the first seven decades of the 19ᵗʰ century were behind them. The Capital City that Andrew Johnson returned to as senator in 1874 was immensely different from the city he had left only five years earlier. One hundred and fifty local citizens had petitioned for and received from Congress a new form of self-government in 1871. Washington citizens were motivated to extensively improve their city, after Congress had threatened to relocate the government to St. Louis, Missouri. The local citizens, inspired by the leadership of the new territorial governor, Alexander Robey Shepherd, began to transform the city from a muddy, neglected, village in disarray, into a magnificent world capital. By the 1880s, Washington boasted a new "high society" consisting of wealthy, influential people who flocked to the Nation's Capital from all across the country.

3

Wealth, Women, Scandals, & Favors

Neighbors to the Presidents :   Ulysses S. Grant - William McKinley (1869-1901)

Washington society evolved into a "high society" in the latter part of the 19th century, when America's "nouveau riche" of the Industrial Age built opulent their winter residences in the Capital City. Winter entertaining coincided with the winter congressional sessions. Washington's social season commenced on the first of January and ended in the spring with the beginning of Lent. The entertainments that were offered by the members of this new society were more than excessive displays of ego. Lavish dinner parties and receptions were hosted primarily to solicit political favors and to influence the opinions of members of Congress on future legislation. Washington's social life became entrenched in national politics.

Scholars, scientists, inventors, artists, literary figures, and explorers were attracted to Washington in the late 19th century. They added another dimension to the city's new sophisticated societal mix, joining the investment bankers, wealthy manufacturers, and retired military and diplomatic officers. Many new residents came to the city to work for the new governmental departments of interior, agriculture, and justice, as well as the departmental bureaus of statistics, education, immigration, fisheries, weather, and Indian affairs. Intellectuals were drawn to Washington by new institutions devoted to research and learning, including the Library of Congress, the Medical Library, the Smithsonian Institution, the National Academy of Sciences, the National Geographic Society, the many universities, and the artistic and literary societies.

Living and entertaining in Washington in the late 19th century could be very expensive. Competition for a proper place in the social strata was fierce. Washington's population had more than doubled during the Civil War. Many new states were admitted to the Union and, the number of new representatives and senators vying for power in the city increased proportionately. The diplomatic community in Washington tripled, to include nearly thirty foreign legations. Washington's society, which was formerly a male-dominated society, was now graced with the presence of many wives, daughters, and nieces.

The women who moved to Washington in the last part of the 19th century influenced society more than any other group in the Nation's Capital. Because few women inherited wealth, and even fewer had an opportunity to earn their own fortune, a woman generally made her reputation through her husband's position in society.

Ulysses S. Grant, the 18th President, 1869-1877

Great optimism and high hope preceded General Grant to the White House. People had high expectations for Grant because he was a military hero; they wanted to equate him to General Washington. However, in Grant's case, expertise in military strategy did not lead to political savvy. Grant was a West Point graduate who fought in the Mexican War. He resigned from the military in 1854, to go into business. Unfortunately, he proved to be a poor businessman, so he rejoined the army. Grant was a colonel when the Civil War began and he quickly rose in rank. In 1863, he was appointed lieutenant general and commander of the Northern Forces. Two years later, in April 1865, General Grant accepted Lee's surrender, ending the Civil War.

Good times filled Grant's first presidential term. The Grants had many friends who helped keep their social calendar very full. Grant's wife, Julia, commented that the time she spent in the White House was "the happiest period" of her life. By contrast, during the early years of their marriage, Julia accompanied her husband on military assignments, struggled beside him through business misfortunes, endured separations during the war years, all the while raising their four children. Good-natured and friendly, though somewhat shy, Julia was as popular as her husband. She relished her new role in society as first lady so much that she was not at all offended when a social reporter described her as "fair, fat and forty." "Life at the White House was a garden spot of orchids, a constant feast of cleverness and wit,"[1] she wrote.

Julia Grant hosted Tuesday afternoon receptions that were so popular that an overwhelming number of callers attended them. She was innovative and managed the crowds by inviting the wives of other officials to assist her in receiving the many guests. The press reported in detail on these social events in the White House, and Julia consented to giving an occasional interview to journalists, making her the first first lady to do so.

The journalists also reported on Nellie Grant, the president's teenage daughter, who was said to be far too popular with the boys. The Grants decided to send Nellie to Europe in 1873, chaperoned by Secretary of the Navy and Mrs. Adolph Borie. While visiting England, Nellie was received by Queen Victoria. On the return voyage, Nellie fell in love with Algernon Sartoris, a British subject whom she met onboard ship. Against the better judgement of her parents, she married Sartoris in May 1874. The ceremony was reported, at the time, as the most lavish and expensive wedding ever held in the White House.

Grant was elected to a second term, but, whether through innocent trust or political blunder, his second administration was rife with scandal. Though Grant was an honest man, he seemed unable to discern dishonesty in others. Some of the men he appointed could not resist the temptation to accept bribes. Grant's first vice president, Schuyler Colfax, was involved in skimming profits made from the construction of the transcontinental railroad in the Credit Mobilier Scandal. Grant's private secretary, Orville Babcock, was involved with a bribery scheme to avoid taxes on liquor in the Whiskey Ring Scandal. Grant's secretary of war, William Belknap, also accused of accepting bribes, resigned before Congress could impeach him.

A territorial government was set up in Washington during President Grant's first term. Grant appointed Alexander Robey Shepherd to head the Board of Public Works and, a year later, to serve as the territorial governor. During his two years as governor, Shepherd implemented programs that resulted in paving eighty miles of roads; planting 50,000 shade trees; filling parks with gardens and statues; building new schools, churches, markets, and office buildings; and establishing a sewer system unequaled in the country. Shepherd also installed gaslights that illuminated the streets and changed the way Washingtonians socialized, allowing them to safely enjoy late evening activities. However, for his efforts, Shepherd was accused of causing a financial disaster in Washington. Congress appropriated $6 million for Shepherd's city budget, and in three years, Shepherd spent $20 million on the city improvements. Congress thoroughly investigated Shepherd for what they considered to be excessive overspending, resulting in a 3,000-page document of the proceedings, however, he was never convicted of any wrongdoing.

When Grant left office, he and his wife departed on a two-and-a-half year journey around the world. Grant's good reputation preceded him and he was welcomed as a hero wherever he visited. Upon his return to the U.S., his popularity was renewed and many suggested that Grant be nominated to a third term for the presidency in 1880. However, the Republican presidential nomination eventually went to a compromise candidate, James A. Garfield. Four years later, Grant was diagnosed with cancer. He worked until four days before his death in 1885, completing his memoirs, of which, more than 300,000 copies were sold, earning his widow almost $500,000 in royalties.

Ewell House — *the continuing story* —

722 Jackson Place, NW

©EDWARD F HOGUE EFT

President Grant's first vice president was Schuyler ("Smiler") Colfax, who occupied the Ewell House on Lafayette Square from 1869 until 1873. He was Speaker of the House of Representatives before becoming vice president.

He was as politically powerful as he was handsome and, he was known as a kind man, who often said, "I consider that day wasted in which I have not done some good to some human being or added somewhat to somebody's happiness."[2] His mother and sister served as hostesses in his home for several years, before Colfax married Nellie Wade, the niece of Senator Benjamin Wade of Ohio. Receptions at the Ewell House were among the most popular in the city because of Colfax's friendly and accommodating hospitality. His popularity faded however, when it was rumored that Colfax purchased stock at a deep discount, as a bribe, in Credit Mobilier Corporation, which constructed the Union Pacific Railroad. Although he finished his term as vice president, President Grant did not ask Colfax to serve a second term with him.

In 1874, the next resident of the Ewell House was Senator William Julian Albert, from Maryland. During the year that he and his family occupied the Ewell House, they continued the tradition of entertaining extravagantly. Albert's daughter married Colonel Bliss, the stepson of George Bancroft, former secretary of the navy.

Anna Stockton, who inherited the Ewell House after her husband death, sold the house in 1876 to her cousin, Augusta Twiggs Shippen. Both Anna Stockton and Priscilla Decatur Twiggs (Mrs. Shippen's mother) were nieces of Commodore Decatur. Mrs. Shippen did not live in the Ewell House; instead, she leased the property to Senator Stephen W. Dorsey, of Arkansas. Dorsey became a wealthy businessman, after he left Washington. He followed his business interests to New Mexico, where he made a fortune in ranching and railroad investments. Dorsey stayed involved in politics and, in 1880, he managed James Garfield's presidential campaign.

In 1878, Richard Wigginton Thompson, President Hayes' secretary of the navy, was the next person to lease the Ewell House. Thompson was a Virginian who moved to Indiana, where, in 1841, he was elected to serve in the House of Representatives. He and his wife were said to have ridden on horseback from Indiana to Washington. Presidents Taylor, Fillmore, and Lincoln were very fond of Thompson and had offered him a number of official positions. However, he declined all of the offered appointments until Hayes' asked him to serve as secretary of the navy. Unfortunately, Thompson seemed indifferent to the appearance of conflict of interest, when he also agreed to accept a salaried position as Chairman of the American Advisory Committee on the Panama Canal Company of France. Hayes dismissed him.

Representatives of two foreign countries occupied the Ewell House in the 1880s. The Chilean Legation leased it from 1879 until 1881, and the Spanish Legation leased it from 1883 until 1885. During the two intervening years, 1881 through 1883, Brigadier Major General D. B. Sacket leased the house. Sacket's Harbor, New York was named in honor of General Sacket because his homestead was located there.

————

Augusta Shippen sold the Ewell House in 1884 to Mrs. Washington McLean, who immediately spent $8,000 to improve the home, adding a two-story brick bay window, a third story to the main house, and a two-story extension in the rear. Washington McLean also added a stable in the rear for his fine horses and carriages. When the McLeans completed the renovations, the Ewell House boasted sixteen rooms, two reception halls, and two cloakrooms. Mrs. McLean spared no expense in decorating and furnishing her new home.

Washington McLean was the editor and owner of the *Cincinnati Inquirer*. He was a very wealthy man by the time he moved to Washington with his wife and son, John R. McLean. For several years, the McLeans continued to live and entertain extravagantly in the Ewell House. In 1891, they leased the house, and four years later, they sold it to their son John.

————

In 1891, Representative John Sanford of New York rented the Ewell House for one year. He was independently wealthy and, socially he was very active in many of Washington's popular gentlemen's clubs. The house was next leased to William J. Boardman in 1892, who was associated with the Standard Oil Company of Ohio. Boardman was a man of great wealth and was known for his philanthropic endeavors. He assisted in advancing the work of the American Red Cross, which Clara Barton, in 1881, had established and successfully directed for nearly a quarter of a century.

Boardman's daughter, Mabel Boardman, succeeded Clara Barton in 1904, as chairman of the American Red Cross. Miss Boardman helped enhance the effectiveness of the Red Cross by working with members of Congress to revise the organization's charter in 1905. The responsibilities of the Red Cross were expanded, to include offering domestic disaster relief and special services to members of the military and their families. The San Francisco earthquake and fire, in 1906, brought the first major challenge to Miss Boardman, as head of the organization. The success of the volunteers in tending to the injured and homeless renewed public confidence to the American Red Cross.

Rodgers House — *the final story* —
17 Madison Place, NW

When former Secretary of State William Seward and his family moved out of the Rodgers House in 1869, General William Worth Belknap and his family moved in. Belknap was President Grant's secretary of war, succeeding

General John Rawlins who had recently died in office of tuberculosis. During the Civil War, General Belknap had served with distinction under General Sherman's command, during Sherman's "March to the Sea."

Mrs. Belknap was socially ambitious and her obligatory entertaining in Washington cost her husband twice what he earned with his government salary. Mrs. Belknap prevailed upon her husband to appoint their friend, Caleb P. Marsh, to the position of Indian Post Trader at Ft. Sill, Oklahoma. (The Post Trader granted civilians permission to sell merchandise on military installations and, the position could be quite lucrative.) The Post Trader at Ft. Sill, whom Marsh was to replace, wanted to keep his position so the two men negotiated a deal that was to their mutual benefit. The Post Trader kept working, but he sent Marsh an annual payment of $12,000 from his profits. Marsh, in turn, sent half of the payment to Mrs. Belknap. This annual "bonus" of $6,000 in payoffs sent by Marsh doubled the Belknap's income.

Mrs. Belknap died in 1870, shortly after the deal was finalized. Shortly after the death of his wife, Belknap moved from the Rodgers House to the Arlington Hotel. Mrs. Belknap's sister, Mrs. Bowers, a widow, moved to Washington to help care for Belknap's young child. Sadly, the child died the following June. Mrs. Bowers, however, inherited her sister's "spoils of war" payment and, in 1873, she married Belknap.

In 1875, five years after the Post Trader deal was made, allegations of impropriety were brought against Secretary of War Belknap, which resulted in the House of Representatives passing a vote to impeachment him. Belknap's counsel was Montgomery Blair. In March 1876, before the impeachment trial could take place in the Senate, Belknap resigned. Alphonso Taft (William H. Taft's father) became Grant's next secretary of war, followed by Don Cameron. Belknap remained in Washington and revived his law practice. In 1890, he died and was buried with honors in Arlington Cemetery.

For fifteen years, beginning in 1874, the government leased the Rodgers House for storage of records. When James Gillespie Blaine rented the house in 1889, it was in need of renovation. Mrs. Blaine worked to refurbish the house, rearranging rooms, adding a new kitchen, and having new windows cut into the brick walls. A wonderful party was held to welcome the Blaines to their new home in November 1889. President Benjamin Harrison, who had just appointed Blaine to be secretary of state, was among the many invited guests. Within just a few months of moving into the house, however, two of the Blaine's children, a son and a daughter, unexpectedly died. Blaine reacted to the misfortune by throwing his heart and soul into his work.

Blaine came from Maine, and was described as self-confident, energetic, and undaunted by any difficulty. He was an immense power in politics for more than a quarter of a century and he had worked hard to help establish the Republican Party. Blaine was nominated as the Republican candidate for president, several times. The first time was in 1876, when Colonel Robert Ingersoll, an eloquent speaker, introduced Blaine as "The Plumed Knight." This title stayed with him throughout his life. In 1884, Blaine was nominated again for president, but his bitter enemy, Roscoe Conkling, successfully wielded his power in the House of Representatives to work against Blaine. Twenty years before, Blaine and Conkling were engaged in a battle of words that Blaine may have initially won, but for which Conkling forever held a grudge. In 1892, when Blaine was again considered for the nomination as the Republican presidential candidate, he was well past his prime. The nomination went to the incumbent president, Benjamin Harrison, who was defeated in the election by Grover Cleveland.

While Blaine served as President Harrison's secretary of state, his foreign policy strategy included hosting a Pan American Conference in Washington to "consider and discuss the methods of preventing war between the nations of America."[3] In the winter of 1889-90, the countries of Central and South America received Blaine's invitations to the conference. Seventeen nations accepted. The gathering served to reinforce the philosophy of the Monroe Doctrine. Blaine presided over the conference, where a resolution was passed to create a Commercial Bureau of the American Republics. The purpose of the new bureau would be to "collect and distribute commercial and general information among all the republics and so not only foster the exchange of trade but remove the great ignorance of each other which existed among their respective people."[4] The Pan American Conference accomplished the visionary goal, which Henry Clay had advanced sixty-three years earlier, of peacefully organizing cooperation among the American Republics. The Bureau of Latin American Affairs became known as the Pan American Union and later, the Organization of American States.

In 1892, Blaine resigned as secretary of state and traveled for several months. He returned to Washington, became seriously ill and died. In 1895, the Rodgers House was razed to make way for the construction of a theater.

Sumner House — a story —

©EDWARD F POGUE EFF

In 1868, Charles Sumner, the distinguished senator from Massachusetts, moved into the house he built on H Street, facing Lafayette Square. The last nine years of his life were spent there. The four-story brick home was square and dignified. In every room, the walls were covered with valuable engravings, paintings, and photographs. Sumner collected unusual treasures, including medieval manuscripts, priceless autographs, rare books, bronzes, porcelains, and lace, which were carefully displayed on his tables and shelves.

Sumner had studied law at Harvard in the 1830s under Joseph Story, the former Supreme Court justice. The two men became good friends. After a few years of law practice, Sumner went on an extended journey to Europe, planning to study European law. Three years later, in 1840, he returned with a broad base of knowledge relating to European governments and with the ability to speak French, Italian, and German. On this trip, Sumner formed lasting friendships with some of the leading figures of the day, such as Thomas Carlyle, Baron von Humboldt, and Alexis de Tocqueville.

Charles Sumner was as tall as Abraham Lincoln and was physically striking, with classic features and thick, dark-brown hair. He was elected to the Senate in 1850, as a Whig, supporting anti-slavery issues and territorial expansionism. He continued to serve in the Senate until his death in 1874.

Though initially Sumner had few allies on the anti-slavery issue, he had the courage and eloquence to speak out against the Southern senators. Sumner argued that freedom was national and slavery was sectional and, that no federal act should recognize slavery's barbaric curse. In May 1856, Sumner delivered a speech called "The Crime Against Kansas," denouncing the Kansas-Nebraska Act (which would allow territorial settlers to decide the fate of a new state as free, or slaveholding). In that speech, Sumner called Senator Andrew Pickens Butler of South Carolina a Don Juan who wooed, "the harlot, Slavery." He called Stephen A. Douglas, the sponsor of the Kansas-Nebraska Act, a Sancho Panza and "the Squire of Slavery."

A few extreme anti-slavery men in the Senate praised Sumner for his strongly worded abolitionist speech, but Lewis Cass represented the moderates who branded the speech "un-American and unpatriotic." Two days later, while Sumner sat at his desk after the close of the workday, Representative Preston Smith Brooks of South Carolina approached Sumner from behind. They exchanged a few harsh words. Brooks blamed Sumner for libeling both the South and his relative, Senator Butler. In a fit of anger, Brooks slammed his cane across Sumner's head. When Sumner tried to rise, Brooks hit him again and continued to brutally assault Sumner until he lay unconscious and bleeding on the floor of the Senate; then Brooks walked solemnly away.

Sumner's Senate seat was vacant for more than three years while he recovered from the severe wounds inflicted upon him. The empty seat in the Senate was a constant reminder of the wickedness of slavery and Sumner's misfortune evoked tremendous sympathy from the Northerners. When the Civil War began in 1861, Senator Sumner was appointed chairman of the Foreign Relations Committee. His earlier friendships with European leaders helped him plead the case for the North. He was privy to the unofficial European opinions concerning the war, which he confided to President Lincoln.

After the Civil War ended, Sumner became one of the Radical Republicans that felt the South committed suicide with its attempt to secede. He and other Radical Republicans urged total reorganization for the South. Sumner vehemently opposed President Johnson's lenient reconstruction policies and, he voted to remove Johnson from office during Johnson's impeachment trial. Sumner became even more extreme in his political views, as the years went by.

Sumner's influence over foreign affairs was immense. He became deeply involved with the *Alabama* claims settlement, in which the U.S. Government filed claims against Great Britain. These claims were for damages inflicted during the Civil War to U.S. shipping, by the *Alabama* and other Confederate ships, which had been built or armed by the British. The Claims Commission assembled in Washington in 1871, and Senator Sumner's house was proposed as an appropriate place to meet. Sumner courteously obliged. The night before the official meetings began, Sumner, who understood the diplomatic qualities of a good meal, served a superb dinner to the commission members and their wives, with rare wines and even rarer mandarin tea (a gift Sumner had received from the Chinese minister). The following day the commission returned to Sumner's home to engage in deliberations that extended well into the night. Sumner's personal influence over the statesmen, some of whom were his close friends, helped determine the positive outcome of the negotiations.

Diplomats and prominent men in politics, art, and literature often met at Senator Sumner's home. Sumner was known to monopolize conversations and his guests were expected to be good listeners. In spite of Sumner's loquaciousness, his dinner parties were legendary. Henry Wadsworth Longfellow, a friend of Sumner, once wrote to him, "One returning traveler reports that you are the leader of the Senate, and have more influence than any man there. Another reports that you have the best cook in Washington!"[5]

On March 10, 1874, after Sumner had spent the day in the Senate, he returned home and suffered a fatal heart attack. Sumner's death was mourned around the world. His body lay in state in the rotunda of the Capitol where his friends and colleagues came to offer a final tribute to this advocate of freedom.

Vermont Avenue Houses — the final story —

Arlington Hotel — the first story —

<u>Vermont Avenue between H and I Streets, NW — west side</u>

In 1869, W. W. Corcoran razed the residences on Vermont Avenue, which had been leased by William Marcy, Lewis Cass, and Reverdy Johnson. Corcoran (who had originally built the houses in the early 1850s) replaced them with the Arlington Hotel, which was called the most extravagant post-war hotel in the city. The hotel was six stories tall, designed in the architectural style of the French Second Empire and topped with a Mansard roof. Corcoran had used the same architectural style for his nearby Gallery of Art. The first floor of the Arlington Hotel accommodated five dining rooms, several private parlors, and a billiard room. The hotel boasted a new elevator system and 325 suites (of up to ten rooms each) with private baths. The rent could easily be over $1,000 a month, when an average senator's salary was $5,000 a year. In 1889, Corcoran bought the Sumner House on the corner of Vermont Avenue and H Street, NW, as well as the Pomeroy House next door, and connected them to the hotel. The Sumner-Pomeroy Addition was called the Arlington Annex.

Many famous international guests stayed at the Arlington Hotel, including Prince Albert of Belgium, the Grand Duke Alexis of Russia, the emperor of Brazil, Hawaii's King Kalakaua, and Li Huang Chang, the viceroy from China, whose chef invented "chop suey" for President Cleveland. Adelina Patti, the celebrated soprano, was another notable guest at the Arlington Hotel. Patti first sang in Washington in 1859, when she was only sixteen years old. Almost thirty years later, in 1887, she came back to Washington for her "farewell" performance. Patti was so popular that people waged personal battles to hear her sing in the theater and the best box seats for her performances were auctioned to the highest bidder. In 1890, the most expensive dinner was the ever given at the Arlington Hotel was hosted by Andrew Carnegie. The cost was more than $10,000.

The Arlington Hotel was nicknamed the "Extension of the Capitol" because so many members of Congress made the hotel their home. Presidents, too, briefly resided at the Arlington Hotel. Between 1870 and the turn of the century, nearly all presidents left from the Arlington Hotel to go to the Capitol for their inauguration. Grover Cleveland leased an entire suite of rooms in the Arlington Annex before his first inaugural.

The reputation of the Arlington Hotel never declined. Mr. Theophile E. Roessle, the hotel's highly respected manager, was always seeking ways to improve himself and improve the hotel. In order to better understand the management of the best hotels abroad, Roessle went to Europe every summer to study. While he was overseas, he would also purchase European art and antiques for the hotel. Roessle maintained an impeccable reputation and hotel guests came to expect the impossible from him. When noisy horse and carriage traffic, on the rutted avenue nearby, created an unpleasant nuisance for the guests, Roessle found a solution. He supervised the placing of asphalt on that section of Vermont Avenue, NW, in front of the Arlington Hotel. This was one of the first major uses of street asphalt in Washington.

Rutherford B. Hayes, the 19th President, 1877-1881

Rutherford B. Hayes followed Ulysses S. Grant as president. Like his predecessor, Hayes won his reputation as a military man. He had shown his devotion to duty and bravery in battle when, more than once, he joined his troops in hand-to-hand combat. After the Civil War, Hayes served two terms in the House of Representatives. Later, he served as governor of Ohio. Both Hayes and James G. Blaine were possible presidential candidates for the Republican Party in 1876. The Republicans, however, were very sensitive to the issue of scandals after President Grant's second term, so Hayes, who was scandal-free, was chosen (even though Blaine was more popular).

Hayes competed against the Democratic candidate, Samuel J. Tilden, in the 1876 presidential campaign. On the initial vote count, Tilden won the election. Hayes' supporters, however, accused the Democrats of corruption and challenged the election results in the states of Florida, Louisiana, and South Carolina. They claimed that Democrats had intimidated the voters of African ancestry from going to the polls. After the votes from those three states' Democratic precincts were disqualified, Hayes was declared the winner. Then, the Democrats accused Southern Republicans of corruption.

Citizens protested this unprecedented situation. Congress was forced to compromise and form an election commission to select the president. Five senators, five representatives, and five Supreme Court justices were chosen to be members of the commission. Eight were Republicans and seven were Democrats. Not surprisingly, the Republicans voted for Hayes and the Democrats voted for Tilden. The Democrats had agreed to the committee comprised of a majority of Republicans because, by a secret arrangement, Hayes had assured the Democrats that, as president, he would remove federal troops from Southern states. This action brought an end to Reconstruction and allowed the Democrats to reestablish their power base in the South.

Although Hayes was a strong leader, he faced powerful opposition in Congress. Disgruntled Republican conservatives joined forces with a large Democratic majority to override many of Hayes' vetoes. When Congress voted to issue the first silver dollars, Hayes declared that silver dollars were overvalued and, therefore, would not stimulate the sluggish economy, so he vetoed the bill. Congress overrode Hayes' veto. Congress also thwarted Hayes' efforts at civil service reform, when he tried to abolish the "spoils system," which Andrew Jackson had promoted, nearly half a century earlier. In 1877, however, Hayes was able to act decisively and send federal troops to stop riots in major cities, when railroads went on the first nationwide strike.

Rutherford Hayes met Lucy Webb when he was practicing law in Cincinnati. In his diary he wrote, "Her low sweet voice is very winning . . . a heart as true as steel . . . Intellect she has too . . . By George! I am in love with her!"[6] Rutherford and Lucy were married in 1853 and they had eight children, five of whom lived to maturity. Lucy Webb Hayes was a serene and beautiful woman and, she was the first first lady to be college-educated.

Lucy often visited her husband while he served in the military during the Civil War. Because she assisted the wounded and homesick on the battlefield, the troops called her "Mother Lucy." During Hayes' terms in Congress, Lucy accompanied him to Washington in order to participate in the social seasons. She was also at Hayes' side on his visits to prisons, schools, and asylums. While Hayes served as president, Lucy became a much-admired first lady. Their married life was very happy and they celebrated their twenty-fifth wedding anniversary with a grand reception in the White House.

Intelligent and cheerful, Lucy was popular with the political circles of Washington. She was also very religious and prohibited alcohol from being served in the White House. Although Washington forgave Lucy for the obvious lack of alcohol at government and social functions, Benjamin Perley Poore, a well-known newspaper correspondent at the time, later described Hayes' parties. Poore mentioned that oranges served at White House receptions were secretly spiked with a frozen punch made from "Santa Croix" rum. He also wrote an account of the "Life-Saving Station," wherein, spiked "Roman punch was served about the middle of the state dinners, care being taken to give the glasses containing the strongest mixture to those who were longing for some potent beverage."[7] This was done, of course, without the knowledge of Mrs. Hayes. Lucy took criticism with a sense of humor and, she found it amusing when, several years after leaving the White House, she was nicknamed "Lemonade Lucy."

Octagon House — *the continuing story* —
18th Street and New York Avenue, NW — northeast corner

Benjamin Tayloe bought his brother's half-interest in the Octagon House in 1854, when the neighborhood to the southwest began to deteriorate. Tayloe family descendants continued to occupy the house until 1860. Reverend Charles White, the pastor of St. Matthew's Catholic Church, leased the house for six years, for the St. Rose Technical Institute, a girl's school. St. Matthew's Church offered to purchase the Octagon House but the sale was never finalized. After the Civil War, from 1866 until 1879, the government leased the Octagon House as the headquarters for the Hydrographic Office. When Benjamin Tayloe died in 1868, he left the Octagon House and all of his property, with the exception of his Lafayette Square House, to his daughters. However, Tayloe specified one unusual condition to his daughters, that "none of them live in Washington."[8]

From 1879 until 1898, rooms in the Octagon House were rented for both commercial and residential use. The house had been poorly maintained when Glenn Brown, secretary of the American Institute of Architects (AIA), toured it in 1886. Brown described the house as "almost squalid." Ten years later, he spoke to the executive committee of the AIA about making arrangements to acquire a facility in Washington to be used as their headquarters. At that meeting, Brown recommended that the AIA lease the Octagon House. He described it as "one of the best examples of work done in the year 1800, [and] can be secured for thirty dollars a month; its plan, character of design and workmanship, and location make it peculiarly suitable for the headquarters."[9] The Octagon House was being managed by a trust, in 1898, when Brown revisited it. He found eight to ten families living there, with piles of rubbish several feet high in the drawing room. The AIA immediately agreed to write a five-year lease on the Octagon House. The members appropriated funds to clean and repair the historic home and, in January 1899, they moved in.

Tayloe House — *the continuing story* —
21 Madison Place, NW

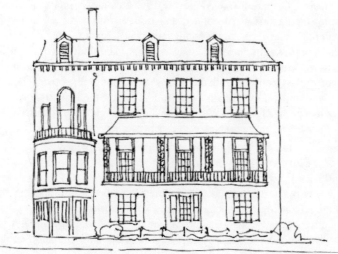

©EDWARD F FOGLE LEFT

Phoebe Warren Tayloe, Benjamin Tayloe's widow, continued living in the Tayloe House on Lafayette Square after her husband died. In 1884, Phoebe died, and the Tayloe's remarkable collection of curios, ornaments, art, and antiques was transferred to the Corcoran Gallery of Art, with the provision that the collection should always be kept and displayed together. In 1898, when the Corcoran art collection was moved to its new gallery building on 17th Street, NW, no special arrangements had been made to display the Tayloes' curios and art. Therefore, after the turn of the century, the trustees of the Corcoran Gallery honored the claims of the Tayloe heirs and returned the items to the family in Troy, New York, which was the birthplace of Mrs. Tayloe and home of her descendants.

In 1887, Senator J. Donald Cameron of Pennsylvania purchased the Tayloe House from Benjamin Tayloe's heirs. Before moving to Washington, Cameron had served as president of the Northern Central Railway Company of Pennsylvania, from 1866 until 1874. For one year, from 1876 to 1877, Cameron served as President Grant's secretary of war. When Hayes became president in 1877, Cameron's father, Senator Simon Cameron, resigned his seat in Congress on the condition that his son, Don, be approved as his replacement.

After Grant returned from his journey around the world in 1880, Senator Don Cameron, together with Roscoe Conkling and John Alexander Logan, felt

Grant should be nominated for the presidency again. Cameron, Conkling, and Logan, who had been powerful men during the Grant administrations, tried to use Grant's military fame to gather support for this nomination to a third term. Grant's campaign slogan was borrowed from Conkling's nominating speech in 1880: "When asked whence comes our candidate, Our sole reply shall be, He comes from Appomattox and her famous apple tree."[10] Grant, however, eventually conceded the Republican presidential nomination to James Garfield.

After the Camerons moved into the Tayloe House, Mrs. Elizabeth Sherman Cameron meticulously redecorated and restored the home's beauty. Outside, she carefully tended the south-facing, walled garden. Inside, she transformed the third floor rooms into the living quarters. The dining room and drawing room were located on the second floor. The kitchen and breakfast room were on one side of the first floor, with the library and parlor on the other. The first floor parlor was known as Cameron's card room, "where the highest games of poker known to a private house in Washington are reputed to have occurred."[11]

"Lizzie" Cameron was the niece of General William Tecumseh Sherman. She was just twenty years old when she married the widower, Don Cameron, who was then forty-four years old with five children, the oldest of whom was Lizzie's age. Lizzie was a slim, tall, gray-eyed brunette. Cameron was taller with a droopy mustache and sand-colored haired. "Beauty and the Beast" is what the gossip columnists called them. Lizzie married Don at the insistence of her relatives, because the man she wanted to marry was suspected of being an alcoholic. She was horrified to later discover that Don Cameron could easily drink a fifth of bourbon in a day. However, Lizzie felt duty-bound to stay with her husband and she tried not to show her disappointment in the marriage. Fortunately, Lizzie had developed a strong and long-lasting friendship with Henry and Clover Adams, a few years earlier. In 1881, the Adams had returned to live on Lafayette Square. They tolerated Don Cameron for Lizzie's sake.

In 1895, the Rodgers House, next door to the Tayloe House where the Camerons lived, was sold and demolished. When a theater was erected in its place, the Lafayette Square neighbors felt their neighborhood had been invaded. However, this was only the first of many changes that would transform Lafayette Square during the 20th century. For two years, the Camerons continued to live in the Tayloe House, but Don Cameron felt compelled to move, when living next door to a theater became intolerable for him.

In 1897, Cameron rented the Tayloe House to Garret Hobart, who was McKinley's first vice president. Hobart was a successful businessman and lawyer. He had amassed a fortune in his lifetime and considered politics to be his hobby. Though Hobart had never held public office before becoming McKinley's vice president, he was unusually influential in the vice president's position. He was McKinley's dear friend and his closest advisor.

The country was suffering from an economic depression when McKinley and Hobart were elected. McKinley, a Republican, blamed the depression on the Democrats. McKinley and Hobart supported a conservative platform, which endorsed the gold standard. Hobart denounced silver dollars, claiming that an honest dollar couldn't be made out of fifty-three cents worth of silver.

Vice President and Mrs. Hobart enjoyed entertaining in the Tayloe House on Lafayette Square. Unfortunately, Garret Hobart died after a brief illness in 1899, before his term as vice president expired. His wife, Jenny, lived to be 91 years old and died in 1941. In the 1930s, Jenny published two books about her life as the wife of the vice president living on Lafayette Square. The books were entitled *Memories* and *Second Lady*.

From 1900 until 1902, Senator Marcus Alonzo Hanna of Ohio leased the Tayloe House from Cameron. Hanna was a forceful, Cleveland businessman who had made a fortune as an industrialist. He exerted tremendous influence over William McKinley in the early 1890s, when McKinley served, for two terms, as governor of Ohio.

In 1897, Hanna was chosen to succeed John Sherman as senator from Ohio. This was Hanna's first public office. Prior to the Republican National Convention in 1896, Hanna heavily promoted McKinley for the presidential nomination, making many pre-election promises on McKinley's behalf. Some of Hanna's deals caused McKinley great embarrassment, after he was elected. One such promise was to appoint the aging John Sherman as secretary of state, thereby allowing Hanna himself to fill Sherman's vacant Senate seat.

Mark Hanna tried to stop McKinley from choosing Theodore Roosevelt as his running mate in the 1896 election. Hanna thought Roosevelt was unpredictable. He told the Republican leaders that, "To make Roosevelt Vice-President would place but a single life between this madman and the presidency."[12] Although Hanna emphatically disliked Roosevelt at first, the two men eventually became good friends. This was characteristic behavior for Hanna, who was a very congenial, good-natured, and popular man.

The Tayloe House became known as the "Little White House" because McKinley spent so much time there, visiting and conferring with Mark Hanna. Their early morning breakfasts were legendary. Hanna was personally well liked and his wife was a skilled hostess. Because of the many dinner parties and receptions the Hannas hosted in their home, it was also known as the "Little Court." Entertaining on a large scale, however, went out of fashion at the turn of the century. After the death of President McKinley, in 1901, the Hannas moved to the Arlington Hotel. Cameron then leased the Tayloe House to various tenants, over the next fifteen years. Marcus Hanna died at the Arlington Hotel, in 1904, of typhoid fever that had been misdiagnosed as exhaustion.

James A. Garfield, the 20ᵗʰ President, 1881

James Abram Garfield was born in a log cabin in Orange, Ohio. His father died when he was just an infant. Garfield's mother was the sole support of her four children and they learned to survive by farming thirty acres of land. In the winter, Garfield attended school and was a voracious reader. As a teenager, he was known as a good fist fighter. He drove mules for a canal barge and worked as a carpenter to pay for his higher education at Western Reserve Eclectic Institute (later Hiram College), in Hiram, Ohio. He was an eloquent, persuasive speaker. While in college, Garfield was hired as an English teacher for three years. Several years after leaving Hiram, he returned to the college to study law and to serve as the school's president of its five-member faculty.

Garfield was almost thirty years old when the Civil War began. He was commissioned as a lieutenant and promoted repeatedly for his consistent bravery in battle. Eventually, he achieved the rank of major general. In 1862, Garfield was elected to the House of Representatives, though he felt duty-bound to stay in the military until December 1863, when he resigned and took his place in Congress.

For the eighteen years that Garfield served as a representative in Congress, he sided with those who supported harsh reconstruction terms for the South. Garfield was a respected leader and recognized for his outstanding oratory skills. With a one-sentence speech, Garfield stopped an angry mob in Washington, who threatened to destroy the offices of the *New York World* newspaper after Lincoln's assassination, because it had been critical of Lincoln in the past. "Fellow citizens," he said, "God reigns and the government of Washington still lives."[13] In 1876, Garfield was appointed to be one of the eight Republican members of the fifteen-man commission that decided the outcome of the Hayes-Tilden presidential election.

In 1880, the Republicans were divided into two opposing factions. One faction, led by Cameron and Conkling, supported Ulysses S. Grant as the presidential candidate. The other faction strongly supported James G. Blaine. Garfield, who had just been elected to the Senate, was chosen as the Republican's compromise candidate. As a goodwill gesture to the "Stalwarts" (the unwavering Grant partisans such as Conkling, Cameron, and Logan) Chester A. Arthur was selected as the vice presidential candidate. Even though every Southern state in the Union supported the Democrats and their candidate General Winfield Scott Hancock, Garfield, nonetheless, won the election.

Lucretia ("Crete") Rudolph and James Garfield met when they were in college in Hiram, Ohio. They were married in 1858. Whenever possible, Lucretia traveled with her husband, except for his first lonely winter in Washington, when he was a freshman representative in 1863. Together, Lucretia and James Garfield raised five children. One of their sons, James Rudolph Garfield, later served as Theodore Roosevelt's secretary of interior. Lucretia was a conscientious, genuine person. Although she did not relish the duties of first lady, she gave receptions twice a week and held many dinner parties that were very popular events. She was forty-nine years old when she moved into the White House and she would live for thirty-six more years.

The Garfields had lived in a home near 13th and I Streets, NW, before they moved into the White House. While living there, James Garfield would stop nearly every day to play a few games of billiards, at the Riggs House Hotel, located at 15th and G Streets, NW. Charles H. Reed, a Chicago lawyer who was living in Washington for part of the year, was one of Garfield's favorite billiard partners. Ironically, Reed later served as the attorney representing Charles J. Guiteau, a disgruntled, unemployed government clerk. Guiteau shot Garfield in the back, on July 2,1881, as he stood in the Baltimore and Potomac Railroad Station in downtown Washington. The shooting occurred four months after Garfield became president. Garfield's doctors felt compelled to try and remove the bullet from his back. His wound became severely infected as a result of the doctors repeatedly and unsuccessfully probing to dislodge the bullet. In September 1881, Garfield died and Chester A. Arthur became president.

Chester A. Arthur, the 21st President, 1881-1885

Chester Alan Arthur was one of nine children, whose father was a Baptist minister from Ireland. As a student at Union College in Schenectady, New York, Arthur was admitted to Phi Beta Kappa when he was a senior. He graduated from college at the age eighteen and he immediately began studying and practicing law. In 1856, Arthur became involved in politics, supporting the new Republican Party. For his work on behalf of the Republicans, he received several political appointments, rising in rank from brigadier judge advocate to quartermaster general for New York militia during the Civil War. He proved to be an excellent administrator. After the war, he returned to private law practice, while remaining an active supporter of the Republican Party.

"Stalwart" Republican Senator Roscoe Conkling, the New York party boss, urged President Grant to appoint Arthur to a very lucrative position as collector of the port of New York, which earned Arthur a small fortune in 1871. When Hayes succeeded Grant as president in 1878, he fired Arthur from the position as part of his efforts to abolish the "spoils system." Two years later, Arthur was offered and accepted the Republican nomination for vice president, even though he had never before been elected to a public office.

Garfield died 199 days after he was inaugurated and Chester A. Arthur assumed the presidency. Charges were made that Arthur and the "Stalwarts" were somehow involved with President Garfield's assassin, Charles Guiteau. This accusation so distressed Arthur and he disassociated himself from the Stalwarts. To distance himself further from the Stalwart-supported spoils system, of which he had once been a beneficiary, Arthur worked for civil service reform. In 1883, he signed the Pendleton Civil Service Reform Act, which eliminated the old patronage system for many federal government jobs and developed examinations for those federal positions.

President Arthur's wife, Ellen Lewis Herndon Arthur, died just months before he accepted the nomination for the vice presidency. Ellen was only forty-two years old when she contracted pneumonia and died within two days. Arthur was devastated by his wife's death. As a young girl, Ellen had lived in Washington and sang in the choir at St. John's Church on Lafayette Square. President Arthur commissioned a stained glass window for St. John's in memory of his wife. He always kept fresh flowers next to her color-tinted photograph while he lived in the White House. Arthur's sister, Mary Arthur McElroy, served in the official capacity of White House hostess and cared for Arthur's twelve-year-old daughter, Ellen (who had been named for her mother).

Chester Arthur earned a reputation as an agreeable host. While living in New York, he and his wife entertained in a grand and elegant manner. Arthur enjoyed Washington society and renovated the White House before moving in, transforming it into a sparkling, lively place where he served an abundance of good food and wine. Because he was as fastidious with his entertainments as he was with his dress, he was known as "the prince of hospitality."

On February 21, 1885, President Arthur presided over the dedication ceremony of the Washington Monument. Crowds filled the monument grounds and braved arctic weather to hear President Arthur declare that from that time forth, the monument was dedicated "to the immortal name and memory of George Washington."[14]

When Chester A. Arthur left Washington at the end of his presidency, he returned to New York City. He resumed practicing law and he accepted the position of president of the New York Arcade Railway Company, which allowed him to oversee the creation the new subway system in New York City. In 1886, Arthur discovered he had Brights' disease, and within a year he died.

St. John's Church – the continuing story –
16th and H Street, NW — northeast corner

St. John's Church had ministered to the members of Washington society since it was built in 1816. The maintenance of the church had been paid for by the yearly rental, and sale, of pews. The church had been enlarged for the first time in the 1820s to provide for more pews and more income. Half a century later, in the 1870s, the church struggled financially and, the members of the congregation discussed the possibility of replacing the charming, intimate church building, with a huge, Victorian structure. Many members of the congregation, argued against changing or replacing St. John's. Instead, they promoted the notion of building a large, national church, elsewhere in the city.

George Washington first suggested the idea of creating a great, free, national church in the Capital City. Nearly a century later, the initial discussions about establishing such a church were held at St. John's and, in January 1893, the National Cathedral Foundation was chartered by Congress. St. John's pioneered the fund-raising efforts that supported the erection of the Washington National Cathedral, on the hill high above Georgetown. One member of the congregation, Mrs. Phoebe Hearst (the mother of William Randolph Hearst), financed the construction of the first building erected on the cathedral grounds: the National Cathedral Girls School.

After St. John's congregation definitively rejected the idea of razing the church, they voted to modernize it. In the 1880s, James Renwick was chosen as the architect for the renovation, because he had a special attachment to the church. His wife, the daughter of Admiral Charles Wilkes, had long been a member of St. John's congregation.

Renwick proved to be sensitive to Benjamin Latrobe's original church design. He recommended preserving of the intrinsic character of the building. During the renovation, the north, west, and south walls of the church were untouched. Renwick extended the chancel to the east, rearranged the interior spaces, and added a two-story addition for a robing room. He created enough extra space in the church to accommodate an additional 180 people. Openings were cut through the walls on the north and south to accommodate new stained glass windows. Madame Veuve Lorin, the curator of glass at Chartres Cathedral, was contracted to create the colored glass for the windows. Six presidents were memorialized in two of the new windows: Madison, Monroe, and Van Buren were honored in one and, Harrison, Tyler, and Taylor in another. A third new window was installed and dedicated to Montgomery Blair by his widow, Mary Elizabeth Woodbury Blair. President Arthur dedicated a fourth window, in the south transept, in memory of his wife, Ellen.

Slidell House — the continuing story —
1607 H Street, NW

Following the Civil War, W. W. Corcoran leased the Slidell House to Senator John P. Stockton. He was a relative of Francis B. Stockton who had owned the Ewell House, on Lafayette Square. Senator John Stockton was descended from a long line of patriots and public servants. His father, Robert F. Stockton, had been a senator and was the naval commodore in command of the *Princeton* when the "Peacemaker" cannon exploded, killing several members of President Tyler's cabinet. His grandfather, Richard Stockton, had been both a senator and representative, and his great-grandfather, also named Richard Stockton, signed the Declaration of Independence, and served as a member of the Continental Congress.

John Stockton's family connections helped him secure a diplomatic appointment from President Buchanan in 1858, as minister to the Papal States. In 1865, he was elected to fill a vacancy in the Senate and was then reelected in 1869. Senator Stockton lived in the Slidell House from 1871 until he lost his bid for reelection in 1875. He returned to his home state of New Jersey and held the position of state attorney general for twenty years.

Another member of Congress, Elisha Ward, was the next resident of the Slidell House. His political career spanned from 1865 to 1877, during which time he served several, non-consecutive congressional terms. He lived in the Slidell House during his last term as a member in the House of Representatives, from 1875 to 1877. In 1880, W. W. Corcoran leased the Slidell House to his most famous tenants, Henry and Clover Adams.

In 1877, Henry Adams, the grandson of John Quincy Adams, moved to Washington from Boston with his wife of five years, Marian (Clover) Hooper Adams. Adams came to edit the papers of Albert Gallatin, Jefferson's secretary of treasury. Clover dreaded leaving Boston. Even more, she dreaded leaving her father, to whom she was very attached. Henry, on the other hand, looked forward to the change, explaining that Washington reminded him of London and noting, "I gravitate to a capital by a primary law of nature. This is the only place in America where society amuses me, or where life offers variety."[15]

In the spring of 1880, Henry and Clover were traveling in Europe when they wrote to W. W. Corcoran to inquire about leasing a house on Lafayette Square. Corcoran replied that his Lafayette Square rental house was vacant and available, and he would gladly make any changes to the house that they might request. When the Adams arrived in the fall, they stayed in Wormley's Hotel at 15th and H Streets, NW, while the Slidell House was being remodeled for them.

While staying at Wormley's Hotel, the Adams became acquainted with

John Hay and Clarence King, two other residents at Wormley's. Hay was in Washington serving as President Hayes' assistant secretary of state, though his wife Clara remained temporarily in Cleveland, with their children. Clarence King was in Washington lobbying for the creation of the U.S. Geological Survey. Hay and King had met several years earlier while they were both in New York and they were happy to renew their friendship in Washington. These five people, John Hay and his wife Clara, Clarence King, and Henry and Clover Adams, became legendary friends, calling themselves the "Five of Hearts."

In December 1880, Henry and Clover Adams moved into the Slidell House on Lafayette Square, after fifteen wagonloads of furniture arrived from Boston. John Hay and Clarence King were among the first guests the Adams entertained in their new home. Clara Hay soon joined her husband in Washington for the winter social season of 1880-81. The Adams' home was filled with a wonderful art collection that Clover and Henry began acquiring while they were on their honeymoon in Europe. Their dear friend and neighbor, Mrs. George Bancroft, jokingly mentioned to Clover, "I dislike auctions very much, but I mean to go to yours after you die."[16]

Since Henry Adams wanted little to do with official politics, he and Clover chose their company carefully. They entertained lavishly and invitations to their salons were coveted. The Adams' were part of Washington's young, intellectual society and their parties reflected their interests and their elite status. Henry and Clover delighted in ignoring what they called "official society." Because Clover was a clever and witty hostess, multitudes of curious individuals left calling cards for her, hoping, in vain, for an invitation to her exclusive salon.

Secretary of State William Evarts, Adams' friend, granted him access to the normally restricted files in the State Department archives, which Adams used while researching the nine volumes he was writing on the *History of the United States*. When Garfield was elected president, James G. Blaine was appointed secretary of state. Adams and Blaine despised each other. Blaine accused Adams of libeling him in a novel called *Democracy*, which was anonymously published but widely attributed to Adams. Adams never admitted writing the novel, but confessed that, because he and Clover were not part of "official society," they did not have to be polite to those people who were. As secretary of state, Blaine spitefully prohibited Adams from continuing his research in the restricted State Department archives.

After the death of Garfield, President Arthur replaced Blaine as secretary of state with Frederick Frelinghuysen, an old friend of Adams who reopened the archives to him. Adams boasted about his triumph over Blaine in a letter to British friend: "I assure you that to stand alone in a small society like this, and to cut the Secretary of State for Foreign Affairs, without doing it offensively or with ill-breeding, requires not only some courage but some skill."[17]

The Adams spent their winters in Washington where Henry continued his research and writing, and Clover pursued her passion for photography. During the summers, the Adams stayed at their Beverly Farms home in Massachusetts. In February 1883, Adams and his friend, John Hay, decided to build permanent homes in Washington, after purchasing the lots next door to the Slidell House on Lafayette Square.

After Adams left the Slidell House, three different residents were listed as living there, before the turn of the century. In 1889,Walter Abbott Wood occupied the house for a year, though his occupation was not listed in the city directory. Ten years earlier, Wood had lived nearby on I Street, NW, when served two terms in Congress. In the interim years, Wood had returned to his home in New York. He was an inventor and manufacturer whose company produced reapers, mowers, and binders. Wood's company was so successful in the United States that he began selling his machines in Europe and greatly enlarged his business, prior to returning to Washington.

Daniel Scott Lamont, President Cleveland's secretary of war, was the next resident of the Slidell House in 1893. Cleveland and Lamont met and became friends, while Lamont was working for the *Albany Argus* newspaper covering Cleveland's campaign for the governorship of New York. When Cleveland was elected governor, he asked Lamont to be his private secretary. In 1885, when Cleveland was elected president, he asked Lamont to accompany him to Washington and appointed him to serve as a cabinet official.

Lamont's business interests involved financing street railroad systems (streetcars) and, his business was prospering in 1893, when President Cleveland asked him to be secretary of war. In 1897, Lamont retired from public life and served as vice-president of the Northern Pacific Railway Company. In the last years of his life, he became a very successful businessman. Lamont is credited with inventing the phrase "A public office is a public trust."

During the Spanish-American War in 1898, President McKinley's secretary of war, Russell Alger, moved into the Slidell House. Fifteen years earlier, in 1883, Alger had been elected to serve as governor of Michigan. Alger was an astute Michigan businessman who made his fortune in the lumber industry. However, Alger's mishandling of the War Department during the Spanish-American War caused McKinley to ask for his resignation. Several years later, Alger returned to Washington, when he was appointed to fill the Senate seat left vacant by the death of Senator James McMillan of Michigan and he was re-elected to the Senate when that term expired.

Hay & Adams Houses — the first story —
16th and H Streets, NW — northwest corner

When Henry and Clover Adams were living at the Slidell House, they were appalled to learn that the lots next door to them were sold to Frederick H. Paine, who wanted to construct an apartment building on the property.

Adams' good friend, John Hay, had recently become a millionaire through an inheritance from his father-in-law, Amasa Stone. Adams wrote to Hay, proposing the possibility of purchasing the Lafayette Square lots from Paine and building homes for themselves: "I need not say how eager I am to spend your money to have you next door. I would sacrifice your last dollar for such an object."[18] In December 1883, John Hay purchased the lots, providing Paine with a huge, quick profit.

Adams contacted his former Harvard classmate, the successful architect H. H. Richardson, to design his and Hay's new homes. Richardson had just completed designing Nicholas Anderson's home near Lafayette Square on K Street, NW. Richardson was an enormous man whose tremendous size was said to be a result of a chronic kidney disease combined with a huge appetite. He weighed 345 pounds, by the time he was working with Hay and Adams. "Richardsonian Romanesque" was the nickname applied to the style of his buildings and it was imitated in cities across the United States. Richardson's architectural style was likened to his rotund physique: it was monumental, masculine, and massive in scale.

The Hay and Adams houses were built of specially molded, elongated red bricks and the fronts of the homes were ornamented with a lighter colored, decoratively carved sandstone. Hay's home was larger than Adams' house, measuring 99-feet wide by 54-feet deep, with a front door facing 16th Street. Adams' house faced H Street and measured a more modest 45-feet wide by 48-feet deep.

In April 1885, Clover Adams' father, Dr. Robert Hooper, died. Clover was devastated. Nonetheless, she was determined not to openly mourn and as a result, she slipped into a depression that became overwhelming. Clover and Henry traveled during the summer of 1885, before settling at Beverly Farms, Massachusetts. By late fall, they were back in Washington, but Clover was still suffering from a serious depression. On the morning of December 6, Henry found Clover dying from ingesting a fatal dosage of a photographic chemical, potassium cyanide. Adams was overwhelmed with grief but, like Clover, he refused to outwardly show his feelings. Within three weeks Adams moved into his new home, determined to start a fresh life. Although Hay's home was not yet completed, Hay decided to move in, to provide companionship for Adams.

John Hay had been anxious to return to Washington and the intellectual climate of the East Coast. He had spent the Civil War years working in the capital city, as close to the center of power as one could get. Hay had first come to Washington in 1861 from Springfield, Illinois, where he had been working as a lawyer. While in Springfield, he was introduced to President-elect Lincoln through a mutual friend, John Nicolay. Lincoln was impressed by Hay and asked him to serve as his private secretary. Hay was a great admirer of Lincoln and years later, when Hay lived in the house on Lafayette Square, he completed writing his famous ten-volume biography documenting Lincoln's life.

After the war, Hay served as secretary to the legations in Paris, Vienna, and Spain and later, he became a journalist with the *New York Tribune*. In 1874, he married Clara Stone, the daughter of the Cleveland industrialist, Amasa Stone. The long hours Hay devoted to writing took its toll on his health, so he quit journalism and joined his father-in-law's business. Hay moved to Cleveland where he continued lived, on and off, for ten years, from 1875-85.

Although Hay turned down several political appointments after moving to Washington, he accepted President William McKinley's request to serve as ambassador to Great Britain in 1897. During the 1898 Spanish-American War, Ambassador Hay won British support for the United States' cause. Hay detested war and satirically branded the Spanish-American War with a moniker that was often misinterpreted a genuine sentiment. He called it, that "splendid little war."

In 1898, Hay became McKinley's secretary of state. His negotiations with China established the "Open Door" policy. Hay signed the Hay-Pauncefote treaty with Britain, allowing the United States to construct the Panama Canal. Hay also served as Roosevelt's secretary of state, but his poor health caused him to cut back on his duties. In 1905, Hay went to Europe hoping to find a cure for his ailments. His stay was brief and he died soon after his return to the U.S.

Henry Adams' life was very different from the life of John Hay. After college, Adams traveled through Europe where he visited Italy, met Garibaldi, and published his impressions of their encounter in the *Boston Courier*. His father, Charles Francis Adams who was a representative in Congress, asked Henry to serve as his secretary in Washington. Later, when his father was appointed minister to Great Britain in 1860, he asked Henry to serve as his secretary in London, thus allowing him to spend the Civil War years in Europe.

When Adams moved to Washington after the Civil War, he despised the atmosphere created by President Grant's administration, so he returned to Massachusetts. For seven years, he worked as an assistant professor of history at Harvard (a career he did not enjoy). His marriage to Marian (Clover) Hooper, in 1872, pleasantly transformed his life. Henry and Clover traveled extensively through Europe and North Africa before they moved to Washington in 1877. Adams chose to remain in Washington for the rest of his life.

In 1885, after Adams settled into his new home following the sudden death of his wife, he decided to travel outside the United States for a while in search of a sense of inner peace. He spent a year traveling in the Orient before returning to the United States in 1886. Adams was unsure whether or not to remain in Washington until his dear friend across Lafayette Square, Lizzie Cameron, encouraged him to stay. Lizzie often urged Henry to dine with her and her family, and gradually, she coaxed him back into society. Adams and Lizzie remained close friends for the rest of his life.

Adams renewed his old friendships and opened his home to any friends who would join him for his famous late breakfasts. At these breakfasts, Adams made two requests: he required his guests to invite themselves and he allowed his friends to bring other friends if they were not boring. Adams' house became "the haunt of all the most charming women going."[19] Included among his friends were many young people whom he regarded as nieces and nephews and, who referred to him as "Uncle Henry."

Adams spent his time traveling, observing, and writing. He finished his nine-volume *History of the United States* in 1890. Adams later wrote *Mont-Saint-Michel* and *Chartres*, followed by the book he claimed was not an autobiography, entitled, *The Education of Henry Adams*. Henry Adams had booked passage to Europe, for April 20, 1912, aboard the new English oceanliner, *Titanic*. Upon hearing the news of April 14, that the ship sank on its maiden voyage from Europe to America, six days before he was to have sailed, Adams suffered a mild stroke.

By the fall of 1912, Adams had recovered from his stroke. For six more years he lived in his home on Lafayette Square, until his death in 1918. The chaos of The Great War (World War I), however, overwhelmed him. Adams despised war. Just before he died, he heard about the "Big Bertha," a new weapon developed by Germany that was capable of firing bombshells from a distance of seventy-five miles. He was outraged by the weapon's destructive capability. He commented to a friend, "Life has become intolerable. This is no world for an old man to live in when the Germans can shoot to the moon."[20]

Henry Adams was buried in Washington's Rock Creek Cemetery, next to his wife Clover. Their graves are not marked with words, but rather with the most famous funeral sculpture in the United States, which Adams had commissioned as a memorial to his wife. The sculpture, by Augustus Saint Gaudens, is called "Peace." Adams' friend, John Hay, had first visited the memorial in March 1891. Hay described his impressions to Adams in a letter, saying, the statue represents "a past without beginning, and a future without end; a repose, after limitless experience; a peace, to which nothing matters."[21]

Decatur House — *the continuing story* —
748 Jackson Place, NW

At the close of the Civil War, General Edward Fitzgerald Beale purchased Decatur House to use as his Washington residence. After years of abuse by the military during the war, Decatur House required extensive renovation, which included replacing some of the floors. Gradually, the lovely old federal-style house took on the fashionable Victorian look of the times.

General Beale was born in Washington and, from a young age, wanted to join the navy. His maternal grandfather was Commodore Thomas Truxton, a hero of the first American naval force. When he was fourteen years old, Beale was awarded a naval appointment by President Andrew Jackson. During the Mexican War, Beale and Kit Carson, assisted in the rescue of General Philip Kearny, when Kearny's troops were surrounded at Santa Fe. Beale and Carson traveled from Santa Fe, across enemy territory to San Diego, in order to secure aid from Commodore Robert F. Stockton. The two men were awarded the privilege of traveling to Washington with the news that California had been conquered. Four-months later, after surviving several dangerous adventures on their cross-country journey, Beale and Carson arrived safely in the Capital City.

Beale returned to California aboard the ship *Ohio,* in 1848. Soon after he arrived, he was chosen to go back across the United States with the news of the discovery of gold. A race across the continent was arranged, between the army and, the navy (represented by Beale). Each wanted to arrive first in Washington with the exciting news. Beale's journey, dubbed the "Gold Dust Derby," took him to Mexico City, where he met Ulysses S. Grant. This meeting was the beginning of a lifelong friendship. Beale traveled to Veracruz, from Mexico City. He then sailed to Mobile, Alabama and secured passage on a stagecoach, for the balance of the journey that would cover 4,000 miles. He finished in a record-breaking, forty-seven days. As proof of the discovery, Beale brought a vile of gold dust to Washington. The gold was divided in half. Half of the gold was donated to the U.S. Patent Office. The remainder was made into a wedding ring for Beale's fiancé, Mary E. Edwards, the daughter of Representative Samuel Edwards. Edward and Mary were married in June 1849.

In 1851, Beale and his new wife traveled to California. Beale had been appointed the Superintendent of Indian Affairs. He believed in the rights of the Native American Indians and tried to protect them from ruthless attacks. In 1857, Beale purchased land in California and established a ranch that he named *Tejon Ranchero*. He described it as "having considerable grass and wild game, but not a single human being . . . At Elizabeth Lake the ducks and geese were so thick that I killed three ducks with one shot of my rifle. . . . I bought this forty thousand acre tract and started to raise cattle. In those days my nearest neighbors were at Visalia on one side and at Los Angeles on the other."[22]

Beale had an idea for transporting supplies to the newly established army forts in the Southwest territory. Having read about the heartiness of camels in the desert, Beale suggested that Secretary of War Jefferson Davis authorize the purchase of camels for pack animals. Seventy-seven camels were brought from Smyrna, Egypt, and Tunis by Commodore David D. Porter, in two trips. In 1857, Beale convoyed the camels from Texas to California. However, the army troops neglected and abused the animals. With the outbreak of the Civil War, all army efforts in the Southwest were suspended and the camels were sold or set free. Beale bought a few of the camels for his California ranch. During the war, Beale volunteered for active duty, however, President Lincoln requested that he remain in California to help keep the West loyal to the Union.

When Beale moved back to Washington, he renewed his friendship with the newly elected president, Ulysses S. Grant. The Beales entertained President Grant often at Decatur House. Grant's visits were known to extend late into the evening. Likewise, the Beales were often invited to the White House. In 1876, Grant appointed Beale to be minister to Austria-Hungary, an enviable position. After a year of diplomatic service, Beale returned to Washington.

When President Grant left Washington after his second term, he traveled extensively throughout Europe, corresponding regularly with Beale. Upon his return, Grant and his wife stayed with the Beales at Decatur House for several weeks. During one of Grant's later visits, in 1884, Decatur House became a place of reconciliation between Grant and James G. Blaine (Beale's Lafayette Square neighbor). For years, Grant and Blaine had maintained a personal feud that threatened to split the Republican Party. Beale brought the two men together and acted as a mediator to smooth over the difficulties, which resulted in reuniting the Republican Party. In 1893, Edward Beale died. His wife, Mary (who died in 1903) and, his son, Truxton Beale, inherited Decatur House.

Marcy House — the continuing story —
736 Jackson Place, NW

James G. Blaine occupied the Marcy House for a year, from 1883 to 1884. During his many years of public service in Washington, Blaine lived in several homes on and near Lafayette Square. Colonel William L. Scott was the next tenant to lease the Marcy House. His daughter, Mary Scott Townsend, her husband, Richard H. Townsend, and their daughter, Mathilde, also resided in the house with Colonel Scott. Richard Townsend was the president of the Pittsburgh and Lake Erie Railroad. Richard, Mary, and Mathilde remained in the Marcy House for several years while their new home was being constructed at 2121 Massachusetts Avenue, NW. The Townsend's palatial, new mansion was built around the old Hillyer residence because of Mary's childhood superstition that, she would experience terrible misfortune, if she were ever to live in an entirely new house.

Richard Townsend came to Washington to retire with the fortune he had made in his railroad business. In 1900, the family moved into their new home, where Mary Townsend entertained in a grand style. A year later, Richard fell from a horse, fractured his skull, and died. His widow, Mary, continued to live in the house and entertain lavishly, for many more years. The expenses for her gala social events often exceeded $240,000 a year (including expenditures for the servants' salaries, household maintenance, florists, and food). When Mary died, Mathilde inherited an enormous fortune, along with the Massachusetts Avenue mansion. In 1925, Mathilde had obtained a divorce from her first husband, Senator Peter Goelet Gerry of Rhode Island. She then married her second husband, Sumner Wells, and moved back into the mansion. President Franklin Roosevelt appointed Wells to be under-secretary of state. Mathilde was said to be the richest woman in Washington, in her time. After her death, the Cosmos Club purchased the home.

Jackson Place Row Houses – the continuing story –

700 - 734 Jackson Place, NW — (formerly 2 - 20 Lafayette Square)

In 1880, Charles Carroll Glover, Sr. built the house at 734 Jackson Place (formerly #20). Thirty years earlier in 1850, when Glover was only four years old, he had been sent from North Carolina to live in Washington, after his father died. He lived at 1331-33 F Street (once the home of John Quincy Adams), with his grandmother, grand-aunt and grand-uncle. Glover's grand-uncle was a bookkeeper with the Riggs Bank and, in 1872, Glover began working as a teller at Riggs. Two years later he became a cashier. He was a dedicated worker and proved to be an astute banker. Glover revolutionized the bank's methods of conducting business, and doubled the deposits at Riggs within a few years. He worked his way up to becoming a partner in the banking firm and, in 1894, he was named president of Riggs Bank.

In 1878, Charles Glover married Annie Cunningham Poor, the daughter of Rear Admiral Charles H. Poor. Glover then built his new home for himself and his bride, in the center of what he felt was the best section of the city, Lafayette Square. Charles and Annie respected and collected fine art. They filled their elegant new home with wonderful paintings and sculpture.

In 1887, Glover's appreciation of art led to his appointment as a trustee of the Corcoran Gallery of Art. He later served as treasurer, vice president, and then president of the Corcoran. In the 1890s, he was responsible for choosing the site for the Corcoran Gallery of Art's new building, on the southwest corner of 17th Street and New York Avenue, NW.

Glover supported Senator William Andrew Clark's idea of establishing the William A. Clark prize, to be awarded during the Corcoran Gallery's "Biennial Exhibitions." Clark later bequeathed his eclectic, personal art collection to the Corcoran Gallery. Glover also inspired and influenced his two friends, Charles Lang Freer and Andrew W. Mellon. Both men donated their art collections to the people of the United States and, they established and endowed galleries in Washington to house their fabulous collections. With Glover's encouragement, Henry Clay Folger, established the Folger Shakespeare Library, on Capitol Hill. Folger donated his remarkable Shakespearean rare books and memorabilia collection, including his numerous first folios, to this library.

Glover's love for the city of Washington was legendary. He struggled for nearly a quarter of a century to save Rock Creek Park from development. In 1888, he suggested a plan to designate 1,750 acres of parkland in the city for recreational use. Glover personally donated an eighty-acre tract of land to the city, between N Street and Massachusetts Avenue, NW, which became part of the Glover-Archibald Park, further expanding Washington's park system. He also donated land that would become part of the National Cathedral grounds.

Glover's efforts to improve Washington brought the top community leaders to his Lafayette Square home, where they discussed and tried to solve civic problems. Glover's close friend, Crosby Noyes, who was the editor of the *Washington Star,* came to listen to, as well as discuss and report on, these civic concerns. John Clagett Proctor, a Washington historian, noted, "Of the many spoken and written tributes that have been given to Mr. Glover as a representative of the ideal citizen, one of the finest was that uttered by the late Theodore Roosevelt, President of the United States, who termed him: 'A man whose name has always been a synonym for all that is honorable, and high minded, and patriotic.'"[23]

William J. Murtaugh, a newspaper editor, occupied the house to the south of Glover's home, at 730 Jackson Place (formerly #18). Murtaugh's newspaper, the *National Republican*, heartily supported Abraham Lincoln for the presidency during his campaign. General Frank Steele was a later occupant of the home, at the end of the 19th century. The row house next door, at 726 Jackson Place (formerly #16), between the Murtaugh residence and the Ewell House (722 Jackson Place), was the home of General J. G. Parke. Parke was a Civil War hero, who had served as the superintendent of West Point.

The two houses south of the Ewell House, at 718 and 716 Jackson Place (formerly #12 and #10), belonged to Mrs. Mary Jessup Blair for many years. Mary Jessup Blair was the daughter of General Thomas Sidney Jessup. Her husband, James Blair, was a son of Francis Preston Blair. As a naval officer, James Blair accompanied Admiral Charles Wilkes on his famous Antarctic Expedition of 1838-1841. After resigning from the navy, Blair's adventurous spirit led him to California in 1849, where he developed a successful steamboat transportation business that made him a very wealthy man.

Unfortunately, James Blair died young. In the 1860s, his widow, Mary, moved into the house she built at 718 Jackson Place. She resided until her death. Her daughter, Violet Blair Janin, continued to reside there well into the 20th century. The row house next door, at 716 Jackson Place, was smaller and less elegant. Mrs. James Blair had it built as an investment property. She leased this rental property over the years to many interesting individuals, including Senator Arthur P. Gorman and George F. Appleby.

The house south of Mrs. Blair's rental property, at 712 Jackson Place (formerly #8), had been leased by Major Henry Rathbone, who accompanied the Lincolns to Ford's Theater on the night of Lincoln's assassination. In the late 1860s, after Rathbone moved out, the house was leased to Admiral Alden. Nicholas Longworth Anderson and his wife later leased 712 Jackson Place. They were living in the house in 1879, while their new home, which was designed by H. H. Richardson, was being built nearby, on 16th Street, NW.

Nicholas Longworth Anderson grew up in Cincinnati. He served in the Civil War and rose to the rank of major general at the age of twenty-six, making him the youngest major general in the army. Anderson's maternal grandfather, Nicholas Longworth, I, was called "the first millionaire in the West" because of his extensive real estate holdings in the Western states. Longworth's grandson (Anderson's first cousin once removed) served for many years as Speaker of the House of Representatives. He was Nicholas Longworth, III, who became President Theodore Roosevelt's son-in-law, when he married Roosevelt's oldest daughter, Alice.

Anderson and his wife were wealthy and sophisticated. They entertained generously while they lived in the Jackson Place Row House. H. H. Richardson stayed with the Andersons at 712 Jackson Place, during the last months of the construction of their new 16th Street home. Richardson evidently caused Mrs. Anderson some frustration, because she wrote to her son, Lars, complaining that she "found him [Richardson] to be a great deal of trouble. He bullies and nags everybody."[24]

In 1905, the Anderson's son, Lars, built a fifty-room mansion across from the Townsend House at 2118 Massachusetts Avenue, NW. Lars was a career diplomat who served as U.S. ambassador to Belgium and Japan. His great-grandfather was Colonel Richard Clough Anderson, a Revolutionary War officer and founding member of the first military beneficial society, called the Society of the Cincinnati. Society membership is inherited. Lars Anderson, who inherited his membership, designed his house so that it would be used as the headquarters for the Society of the Cincinnati, after his death.

At the southern most end of the Jackson Place Row Houses are two homes, 700 and 704 Jackson Place (formerly #2 and #4), which were combined in the

1890s and used by the International Bureau of American Republics, later named the Pan American Union. The bureau's first president, William E. Curtis, resided at the corner house, (700 Jackson Place). Curtis was a newspaper correspondent on the staff of the *Chicago Record-Herald.*

Andrew Carnegie was a participant in the first International Conference of the American Republics, which was held in Washington due to the efforts of Secretary of State James G. Blaine. Carnegie purchased the two houses on Lafayette Square, so that the bureau could have its offices in a prominent Washington location. A decade later, Carnegie gave the money to build a new headquarters building for the Pan American Union, on the property where the old Van Ness House stood (at 17th Street and Constitution Avenue, NW). The conversion of these two Lafayette Square private residences into an office building started a trend. Gradually, one by one, the Jackson Place Row Houses were transformed from residential to commercial use.

Blair House — the continuing story —

1651 Pennsylvania Avenue, NW

Montgomery Blair continued to live and entertain in the Blair House after the Civil War ended. He and his wife renewed their old friendships with Southern leaders. The Blair family gave their support to President Johnson's lenient reconstruction policy. However, as the Radical Republicans gained more power in the Congress, the Blairs abandoned their Republican affiliation and supported the Democrats. Blair's younger brother, General Frank Blair, returned to Washington in 1867, when he was elected as the Democratic senator from Missouri. In 1868, Frank Blair was the Democratic vice presidential running mate to presidential candidate Horatio Seymour, however, they lost the election to Ulysses S. Grant. In 1873, Frank Blair was stricken with paralysis and he died two years later, at the age of fifty-four. The next year, Frank's father, Francis Preston Blair, died. Frank Blair was a hero to Missourians because he saved the federal arsenal at St. Louis for the Union, during the Civil War. The Missouri state legislature voted to send his statue to the Capitol for display in National Statuary Hall.

In the presidential election of 1876, Montgomery Blair supported the Democratic candidate, Samuel J. Tilden, over Rutherford B. Hayes. The election result, which gave neither candidate a true victory, was challenged and eventually decided by a special commission in favor of Hayes. Montgomery Blair never accepted the outcome of the election and refused a political appointment offered by Hayes, because he felt Hayes was not the legal president. Blair lost prestige in Washington over his moral stand on the issue of the legality of the presidency. Montgomery Blair died in 1883. His widow, Elizabeth Woodbury Blair, continued to live in the Blair House, often sharing it with members of the next generation of Blairs. However, for the rest of the 19th century, no Blair family members participated directly in the politics of the day.

Grover Cleveland, the 22nd & 24th President, 1885-1889 & 1893-1897

Grover Cleveland was the first Democrat to be elected to the presidency since Buchanan's administration in the late 1850s. Cleveland, a self-made man, was one of nine children whose father was a Presbyterian minister. He studied to be a lawyer and later, served as mayor of Buffalo, New York. In 1881, he was elected to serve as the governor of New York.

Cleveland was independent, courageous, and honest. His reputation as a reformer led the Democrats to choose him as their presidential candidate, in 1884, to oppose the Republican candidate, James G. Blaine. During the presidential campaign, the Republicans learned that Cleveland had been supporting an illegitimate child. When the accusation was made public, Cleveland admitted to it and told his campaign workers to "tell the truth." The Republicans also criticized Cleveland for having paid three hundred dollars rather than being drafted during the Civil War, which was common policy. He avoided military service so he could work and support his mother and younger siblings. The Democrats soon learned, however, that James G. Blaine had done the same thing. Cleveland won the presidential election by a small majority.

During his first year in office, Cleveland enacted the Civil Service Act, which placed government jobs on a merit system of hiring, rather than patronage. During his second year in office, he created a sensation by marrying Frances Folsom. Cleveland was the first bachelor president in office since Buchanan and, the first to have a White House wedding. Cleveland had known Frances all her life. She was the daughter of Cleveland's close friend, Oscar Folsom, who died when Frances was just a small child. Before he died, Folsom had asked Cleveland be his child's legal guardian.

Like earlier first ladies, Frances set the trend in fashion and entertaining. She was greatly admired for her public receptions, which she held in the evenings and Saturdays so that working women could attend. Public curiosity about the newlyweds became so overwhelming that the Clevelands rented a second residence, located above Georgetown called Red Top, which they used mostly in the summer. The neighborhood surrounding their summer home was later named Cleveland Park, in honor of President Cleveland.

When Cleveland left Washington in 1889, after losing the presidential election to Benjamin Harrison, he and Frances vowed they would return. In the 1892 presidential election rematch, Cleveland won over Harrison by a large number of electoral votes. When Cleveland was inaugurated for the second time, the country was in a state of economic panic. Five hundred banks had failed, numerous businesses were bankrupt, and unemployment was soaring.

Cleveland attributed the distressing financial situation to inflation caused by the Sherman Silver Purchase Act of 1890. The Silver Act required the U.S. Treasury to purchase 4.5 million ounces of silver a month at market value, causing a near depletion of the Treasury's gold reserves. Silver was overvalued and Cleveland convinced Congress to repeal the Silver Act and reestablish the gold standard. Unfortunately, this did not solve the problem, which was much more complex and, Cleveland was blamed for a situation he had inherited.

The annexation of Hawaii was a controversial issue during Cleveland's second term. A revolution in the Hawaiian Islands by non-Hawaiians under the leadership of Stanford B. Dole, led to the overthrow of Hawaiian Queen Liliuokalani. Dole, who had significant business interests in Hawaii, set up a provisional government, gained protection from 300 U.S. Marines stationed in Honolulu's harbor aboard the cruiser Boston, and asked the United States government to annex the islands. Queen Liliuokalani protested to President Cleveland, who believed the annexation treaty to be unfair and withdrew it.

Happiness filled the White House with the birth of Cleveland's second daughter Ester, the first child of a president to be born in the White House. His first daughter, Ruth, (for whom the Baby Ruth candy bar was named) was born in 1891, between Cleveland's two non-consecutive terms. Another daughter, Marion, was born in the White House, and two sons, Richard and Francis Grover, were born in 1897 and 1903. Frances Cleveland entertained less frequently in the White House after the children were born.

In 1889, the Clevelands retired to Princeton, New Jersey, where Grover Cleveland lectured and wrote articles and books. The board of trustees of Princeton University appointed him to be a board member and, in 1904, he was elected president of the board. At the same time, Woodrow Wilson was serving as president of Princeton University. Grover Cleveland died of a heart attack, in 1908. Frances remarried several years later. Her second husband, Thomas J. Preston, Jr., was an archaeology professor. Frances died in 1947 and, she was buried with her first husband, Grover Cleveland, in Princeton, New Jersey.

Benjamin Harrison, the 23rd President, 1889-1893

Benjamin Harrison was one of ten children who descended from men active in public service. His great-grandfather was a signer of the Declaration of Independence. His grandfather, William Henry Harrison, was elected president when Benjamin was only seven years old, but died after only one month in office.

While attending school in Ohio, Benjamin Harrison chose to study law. After school, he moved to Indianapolis and started a very successful law partnership. During the Civil War, Harrison commanded a regiment that guarded the railroads and, he later joined the Sherman's Atlanta campaign. He was a strict, military disciplinarian and unpopular with his men, but through their successes in battle, Harrison earned a promotion to brigadier general.

After the war, Harrison became one of the most popular men in the state of Indiana because of his war reputation, legal skills, and speeches in favor of the Republican Party. In 1881, Harrison was elected to the U.S. Senate from Indiana. Six years later, the Democrats had gained control of the state legislature and he was not reelected. However, in 1888, Harrison received the Republican presidential nomination. When he won the election, both houses of Congress were controlled by Republicans, which helped make his presidential term successful. He easily persuaded Congress to pass the Sherman Silver Purchase Act, which was repealed by Cleveland four years later.

Harrison raised tariffs to help protect U.S. industry, resulting in rising costs for consumer products and inflation. Although Harrison's economic policies were disastrous, he enjoyed a measure of success with his foreign policy through James G. Blaine, his secretary of state. Blaine presided over the 1889 Pan American Conference in Washington, which led to the establishment of the Pan American Union.

Harrison's wife Caroline was well educated. She met Benjamin when they were both students at Farmer's College in Cincinnati. After completing their educations, they were married military four years later, in 1853. Caroline was a cheerful person who was artistically talented and musically inclined. Rather than developing her own talents, however, she gave much of her time to assisting her husband in his civic endeavors.

When the Harrison's moved into the White House, Caroline had great hopes of renovating the executive residence. She presented three different remodeling plans for congressional approval, but Congress appropriated only enough money for paint and minor repairs. Caroline was responsible for having electricity installed in the White House for the first time, but was horribly afraid of it. She is credited with designing her own White House china pattern and, she started the White House china collection by bringing together pieces of china from earlier administrations.

During the Harrison's second presidential campaign in 1892, Caroline became seriously ill with recurring attacks of tuberculosis. She was so sick that Harrison refused to actively campaign. Consequently Cleveland, out of respect for Caroline, also declined to campaign. Caroline died two weeks before the election.

In March of 1893, Benjamin Harrison accompanied Grover Cleveland to the inaugural ceremonies, just as Cleveland had accompanied Harrison four years before. After leaving Washington, Harrison returned to his law practice in Indianapolis. Three years later, he married his wife's niece, Mary, and they had one child who was born when Harrison was sixty-three years old. Harrison and Mary toured Europe in 1899 and 1900. Not long after their return, Harrison contracted pneumonia and died in 1901.

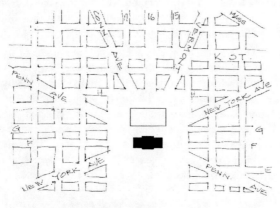

Lafayette Square — *the continuing story* —

During the Civil War because, just as during the War of 1812, Lafayette Square served as a mustering place for the military troops protecting the White House. The soldiers who camped in the park cut down all the trees for firewood and irreverently hung their clothes to dry on the fences and on the equestrian statue of Andrew Jackson.

Beginning in 1871, the city parks throughout Washington were improved under the new territorial government and, through the leadership of Alexander Robey Shepherd. Congress appropriated funds for landscaping Lafayette Park, in 1872. Flowers were planted and W. W. Corcoran donated ornamental foliage and decorative palms to beautify the park. Various animals, many of which were gifts to the United States by foreign ministers, were caged and displayed in Washington's parks, many years before the National Zoological Park was established. A pair of caged prairie dogs became an attraction when they were displayed in the center of Lafayette Square.

Two bronze urns, each about seven feet tall and cast at the foundry of the Washington Navy Yard, were placed on granite pedestals in Lafayette Square and filled with flowers. Gas and water connections were brought to Lafayette Square in 1872, when eight lampposts were installed (two of which also had drinking fountains). Electric lights replaced all but two of the gaslights in 1896. The two old lampposts that remained were the combination units with gaslights and drinking fountains.

The park was enhanced by other amenities. Walkways were laid out in gravel and then later were replaced, in 1888, with smooth asphalt. Congress appropriated money to purchase and install park benches in Lafayette Square, because it was the most popular park in Washington. In 1856, the first twelve settees were placed in Lafayette Square. Ten more were added in 1875 and by 1887, there were 172 settees in the park.

Another improvement to the park was the addition of a lodge building used by the watchman on duty in Lafayette Square, during the evening hours. One room of the lodge was designed for the storage of tools. Two restroom facilities were added to the lodge: one with accommodations for gentlemen and a second for nurses caring for young children. The lodge stood on the north side of the park, partly shielded from view by tall evergreens.

In the late 1880s, a decision was made to place a statue of the Marquis de Lafayette, in the park. At that time, the iron fence that had been placed around the park when the Jackson statue was erected in 1853 was finally removed in 1888 to make the park more accessible to the public. The fence was taken to Gettysburg, Pennsylvania and installed at Culp's Hill on the Gettysburg Battlefield. The Seneca sandstone footing piers for the fence were covered over and forgotten until October 1999 when they were accidentally rediscovered by a work crew installing a new security fence. The historic piers were removed and taken to the site of the original Seneca stone quarry in Maryland.

Marquis de Lafayette Statue — a story —

Lafayette Square — southeast corner

In 1891, a monument was dedicated, in Lafayette Square, to General Marie Jean Paul Roch Yves Gilbert du Motier, the Marquis de Lafayette (his fellow officers called him "Gil"). In 1777, at the age of nineteen, Lafayette set sail for America from France in defiance of King Louis XVI. He had outfitted his own ship, *La Victoire*, and his mission was to assist the Americans in their fight for independence. Lafayette was appointed major general in the Continental Army and he served as an aide-de-camp to George Washington at Valley Forge.

Upon his return to France in 1778, Lafayette persuaded Louis XVI to send French troops and officers to aid the Americans. Among the great French military leaders who came to America were Major General Comte Jean Rochambeau and Comte François de Grasse. During the war years, Lafayette returned to serve with the American military and, he invested $200,000 of his personal fortune to help the war effort. (Forty years after the war's end, in 1824, Congress repaid him.) Lafayette is credited with maneuvering British Lord Cornwallis into a position of surrender at Yorktown, thereby significantly contributing to the Revolutionary War victory.

Congress appropriated money for the monument to Lafayette and awarded the sculptural contract to a French firm. The artists who created Lafayette's statue were Jean Alexandre Joseph Falquière and Marius Jean Antonin Mercié. A site for the statue was chosen directly across Pennsylvania Avenue from the White House. In March 1890, work on the foundation for the monument began.

The statue's pedestal was erected due south of the Jackson statue at the park's edge, in direct line with the White House. This blocked the view of Jackson's monument from the White House. There was even talk of removing the Jackson statue, but to do so required an act of Congress.

The site for the Lafayette statue was so controversial that, after the bronze pieces of the statue arrived from France, they were put in storage in the Senate stables while discussions continued concerning the statue's placement. For months, the pedestal stood without a statue. Several new locations were considered for the Lafayette statue, including the west lawn of the Capitol, south lawn of the White House, and southeast lawn of the Treasury Department. Finally, in December 1890, a site was chosen at the southeast corner of Lafayette Square. Transferring the stones of the pedestal proved difficult because they had been well anchored into the first location, in front of Jackson's statue.

On April 6, 1891, the erection of the Lafayette statue was completed. There was no official dedication ceremony because the statue was not a gift of the French government. The statue was authorized, as stated in the inscription on the north face of the pedestal, "By Congress, in commemoration of the services rendered by General Lafayette and his compatriots during the struggle for the independence of the United States of America."

The statue portrays Lafayette petitioning the French National Assembly to send aid to the Americans. Below the statue, on the south face of the base, is a female figure representing *America* offering a sword to Lafayette. On the east face of the pedestal are two portrait statues in bronze of Comte d'Estaing and Comte de Grasse, with an anchor representing the French Navy. On the west face of the pedestal are two portrait statues in bronze of Comte de Rochambeau and the Chevalier du Portail, with a cannon representing the French Army. The Lafayette Statue has been described as "not a portrait but a gallery."[25]

Dolley Madison House — the continuing story —

1520 H Street, NW

Admiral Wilkes' widow, Mary Wilkes, leased the Dolley Madison House until 1884, when she began the negotiations to sell the house to a new scientific club in Washington. Major John Wesley Powell had started the club in November 1878. Powell drew upon the intellectual elite in Washington for the club's membership. Among the club's founders were Henry Adams, Clarence King, Spencer Baird, and Edward Gallaudet. Powell sent a circular to various individuals who were proposed as possible candidates for membership, stating, "The Scientific Club of Washington" is to be composed of "men, devoted to or interested in science, professionally or otherwise."[26] He later expanded this idea, further defining it as a scientific and literary club "which unites the love of study and of books with the fellowship of men."[27]

At a meeting in December 1878, the club's name, *Cosmos Club*, was chosen. Although one member suggested using the Greek spelling *Kosmos*, the idea of then spelling "club" with a *K* for symmetry was rejected. The club was incorporated and the object of the association was stated as "the advancement of its members in science, literature, and art, their mutual improvement by social intercourse, the acquisition and maintenance of a library, and the collection and care of materials and appliances relating to the above objects."[28]

The Cosmos Club chose a prestigious location in which to meet during its first few years. In 1879, a suite of rooms was leased on the third floor of Corcoran's office building at 15th Street and Pennsylvania Avenue, NW, across from the Treasury building. In 1882, the club moved to an even more distinguished address on Lafayette Square. The Cosmos Club leased the Ingersoll House at 23 Madison Place, which was built in the late 1870s between the Tayloe House and the Dolley Madison House. The Ingersoll House was leased by the club for twenty-five years until the club's members were finally able to arrange for its purchase.

By 1884, the Cosmos Club needed more room for its growing membership and negotiations began for the purchase of the Dolley Madison House. The purchase was finalized in June 1886. A one-story assembly room was built on the lot south of the house facing Lafayette Square and, within a few years, two more stories were soon added to the assembly room. At the same time, the partial upper level of the Dolley Madison House was raised to a full story.

The National Geographic Society was an outgrowth of the Cosmos Club's membership. In January 1888, thirty-three gentlemen were invited to meet at the Cosmos Club to discuss "the advisability of organizing a society for the increase and diffusion of geographical knowledge."[29] Many exceptional men joined this group, including meteorologists, geographers, explorers, cartographers, naturalists, biologists, engineers, geodesists, and inventors. One member proudly described a few of his fellow members as being the "first explorers of the Grand Canyon and the Yellowstone, those who had carried the American flag farthest north, who had measured the altitude of our famous mountains, traced the windings of our coasts and rivers, determined the distribution of flora and fauna, enlightened us in the customs of the aborigines, and marked out the path of storm and flood."[30] A separate entrance for the National Geographic Society was added to the clubhouse in 1891 and numbered 1518 H Street, NW. The Cosmos Club continued to use the Dolley Madison House address of 1520 H Street, NW.

Ingersoll & Windom Houses —a story—
23 and 25 Madison Place, NW

In the late 1870s, two houses were erected on the lots between the Dolley Madison House and the Tayloe House. The two were similar in appearance, each three-stories tall with a gabled attic and built of brick. William Windom, the secretary of the Treasury during President Benjamin Harrison's administration, occupied the house closest to the Dolley Madison House, at 25 Madison Place.

Windom was from Minnesota and served in Congress from 1859 to 1869. In 1870, he was appointed to the Senate to fill a seat that had been vacated and, when his appointed term expired, he was reelected. In 1877, Windom had been considered as a presidential candidate for the Republican Party, but he lost the nomination to Hayes. In 1888, Windom resigned his Senate seat when President Garfield appointed him to serve as secretary of the treasury. However, after Garfield died and Chester Arthur became president, Windom resigned his cabinet appointment and returned to the Senate. In 1889, President Harrison appointed Windom, again, to the position of secretary of the treasury. Unfortunately, he did not live through Harrison's term. While in New York in 1891, after delivering a speech to the Chamber of Commerce, Windom became ill and died unexpectedly.

The house at 23 Madison Place, located between the Windom and Tayloe houses, was lived in briefly by Senator Reuben Fenton of New York. Colonel Robert G. Ingersoll next occupied the house, which for years afterwards, carried his name. Ingersoll was known as a great orator and ranked as "the most eloquent man who ever spoke from a public platform."[31] In 1876, Ingersoll gave the presidential nominating speech for James G. Blaine at the Republican convention, which, it was said, "literally froze the delegates in their seats, overcome with emotion."[32] In that speech, Ingersoll coined the nickname that Blaine carried with him the rest of his life, the "Plumed Knight of Navarre."

Ingersoll was a free thinker whom some labeled an atheist. His home was filled with books and sculpture. Oil paintings, engravings, photographs, and pictures of all sorts covered the walls. Ingersoll had a grandly bound volume of Shakespeare with blank pages in which to record important events in his family history. Inscribed in the volume were the birth dates of himself and his wife, their marriage date, and the birth dates of their two children. He spoke lovingly of this volume of Shakespeare, saying, "Here is all the religion I want . . . this is the family Bible."[33] During a lecture given by Ingersoll, he spoke glowingly of Shakespeare, saying, "Shakespeare was an intellectual ocean whose waves touched all the shores of thought."[34]

Corcoran Office Building — the first story —

15th Street between Pennsylvania Avenue and F Street, NW — east side

W. W. Corcoran developed a number of property lots near Lafayette Square, some of which were homes and others, commercial investments. One piece of prime real estate, which Corcoran purchased in the 1840s, was at the southeast corner of 15th and F Streets, NW, across from the Treasury Department. The federal-style row houses built in 1800 on the site were demolished in 1847, when Corcoran constructed a Greek Revival-style, forty-room, five-story office building.

In 1875, Corcoran razed the first office building and constructed a new one on the same site. Corcoran's personal offices were located in the new six-story building, which was twice the size of the building it replaced. In 1879, the Cosmos Club leased a portion of the building's third floor, for three years, before moving to Lafayette Square. The view from windows of Corcoran's building, which faced onto both Pennsylvania Avenue and 15th Street, made it one of the most sought after spots in the city for watching the inaugural parades.

Corcoran was a true patron of the arts and he leased many of the offices in his building to artists who used them for studios and classrooms. Washington art students delighted in having this wonderful location where they could study painting and drawing. One local painter, E. F. Andrews, leased space in Corcoran's building. He was later appointed as the art director for the new Corcoran School of Art, which was built behind the old Corcoran Gallery.

Freedman's Savings Bank — a story —
Pennsylvania Avenue and Madison Place, NW — northeast corner

In 1869, on the site where the Gunnell House once stood, a magnificent five-story building was erected for the Freedman's Savings Bank. Congress chartered the savings institution on January 27, 1865, for former slaves and their descendants. The bank's deposits were to be invested in "stocks, bonds, Treasury notes, or other securities of the United States."[35] No loans were to have been made and the depositors were to have been the owners of the assets.

The idea of a deposit bank for freedmen is credited to a Congregational minister, John W. Alvord, who served as a chaplain in Sherman's army. He believed that a permanent banking system could help former slaves advance in society and progress more easily from slavery to freedom. The bank would be operated strictly by and for freedmen. Alvord argued that such a bank would teach thrift and industry in this new community of Americans of African descent. He worked with Senator Charles Sumner, who sponsored the bill in Congress to incorporate the Freedman's Savings and Trust Company. Thirty-seven branch banks were eventually established, most of them in the South.

The first office of the Freedman's Bank in Washington was on Pennsylvania Avenue at 19th Street, NW. By 1869, the bank had purchased the Gunnell House and lot. The house was demolished and in its place was erected the most costly bank building in the city. The new Freedman's Savings Bank building was an extravagant, French Second Empire-style, brownstone structure with a mansard roof. The total cost of the lot and building was $260,000. The bank building was embellished inside with black walnut and marble. Depositors were given leather-covered bankbooks embossed with a likeness of Lincoln. Instructions in the bankbook told the depositor how to become rich on the interest earned on savings accounts. The bank eventually listed more than 70,000 depositors.

In 1870, the bank charter was amended to allow for the deposited money to be loaned, at the discretion of the trustees. One of the trustees, Henry D. Cooke, also served as president of the First National Bank. In 1871, Cooke was appointed as the first territorial governor of the District of Columbia. He aided his own bank by transferring poor securities from the First National Bank to the Freedman's Savings Bank. Cook also allowed the Freedman's Bank to loan huge sums of money to the District Government, collateralized only by worthless securities.

Mismanagement within the bank included poor bookkeeping practices, theft, and incompetence among the workers. In 1873, the United States was suffering from an economic depression and many banks nationwide were ruined. Frederick Douglass was elected as president of the Freedman's Savings Bank in March 1874, unaware of the bank's horrible financial situation. He invested $10,000 of his own savings in the bank and lost much of it when the bank failed. A year later, Douglass described his involvement with the Freedman's Bank, by comparing it to being "married to a corpse."

The Freedman's Savings Bank closed in June 1874. The Comptroller of the Currency, James J. Knox, pleaded with Congress to appropriate money to repay depositors in full, rather than paying them dividends on the assets, as they were sold. Unfortunately, this was but one of many bank failures across the nation. Special interest, however, was extended to repaying only those depositors of African descent; claims filed by Caucasian depositors were not accepted.

The average account at Freedman's Savings Bank was $47.50, though there were 15,000 accounts of $5.00 or less. After the bank's failure, its assets were turned into cash as quickly as possible. The first paid dividend was equal to 20 percent of what was owed. Notice of the dividend payment was published in newspapers and, word was spread through the churches, yet many people did not claim their dividends. A second dividend payment of 10 percent of the deposit amount was paid, and then a third payment of 10 percent, a fourth dividend payment of 15 percent, and a final dividend of 7 percent was made. A total of 62 percent of the amount owed was paid to each eligible depositor who came forth to claim the dividend.

The government purchased the beautiful bank building and used it as an office building for the newly created Department of Justice. The United States Circuit Courts were also housed in this building for a few years. In 1899, the once elegant Freedman's Savings Bank building was razed.

Chamberlain Club — the first story —
15th Street between H and I Streets, NW — east side

Washington hotels were described as a place where "the lobby man dines the Representative; the Representative dines the Senator; the Senator dines the charming widow, and the charming widow dines her coming man. . . . Dining played a great part in American politics."[36] Luxury hotels proliferated in

Washington in the latter part of 19th century. The Willard Hotel's reputation was based on the extravagant meals served to the guests. The Arlington Hotel employed one of the finest chefs in the country. Welcker's Hotel restaurant was internationally famous. Wormley's Hotel was the place to go for a quiet supper. The Chamberlain Club Hotel was said to have the best of everything. By the turn of the century, within five blocks of the White House were more than a dozen grand hotels catering to residents and visitors alike.

The Chamberlain Club, which was started in the late 1870s, was unique: "a mixture of hotel, club, saloon, home, restaurant, and banqueting hall. Gambling was a secondary consideration."[37] John Chamberlain had made a name for himself before he came to Washington. He had been the proprietor of many gambling houses, where stakes were high and everything was done on a grand scale. His glory days were over by the time he established his small hotel, just a few blocks northeast of the White House, at 1409 New York Avenue, NW. Chamberlain leased the building once used by the Washington City Club. Alexander Robey Shepherd had formed that club with a group of powerful businessmen, during the brief time that Washington was self-governed and Shepherd served as the city's territorial governor.

Washington fell under the spell of John Chamberlain and, the Washington City Club's building soon became known as the Chamberlain Club. His business was so good that he moved to a new location, in 1882, at the southeast corner of 15th and I Streets, NW, a little closer to Lafayette Square.

Chamberlain leased several fine row houses (821-825 15th Street, NW) on the east side of 15th south of I Street, NW. Samuel P. Brown, the founder of Washington's Mount Pleasant neighborhood, had built the row of houses in 1866, which filled most of the block. Brown's house, at 812 15th Street, became the meeting place for the local citizens, when they had gathered to draw up the 1871 Act of Congress establishing a tentative form of home-rule government for Washington. This house later belonged to James G. Blaine, whose three children were born there. James Garfield and Chester A. Arthur often visited Blaine in this house, as did Schuyler Colfax and William Seward.

Another of the houses, at 823 15th Street, NW, was the home of Fernando Woods of New York, who was one of the best known Democrats in Congress. Woods entertained liberally, hoping to influence the votes of Democratic members of the House of Representatives in order to achieve his ambition of being chosen as Speaker of the House. But Woods' early political reputation was so unsavory that his courtly manners, faultless dress, and emotionless countenance could never overcome his tarnished image from the past.

The Chamberlain Club occupied three houses, 821, 823, and 825 15th Street, NW, from 1882 until Chamberlain's death ten years later. Part of the center house was made into a restaurant for ladies, with the entrance at 823 15th Street, NW. The cuisine at Chamberlain's was rumored to be the best in town. In the kitchen was a small army of cooks (women of a mature age of African descent) who had learned the perfection of their specialties in the finest aristocratic homes of Maryland and Virginia. The cooks allowed no one in their kitchen, including Chamberlain. Harsh words and frying pans were thrown at anyone who came into their kitchen uninvited. John Chamberlain's chief of staff was the dignified James Gray, who was of African descent. Gray was said to have had no equal in his profession in Washington.

Patrons of Chamberlain's were the bon vivants of the city; they were men who enjoyed, and could afford, the good things in life. The Chamberlain Club became known as "the center of Washington's Bohemian night life,"[38] for men like Henry Adams, John Hay, and their friends, as well as for politicians like Don Cameron, Chester Arthur, and Grover Cleveland. "Chamberlain's was the resort of that class of public men, and their companions and satellites, who loved good things to eat and drink, who enjoyed the companionship of those of their own way of living, and who found pleasure and profit in sitting in the poker game that was conducted virtually on a continuous plan." [39]

So many senators gathered at the Chamberlain Club that someone noted there were often enough senators for a quorum. Roscoe Conkling, James Blaine's nemesis, was a regular. Conkling was a very handsome man who possessed an inflated ego and thought of himself as physically and mentally invulnerable. He took great pride in his appearance, sporting a Van Dyke goatee and a carefully arranged blond curl in the center of his forehead. In a speech before Congress, Blaine criticized Conkling for his "haughty disdain, his grandiloquent swell, his majestic super-eminent, overpowering, turkey-gobbler strut."[40] Conkling never forgave Blaine for those comments.

Chamberlain encouraged newspapermen to write clever stories about those who came to his club. Along with the club members, many journalists attended (and reported on) the traditional afternoon rite of serving of cold apple toddies. Members of Congress adored the publicity. When Chamberlain died in 1892, he was financially overextended and bankrupt. For years after Chamberlain's death, the Old Book Shop, on Pennsylvania Avenue near the Capitol, kept his memory alive. Displayed in the shop window, for sale, were many photographs of his famous patrons, autographed and dedicated to Chamberlain, which had once proudly decorated the walls in the Chamberlain Club.

Wormley's Hotel — the first story —
15th and H Streets, NW — southwest corner

James Wormley grew up in Washington. He was the son of a prominent Washington family of African ancestry. Before the Civil War, Wormley had been a steward at the old Washington Club in the Rodgers House on Lafayette Square, when Philip Barton Key and Dan Sickles were members. While working there, Wormley became an experienced caterer. In 1868, he accompanied Reverdy Johnson to England while Johnson was serving as minister to the Court of St. James. In England, Wormley catered to the many diplomats and dignitaries whom Johnson entertained.

In 1871, James Wormley, at the age fifty-one, opened his own hotel. He chose the location for his hotel: one block away from Lafayette Square. He had a well-established reputation, and foreign visitors, political leaders, and socialites sought him out because they appreciated the special attention he showered upon them. Wormley's Hotel contained a main dining room and several, equally popular, private dining rooms. Spacious halls for receptions and parties were available. The hotel also offered offices for lease. Some of the fine antique furniture in Wormley's Hotel was purchased from the estate of Charles Sumner, when Sumner's effects were auctioned after his death in 1874.

Wormley was only sixty-four years old when he died in October 1884. The great leaders of the political, diplomatic, and social community attended his funeral. Wormley had proven that race was no barrier for a good businessman. The pall bearers at his funeral included Caleb Willard (of the Ebbitt House), T. E. Roessle (of the Arlington Hotel), O. G. Staples (of the Riggs House Hotel), and M. W. Galt, the renowned Washington jeweler.

Shoreham Hotel — *the first story* —

15th and H Streets, NW — northwest corner

The Shoreham Hotel was built on the site of Samuel Harrison Smith's town house. In 1828, Samuel Harrison Smith and his wife, Margaret Bayard Smith, built this house at the northwest corner of 15th and H Streets, near Lafayette Square. Samuel H. Smith was the son of Jonathan Bayard Smith, a member of the Continental Congress. His wife's father, John Bayard, was also a member of the Continental Congress. They were distant cousins. Samuel Smith was a writer and editor who came to Washington in 1800, when Congress arrived. He established the first national newspaper printed in America, the *National Intelligencer*, which ten years later he sold to Joseph Gales. Margaret was also a writer, whose occasional articles were published in *Godey's Lady's Book* and other popular magazines of the times. She wrote thousands of personal letters about her life in Washington, many of which were saved by her son. A selected number of her correspondences were complied and published in 1906 by her grandson, J. Henley Smith, in a book entitled, *The First Forty Years of Washington Society*.

The Smith home was later purchased by Senator Samuel Hooper of Massachusetts. During the Civil War, Hooper rented it to General George McClellan. After Lincoln's assassination, Hooper turned the house over to Andrew Johnson in May 1865, while Johnson waited for Mrs. Lincoln to move out of the White House. In 1880, Congressman Levi P. Morton of New York purchased the Smith house and razed it, to make way for a new hotel.

Morton was the son of an Episcopalian minister and early in his life, he proved to be a successful businessman. The Civil War took its toll on his business, however, because his Southern debtors were unable to pay him, though he managed to pay off all of his own debts. In 1863, Morton started a Wall Street banking firm and amassed a small fortune.

In 1878, Morton entered politics as a member of the House of Representatives from the Manhattan district of New York. He was reelected in 1880, but resigned, when President Garfield appointed him to serve as minister to France for four years. Morton entertained lavishly while he lived abroad. Upon his return to New York, he ran, unsuccessfully, as a contender for a seat in the U.S. Senate. President Garfield had asked Morton to be his vice president in 1880, but Morton had refused. In 1888, when Benjamin Harrison asked Morton to be his vice president, Morton decided to accept Harrison's offer. After serving for four years as vice president, Morton returned to New York and, in 1895, he was elected governor of the state. Although Morton worked hard to try to secure the Republican presidential nomination for himself, in 1896, it was given to McKinley instead. Afterwards, Levi Morton decided to retire from politics and, he returned to New York where he lived to be ninety-six years old.

Morton had built the Shoreham Hotel on the site of the Smith House, as a business investment. He named it after his birthplace: Shoreham, Vermont. The hotel was an apartment-hotel, which catered to members of Congress and, it was especially popular with members of the House and Senate from New York and New England. When the fabulous, new Willard Hotel replaced the old Willard, Morton, in turn, invested huge sums of money to renovate and refurbish the Shoreham Hotel, in order to keep up with the competition. The Shoreham's new dining room was considered the most elegant in the city, with onyx paneling and a gold-gilded ceiling. The hotel was designed in the Romanesque Revival style, with influences of French Baroque and Queen Anne. Architecturally, there was no other building like it in Washington.

Welcker's Hotel — *the first story* —
727 15th Street, NW

John Welcker came to Washington from New York, at the beginning of the Civil War. He was said to have been from Belgian, originally. In 1865, Welcker leased property on Pennsylvania Avenue, NW, near 10th Street, and opened his first restaurant. A few years later, he leased property on 15th Street, NW, and converted it into a hotel. The dining room at Welcker's Hotel was said to be 80-feet long and 16-feet wide, with adjustable screens to adapt the large space for several small, private parties. "Charles Dickens says Welcker kept the best restaurant in the world."[41] Weckler's prices were comparable to the meal prices in the best Paris restaurants. He generally charged between $10 and $12 per plate, although some meals cost as much as $20. During President Grant's inauguration, Welker accommodated 700 people in his restaurant in one day. The best suites of rooms in Welcker's Hotel cost $50 a day, which included food and wine. President Ulysses S. Grant and Algernon Sartoris, who married Grant's daughter Nellie, were often guests at Welcker's. John Welker managed his hotel with the help of his brother, Peter Welcker. When John Welker died in 1875, Peter and his wife, Anna, continued to operate the hotel for a while until Peter opened his own establishment on Pennsylvania Avenue.

Columbian University — the first story —
15th and H Street, NW — southeast corner

Across 15th Street from Wormley's Hotel was the Columbian University building. The Baptist Church had started Columbian University (then called Columbian College), in 1821, to train divinity students. Columbian College was first located on "college hill," between 14th and 15th Streets, Florida Avenue and Columbia Road, NW, (the Adams-Morgan neighborhood). Streets in the "college hill" area were named to reflect a college atmosphere: Euclid Street, University Place, Harvard Street, and Columbia Road. In 1822, John Quincy Adams loaned money to the college for the construction of their first building. During the Civil War, the "college hill" buildings were used by two military hospitals. When the college expanded to include both a law school and medical school, in 1873, it was rechartered and renamed Columbian University. The Medical School was located in a leased building once used for the United States

Army Medical Museum, at H and 13th Streets, NW. In 1865, W. W. Corcoran purchased the Medical Museum building and gave it to the college.

In 1882, the trustees of Columbian University purchased property nearby the Medical School, on the corner of H and 15th Streets, where they planned to erect a new building for the law school. Corcoran gave the school $30,000 to assist them in buying the property. The old "college hill" property was later sold for $200,000. A Washington architect, William Poindexter, who remodeled the Cosmos Club, was hired to design the four-story structure. Fine pressed and molded bricks were used in the building's construction, and terra cotta ornamentations enlivened the facade. The new multi-purpose building, which held classrooms, offices, a 500-seat lecture hall, and two libraries, was completed in 1884 and measured 120-feet long on 15th Street and 64-feet wide.

By 1893, the school's enrollment increased to more than 1,000 students and the university needed to expand. The trustees purchased the Van Ness property on Constitution Avenue and 17th Street. The George Washington Memorial Association offered to build the main administration and classroom building on the site, with the condition that the school change its name to: The George Washington University. The name change occurred. However, the association was unable to raise the necessary funds to construct the promised building. The university was nearly destitute and, their great benefactor, W. W. Corcoran, had died several years before, in 1888. The university trustees mortgaged, and eventually were forced to sell, all of the university buildings. The classrooms were moved into a few rented row houses in the poor Foggy Bottom neighborhood. Throughout the 20th century, George Washington University vastly expanded its property holdings in Foggy Bottom, increased its student enrollment, and raised its academic status, to be scholastically competitive with the top universities in the United States.

YMCA Building — a story —

1409 New York Avenue, NW

Morgan McCleary built his house at 1409 New York Avenue, NW, just after the Civil War ended. The Washington City Club, under the leadership of Alexander Robey Shepherd, bought the house in 1870. When the club went bankrupt, it was taken over by John Chamberlain, who eventually moved his establishment two blocks away, to 15th and H Streets, NW.

In 1888, the YMCA (Young Men's Christian Association) purchased the old McCleary House. The Washington Chapter of the YMCA was started twenty-five years earlier, following the principles set out by its British founder, George Williams, a department store clerk. Williams created the YMCA because he believed that such an association could improve the morale and moral character of working class people. Wealthy businessmen supported the idea, because the improved moral character of YMCA members resulted in the improvement of workers' productivity. In 1895, the YMCA building burned. Mr. S. Walter Woodward, of Woodward and Lothrop's Department Store and the patron of the local YMCA chapter, erected a new building for the YMCA, which was located west of the White House at 18th and G Streets, NW.

St. Matthew's Catholic Church — the first story —

15th and H Streets, NW — northeast corner

The nearest Catholic Church to Lafayette Square was St. Patrick's Church, located at 10th and G Streets, six blocks away. By the mid-1830s, the church was so overcrowded that Reverend William Matthews made plans to build another church several blocks to the west. Father Matthew generously sold a house that he owned (valued at $10,000) and donated the profits from the sale of the house to assist in paying for the new church. The building committee chose "St. Matthew's" as the name of the church, to honor both St. Matthew the apostle and Father Matthew for his work in establishing the new congregation.

By 1838, the construction of St. Matthew's Church was completed. The Greek Revival-style building had a towering steeple and dignified columns aligned on the porch, facing H Street. President Tyler's sister was baptized at St. Matthew's Church in 1841. In 1856, Stephen A. Douglass and Adelle Cutts, Dolley Madison's grandniece, were married in the church. As the congregation grew, a school building was added on the east side of St. Matthew's. The church cemetery was located at 15th and U Streets, NW. (Years later, however, the graves were relocated to Mt. Olivet Cemetery in northeast Washington.) By 1893, towering commercial structures surrounded St. Matthew's so Reverend Thomas Lee chose a new site for a new church on Rhode Island Avenue, NW, between M Street and Connecticut Avenue. The new St. Matthew's Catholic Church was completed in 1898 and the old church was razed in 1910.

McLean House — the first story —

1500 I Street, NW

John R. McLean built an extravagant home near Lafayette Square, completely enveloping an existing older residence. He was the son of

Washington McLean, who had lived at the Ewell House on Jackson Place. In 1884, John bought an existing home near the southwest corner of 15th and I Streets, NW, and several adjoining lots. He combined the lots and added four major additions on the original home, creating an immodest, opulent mansion.

The original home had been built on the site in 1860, by Jonah Hoover. Hoover was a Washingtonian who served as the United States Marshall for the District of Columbia. He was a strong supporter of the Democratic Party and a highly respected local citizen. The Jackson Association Democrats gave Hoover the honor of greeting the Hungarian Revolutionary, Louis Kussoth, on their behalf, during Kussoth's famed visit to Washington in 1852. In 1870, Jonah Hoover died of consumption (tuberculosis), at the age of forty-nine. Among his pallbearers were W. W. Corcoran, G. W. Riggs, and Senator Stockton. The artist Clark Mills made a plaster death mask of Jonah Hoover's face, from which he executed a sculpture for the family.

In 1861, Hoover leased his house to Senator Simon Cameron of Pennsylvania, who was the father of Don Cameron (owner of the Tayloe House). When Simon Cameron was only ten years old, he started working in a newspaper office. As a young man, he came to Washington and worked with Joseph Gales in the office of the *National Intelligencer*. Returning to Pennsylvania, Cameron made a fortune through business ventures and became involved in politics. In 1838, he aided Buchanan in his election campaign to the U.S. Senate. Buchanan rewarded Cameron by appointing him as commissioner to settle the Winnebago Indian claims. Cameron used his position to personally profit from handling the claims. The ensuing problems lead to a scandal, but the effect on Cameron's political career was inconsequential. In 1845, Cameron won the seat in the Senate that had been vacated by Buchanan.

Following two unsuccessful bids for reelection, Cameron switched political parties and became a strong supporter of the Republicans. In 1860, he was considered as the Republican candidate for the presidency, but he made a deal to shift Pennsylvania's votes to Abraham Lincoln. When Lincoln won the election, he appointed Cameron as secretary of war. During Cameron's brief tenure in office, the War Department was filled with corruption. In January 1862, Lincoln appointed Cameron to be minister to Russia. After serving only a few months, Cameron resigned the diplomatic position and he returned to Washington. In 1867, Cameron was again elected to the Senate where he remained for ten more years. He resigned his seat in the Senate on the condition that his son, Don, should be appointed to fill the vacancy.

In 1863, Senator Edwin D. Morgan of New York purchased Jonah Hoover's house. Morgan had established a wholesale grocery business in New York and made a fortune. He then started a successful brokerage firm, E. D. Morgan and Company. In 1858, Morgan served as governor of New York and he proved to be an excellent governor. Four years later, in 1862, Morgan moved to Washington, when he was appointed to fill a vacancy in the Senate.

During the Civil War years, Senator Morgan entertained generously in his new home near Lafayette Square. A newspaper article of 1865 stated that Morgan had "*the finest residence in Washington*," and the city's entertainments were no longer dominated by Southern tradition; rather, the article continued, "the national capital has never had such elegant drawing rooms as northern men are beginning to present there."[42] Twice Morgan was offered the position of secretary of the treasury, but he declined both times. He left Washington in 1869, after he lost his bid for reelection to the Senate. When Morgan died fourteen years later, his estate was estimated to be worth nearly $10 million.

Morgan leased his Lafayette Square house to Hamilton Fish, while Fish was serving as President Grant's secretary of state. The Grants were often entertained in the house, as the guests of honor at Fish's parties. Hamilton Fish's wife, Julia Kean Fish, was an accomplished hostess. She efficiently managed many formal state dinners and receptions, for hundreds of guests at a time. Julia also raised eight children, three of whom continued on in public life.

Hamilton Fish had entered upon a career in politics, after studying law in college. In 1842, he served one term as a representative in Congress. He then served as governor of New York and, in 1851, Fish was elected to the U.S. Senate. During the Civil War, Fish was a trusted advisor to Lincoln. After the war, he was serving as president of the New York Historical Society and trustee of the Astor Library, when he met General Grant. Fish did not seek an appointment from Grant and, at first he turned down Grant's request that he serve as secretary of state. However, Fish finally relented and accepted the appointment. He retained the cabinet position during both of Grant's presidential terms.

Fish assisted in the successful negotiations that settled the *Alabama* claims with Great Britain. The U.S. Government felt that Great Britain should make restitution for damages inflicted upon Union ships by the Confederate ship *Alabama*, which had been equipped by the neutral British Navy. The damages to the Union ships had resulted in lengthening the war. Senator Charles Sumner, who played an important role in the negotiations, wanted Britain to cede Canada to the United States as reparation. Fish's views were far more moderate.

Grant had wanted Hamilton Fish to succeed him as president, but when Hayes was chosen as the Republican presidential candidate, Fish returned to New York. He served as president-general of the Society of the Cincinnati and dedicated the rest of his life to civic interests.

In 1884, the Cincinnati newspaperman, John R. McLean, purchased the old Hoover house from the Morgan estate for $112,500. McLean, who was educated at Harvard but did not graduate, had a passion for sports. He traveled and studied in Europe, then returned to Cincinnati and became one of the original members of the Cincinnati Red Stockings baseball team.

John McLean' father, Washington McLean, was a leader in the Ohio Democratic Party, a successful manufacturer, and owner of the *Cincinnati Enquirer*. Although Washington McLean wanted his son to follow him in the manufacturing business, John showed no interest. He was somewhat attracted to the newspaper business, however. In order to lure John away from baseball, Washington McLean bribed his son with $10,000 to entice him to work for the *Cincinnati Enquirer*. John proved himself in the newspaper trade and the elder McLean sold the paper to his son in 1873. John made the paper a success. Through the paper's continued backing of the Democratic Party, John became involved with politics. In 1885, he was nominated for the Senate but was defeated by Calvin Brice. In 1889, he ran for governor of Ohio but was again defeated. Seven years later, he was an unsuccessful presidential candidate.

John R. McLean married Emily Beale, the daughter of General Edward Beale, who owned Decatur House. Once again, Decatur House was the setting for a fabulous wedding. McLean had purchased Morgan's property (the old Hoover house) a few months prior to their marriage, but the McLeans did not immediately move in. They hired the architects, Joseph Hornblower and J. Rush Marshall, to renovate and updated the home. By 1888, the McLeans finally had moved into their refurbished house. In 1892, architect Harvey L. Page was hired to design a new dining room, 40-feet long and 30-feet wide, for the McLeans. In 1894, the house was further enlarged when a two-story extension with a curved bay window was added. Not until the beginning of the 20th century, however, did the complete rebuilding of the house take place.

The business of banking interested John McLean and he became a director of both the Riggs National Bank and the American Security Bank and Trust Company. He owned the *New York Journal* newspaper, which he sold to his friend William Randolph Hearst. McLean invested profitably Washington real estate and in Washington public utilities. He was part owner of the Washington Gas Light Company, the Capitol Traction Company, and the Great Falls and Old Dominion Railroad.

The Great Falls and Old Dominion Railroad was an electric rail line that connected Washington to Great Falls, Virginia. By the turn of the 20th century, the rail line carried thousands of Washingtonians to Great Falls Park to enjoy the picnic grounds and the merry-go-round. John McLean and his partner, Senator Stephen Elkins, also built a dance pavilion at Great Falls that became very a popular attraction. The operation of the Old Dominion line was a tremendous success for McLean. Many communities along the rail line prospered, as well. One of those rail-line communities was McLean, Virginia, named for the founder of the Old Dominion line, John R. McLean.

The McLeans owned two houses in Washington: the Lafayette Square house at 1500 I Street, NW, which became known as the McLean House and, a country estate, called Friendship, on upper Wisconsin Avenue (the site of the

McLean Gardens apartment/condominiums). The McLeans traveled frequently to Europe where they purchased magnificent art and tapestries. They filled their Washington homes with these fabulous antiques. Mrs. McLean was a lavish entertainer and her parties were often described in detail in the society pages of the newspapers. John McLean was not only a very successful businessman, he was also a student of history and literature, a musician of some merit, and a lover of art. The McLeans' only son, Edward Beale (Ned) McLean, grew up in Washington and was the sole heir to his father's fabulous wealth.

Tuckerman House — the first story —
16th and I Street, NW — southwest corner

In 1886, Lucius Tuckerman built his home on southwest corner of 16th and I Streets, NW, directly behind the John Hay House. The Tuckerman House was one of the great homes built near Lafayette Square by the prominent local architects, Hornblower and Marshall. The house reflected the fashionable and popular Romanesque Revival architectural style of the times, incorporating fancy Roman brickwork with red sandstone trim. On the front of the house, there was a massive, three-story entry bay and, facing the Hay House, there was an unusual rear facade with a two-story recessed porch. The Hay and Adams Houses had just recently been completed and the Tuckerman House was a complimentary addition to the new homes being built in the neighborhood. Hornblower and Marshall also designed the high brick wall that separated the Tuckerman House from the Hay House and surrounded a wisteria-filled garden.

Lucius Tuckerman made his fortune through an iron manufacturing business in New York. He had a great interest in art. In 1870, Tuckerman served as the president of New York's Metropolitan Museum of Art. Over the years, Tuckerman assembled a fabulous personal collection of paintings, which he brought to Washington and displayed in his home. Tuckerman brought his family to live in Washington because the climate was milder than in New York. However, like many late-19th century Washington residents, Tuckerman built a magnificent residence that remained in the family for relatively short period of time — less than twenty years.

Myer House — the first story —
<u>17th and I Street, NW — northeast corner</u>

Elisha Riggs, Jr., the younger brother of banker, George Washington Riggs, built a house for himself, next door to his brother's home on I Street. The house was built before the Civil War in an unusual, Gothic architectural style. However, Elisha lived there for only seven years. In 1865, the home was leased to the British Legation, when Sir Edward Thornton was serving as the British minister. In 1870, a glorious reception was held in the house in honor of the visit of Queen Victoria's youngest son, Prince Albert. Seven years later, in 1877, the house was purchased by Brigadier General Albert J. Myer.

Myer had distinguished himself in the army, prior to the beginning of the Civil War, by applying his thorough understanding of sign language to the creation of a military system of flag signaling. Flag signaling was very valuable for use during combat and, in 1860, Myer became the first Signal Officer of the Army. By 1863, the Army Signal Corps had been organized to instruct men in the use of both the telegraph and flag signaling. After the war, Myer established the first Army signal school at Fort Whipple, in Arlington, Virginia, which was later named Fort Myer, in his honor.

Joseph Henry, secretary of the Smithsonian Institution, became interested in Myer's experiments associated with the collection of data, via the telegraph, and meteorological forecasting. In 1870, Myer was permitted to create a weather bureau. People across the nation would use the telegraph to send precise information to Myer, concerning the weather in their part of the country. He analyzed the information and predicted weather patterns. The experiments were so successful in aiding farmers that, in 1890, the weather bureau was transferred to the Department of Agriculture. Because of Myer's weather forecasting abilities, he became affectionately known as "Old Probabilities." Myer died unexpectedly in 1880 while visiting New York.

Myer's son inherited the Myer House and continued to live in there for many years, while serving as an assistant rector for St. John's Church. His mother and siblings built two more houses on the same block.

Tracy House — the first story —
<u>1634 I Street, NW</u>

In 1889, Benjamin Tracy was appointed to serve as secretary of the navy under President Benjamin Harrison. He and his family moved to Washington and he purchased a house that had been built in 1876, on the southeast corner of 17th and I Streets, NW. For years Don Dickinson had owned the house, while serving as President Cleveland's postmaster general. Tracy was called the father of the modern American Navy, because of his ambitious shipbuilding program. Mrs. Tracey was a well-known hostess who enjoyed entertaining in Washington society. Unfortunately, in February 1890, a terrible fire consumed the house. Although Benjamin Tracey escaped, his wife and his youngest daughter died.

The property was sold after the fire, in 1891, to Augustus Tyler who built a new home on the site. The first floor was said to have been designed after the interior of an ocean liner. Mrs. Tyler, like Mrs. Tracy, became a respected hostess in Washington. Theodore Roosevelt's wife, Edith, was a niece of Mrs. Tyler and a frequent guest at the house. Both Mr. and Mrs. Tyler vehemently denied all the rumors that the house was haunted. However, city tour-guides often delighted in pointing it out to tourists, labeling it "the Haunted House." Mr. Tyler became so offended when he overheard the tour-guides refer to his house as "haunted" that, he occasionally would rush out into the street, insisting that the ridiculous assertion was damaging to the real estate value of his property and, loudly proclaim, "It's all a damned lie."

Shubrick & Bancroft House — a story —
1617 and 1623 H Street, NW

In the 1850s, several free standing, Greek Revival-style houses were built on H Street, across from Decatur House. Although they were built of brick, the facades were plastered and scored to look like stone block. The houses had spacious interiors and were rather majestic, standing three stories tall, three windows wide, with a center doorway on an unornamented, flat façade.

For years, Admiral William B. Shubrick occupied one of the houses, located at 1617 H Street, NW. Shubrick had served in the War of 1812 and commanded the *Brandywine*, which was the vessel that returned Lafayette to France after his visit in 1824. He later commanded the Pacific Squadron during the Mexican War. In 1859, after a U.S. steamer was fired upon in Paraguay, Shubrick was sent there to bring back a proper apology. From 1860 until his death in 1874, Shubrick served on the Lighthouse Board.

Admiral Shubrick's daughter inherited the house after Shubrick's death. She was married to Dr. George Clymer of the U. S. Navy. Dr. Clymer died in

1881, but his widow stayed in the house until her death in 1892. Clymer's widowed daughter, Mrs. Thomas F. Bayard, Jr. inherited the Shubrick House, which was the place of her birth. Her husband, Thomas F. Bayard, Jr., was a respected senator from Delaware. Her father-in-law, Senator Thomas Bayard, Sr., was the grand nephew of Margaret Bayard Smith, the chronicler of social life in Washington, whose home had been located near Lafayette Square.

Mrs. Bayard was said to have presided over the most exclusive diplomatic functions in Washington. One writer noted that, "It matters not that Mrs. Bayard's patrician ancestors and her distinguished husband have left her little beyond a modest competence, and that all around the unpretentious mansion where she was born . . . have sprung up the palaces and almost regal abodes of western millionaires and metropolitan money kings, each vying with the other in the smartness of equipage and entertainment, all Washington recognizes her social supremacy and flocks to pay court at her drawing rooms."[43]

Next door to the Shubrick House, at 1623 H St, was the Bancroft House, where George Bancroft lived during the last seventeen years of his life. Bancroft moved to the house in 1874. Nearly thirty years earlier, in 1845, he had lived at the Blair House as President Polk's secretary of the navy. Bancroft also served as minister to Great Britain and Prussia. After retiring from public life, he returned to Washington and chose to live near Lafayette Square.

Bancroft was a brilliant man. He was considered to be Washington's most distinguished man of letters and America's foremost historian. At the age of thirteen, Bancroft entered Harvard University and graduated with honors at seventeen. A year later, he went to Europe and studied German, French, Italian, and the Oriental languages. Bancroft earned a PhD when he was twenty years old. In his lifetime, he met many great men of the 19th century, including Lafayette, Baron Wilhelm, and Lord Byron. He interviewed or personally knew all the presidents from Adams to Cleveland. President Lincoln often consulted with Bancroft during the Civil War. Bancroft spent more than forty years of his life researching and writing his comprehensive *History of the United States,* which was published in ten separate volumes between 1834 and 1874.

In 1876, Bancroft revised and condensed his *History of the United States* from ten volumes to six for the Centennial second edition, from which he garnered a profit of $12,000 in the first year of sales. While living in his Lafayette Square home, Bancroft wrote the *History of the Formation of the Constitution of the United States,* which was published in 1882. After he finished this monumental work, he was asked if he could suggest what changes should be made to the Constitution. Bancroft replied, "I know of none; if any change is needed it is in ourselves that we may more and more respect that body of primal law."[44] He also wrote a biography of Martin Van Buren and later, a biography of James Polk, which was unpublished at his death.

The house where Bancroft lived was arranged specifically to suit his lifestyle. On the first floor was his parlor, where Bancroft entertained his many friends, who were considered to be Washington's intelligentsia. His guests included his nearby neighbors John Hay and Henry Adams, as well as Henry Cabot Lodge, and Senator John Sherman. Ainsworth Spofford, the Librarian of Congress, and Thomas Nelson Page, the famous antebellum writer, were also frequent visitors to Bancroft's home, as was President Hayes. The second floor of the house was used as Bancroft's study, with four rooms dedicated to his library of more than 12,000 volumes. A fifth room on the second-floor was his workroom, filled with desks and tables overflowing with stacks of books, papers, and documents. The third floor served as his private living quarters.

Growing flowers was more than just a hobby for Bancroft. He was especially fond of roses and lovingly devoted many hours to cultivating and cataloging more than 500 species, in his garden behind the Bancroft House and at his summer home in Newport, Rhode Island. Bancroft is credited with developing and perfecting a type of rose that came originally from France but had also been grown in Germany. Bancroft brought the rose to Washington and grew it in his backyard. He sold cuttings to George Fields, the White House gardener, who, with his brother Thomas, tended to it in their private hothouse. This rose became known as the American Beauty Rose.

Bancroft attributed his longevity to moderation in eating and drinking. He also adhered to a routine of working from dawn until noon on his books, followed by several hours dedicated to his correspondences or tending his rose garden, and later, taking three or four hours of exercise. He enjoyed a walk or, preferably, a horseback ride and, he was able to continue to ride until he was nearly ninety years old. Bancroft was a familiar figure in Washington with his thick white hair and full white beard blowing in the breeze as he rode through the city astride his white horse named Startle. His long horseback rides sometimes extended out into the country as far as Great Falls, Virginia. On Sunday afternoons, he was usually accompanied on his rides by his friend Ainsworth Spofford, the Librarian of Congress.

Bancroft's first wife, Sarah H. Dwight, with whom he had one daughter and two sons, died in 1837. His second wife, Elizabeth Davis Bliss, who had a son by a previous marriage, died in 1886, predeceasing him by only five years. After Elizabeth died, one of his granddaughters served as his companion for a couple of years, until she married. Bancroft's youngest son, John Chandler Bancroft, then brought his family to live in the Bancroft House, much to the delight of George Bancroft. In 1891, Bancroft died at the age of 91. He had rightly earned the title of the "Father of American History."

Corcoran Gallery of Art — *the first story* —
Pennsylvania Avenue at 17th Street, NW

When W. W. Corcoran began collecting art in earnest, he added a room to his Lafayette Square house to accommodate his newly acquired paintings and sculpture. His many works of art soon outgrew the available space in his home, and in the mid-1850s, he decided to construct a gallery specifically to display his collection. Corcoran purchased a large piece of property from the Blair family, next door to the Blair House. In 1858, he hired James Renwick to design the new gallery for this site. The gallery was nearly completed when the Civil War began. Fortunately, when the Union Army commandeered the building for use by the Quartermaster Corps, the art collection had not yet been installed. Brigadier General Montgomery C. Meigs, who commanded the Quartermaster Corps, converted the palatial gallery into a depot for Army clothing and, transformed the finest salons into offices for himself and his staff.

The military continued to occupy the beautiful gallery building until 1869, four years after the Civil War ended. When Corcoran regained possession of the building, he deeded it to a board of trustees who were chosen to oversee the operation of the gallery. The building was in need of a major renovation, after nine years of occupancy by the military. In 1870, the gallery was incorporated as a tax-exempt institution by Congress. The next year, it was finally opened to the public, thirteen years after Renwick designed it. The interior of the gallery was planned so that the southwest hall displayed the unusual assortment of statuary, paintings, bronzes, ceramic ware, and articles of historical interest that had belonged to Corcoran's friend, Benjamin Ogle Tayloe. The collection's pièce de résistance was Hiram Powers' sculpture, the *Greek Slave*, for which the second floor octagon gallery was specially designed. The sculptured nude figure was so controversial at the time that separate visiting hours were arranged for men and women, and children under 16 were not allowed to visit the gallery at all. The general admission fee was 25 cents.

In 1871, the Corcoran Gallery was the largest private gallery of its kind in the United States dedicated solely to art. Renwick's design for the gallery introduced the new French Second Empire architectural style to Washington, influencing the look of Washington's new buildings for the next two decades. The gallery's slate Mansard roof, decorative filigree ironwork at the roof-line, and curved pediments are reflected in the architecture of the old State, War, and Navy Building (the Eisenhower Executive Office Building), which was built between 1871 and 1888, directly across Pennsylvania Avenue.

Renwick added American touches to the ornamental elements of the Corinthian pilasters. Tobacco leaves and ears of corn were carved on top decorative capitals of the attached pilasters and columns. The second-floor exterior niches contained statuary representing eleven "great figures in art," chosen by Corcoran. Ten of the eleven figures were European artists: Michelangelo, Rembrandt, Raphael, Rubens, Durer, Titian, da Vinci, Murillo, Phidias, and Canova. The eleventh figure was an American artist, Thomas Crawford, who was known for sculpting the statue of *Freedom* that stands on top of the dome of the Capitol (cast by Clark Mills).

Moses Ezekiel sculpted the gallery's exterior statues while living in Rome. Ezekiel was born to Orthodox Jewish parents, in Richmond, Virginia. During the Civil War, Ezekiel fought on the side of the Confederacy. After the war, he traveled to Berlin to study at the Royal Academy of Art. He then moved to Rome, where he lived for forty years and, was knighted by the Italian King Victor Emmanuel for his lifetime contributions to art.

On February 22, 1871, Corcoran hosted the grand opening of Corcoran Gallery of Art. The gallery's main salon was 120-feet long and 30-feet wide. On opening night, the salon was lit with 280 gaslights and, filled with caged canaries. President and Mrs. Grant presided over a magnificent ball that was staged in the gallery. Proceeds from the ball were to benefit the Washington Monument Society and assist in completing the construction of the monument, which had stood unfinished, at one-third of its eventual height, since 1854.

Although Corcoran collected many paintings of famous European artists, he preferred to support American artists and the "American genius." In 1877, Corcoran gave the gallery and the surrounding property (valued at $250,000) to the public and, he left an endowment worth $900,000 and a collection of paintings and sculptures valued at over $100,000. Corcoran died in 1888, leaving an amazing, unusual biography in the form of 12,000 personal correspondences that he had saved throughout his lifetime.

By the early-1890s, the Corcoran trustees realized that the art collection had outgrown its space in the charming gallery. Earnest Flagg, a New York architect, was hired to design a new building. The collection moved to its new location, two blocks away, in 1899. The gallery's purpose, however, remains unchanged as an institution for "the perpetual establishment and encouragement of Painting, Sculpture, and the Fine Arts generally."[45]

William McKinley, the 25th President, 1897-1901

McKinley was raised in a large family of nine children. When he was eighteen years old he joined the Union Army and his commanding officer was Rutherford B. Hayes. At the end of the Civil War, twenty-two-year-old McKinley was a decorated major. He studied and practiced law and was elected to Congress in 1876, the same year Hayes was elected president. McKinley served eleven consecutive terms in the House of Representatives, but he eventually lost his place in Congress when he supported civil service reform, high tariffs, and voting rights for people of African ancestry.

McKinley returned to Ohio where he was twice elected as governor. In 1896, while McKinley was still serving as governor, his influential friend, Marcus Hanna, the Republican Party boss, strongly promoted him as the presidential candidate. McKinley won the nomination and the presidency. His Democratic opponent was the great orator William Jennings Bryant. This would be Bryant's first of three unsuccessful bids for the presidency.

In 1898, during McKinley's first term, the U.S. battleship *Maine* was sunk, due to an explosion. The ship had been stationed in Havana Harbor to watch the developments in Spain's brutal treatment of Cuban revolutionaries. The United States declared war against Spain and, although the U.S. military was not prepared to fight, the U.S. won the war within just a few months. Spain signed a treaty freeing Cuba and ceding the Philippines, Puerto Rico, and Guam to the United States. That same year, McKinley oversaw the annexation of Hawaii. In 1899, McKinley replaced his first secretary of state, John Sherman, with John Hay. Hay later negotiated the "Open Door Policy" with China, assuring equal trading rights among all nations dealing with China.

McKinley's wife was Ida Saxton McKinley, who, as a young woman, was described as attractive, intelligent, educated, and headstrong. She and William McKinley met while she was working in her father's bank. They married in 1871 and their first child, Katie, was born the next year. A year later, Ida suffered a sorrowful shock when her mother died suddenly and unexpectedly. Her mother's death was soon followed by the loss of their second daughter, who died in infancy. The McKinleys' first daughter, Katie, died less than two years later. Ida never recovered from the emotional stress of these tragic events. She suffered epilepsy, phlebitis, and migraine headaches the rest of her life, causing her to be an invalid who was unable to walk without the aid of a cane.

Despite her illness, Ida insisted on presiding over official functions at the White House. The president always sat next to her at state dinners, going against the established rules of protocol, because she frequently suffered seizures. He was always prepared to come to Ida's aid and, at the first sign of an epilepsy attack, he threw a napkin over her face (which became horribly distorted), lifted her gently, and carried her quickly out of the room. He would then return to his guests as if nothing had happened. McKinley was devoted to his delicate wife Ida and she worshiped him.

In 1900, McKinley was nominated again for the presidency. His first vice president, Garrett Hobart, had died in office in 1899. McKinley's new running mate was Theodore Roosevelt, who had distinguished himself during the war with Spain. Again, the Democrats selected William Jennings Bryant to run against McKinley and again, McKinley won.

Six months after his second inaugural, McKinley traveled to Buffalo, New York, to deliver a speech for the opening of the Pan-American Exposition. While he was shaking hands with thousands of well-wishers, a self-proclaimed anarchist named Leon Czolgosz, approached McKinley and fired two shots at the president with a concealed gun. Both bullets hit McKinley and, at first, it was thought the president's wounds were not mortal. McKinley worried more about Ida than himself. He begged that she not be told of his wounds, for fear of how the news would affect her delicate health. However, the gun shot wounds proved fatal and, eight days later, McKinley died. His body was brought to Washington to lay in state in the Capitol, before being returned to his home in Canton, Ohio, for burial. Ida gave the appearance of being terribly strong throughout the ordeal, but afterward it was said that she prayed daily to die. Six years after McKinley's death and, just a few days prior to the dedication of the McKinley Mausoleum in Canton, Ohio, Ida died. She was buried beside her beloved husband.

The turn of the century brought extraordinary change to the neighborhood surrounding Lafayette Square. Those residents who remained in the once exclusive and elite community considered the changes to be distasteful and undesirable. Real estate values skyrocketed near Lafayette Square and commercial ventures engulfed the area. Banks, associations, and powerful organizations that sought to bring attention to their establishments by leasing or purchasing Lafayette Square addresses. No longer did the new elite members of Washington society seek to live close to the president. Among the incentives luring them away from the heart of the city were clean air, cheap land, and new modes of transportation. Government departments and commercial enterprises seeking their own proximity to power came to dominate the neighborhood near the White House in the 20th century.

4

Bull Moose, Beaux Arts &
Backdrop Buildings

Neighbors to the Presidents :   Theodore Roosevelt - John F. Kennedy (1901-1963)

By the turn of the century, the neighborhood surrounding Lafayette Square was an odd mix of old structures readapted for the use of new commercial ventures and bold, new buildings designed in the Victorian and Beaux Arts styles. The new buildings were showcases for associations, unions, law and real estate offices, department stores, investment firms, and banks. Only a few private residences remained.

Concerned about the hasty and haphazard growth in the city, Senator James McMillan of Michigan established a senate commission (the McMillan Commission) initially, to study the park system; but later, it expanded its role to revising the city plan and suggesting the architectural style and placement of future federal buildings. Commission architects, Daniel Burnham and Charles McKim, proposed replacing all the buildings on Lafayette Square with several neoclassical, white marble structures to be used by the executive departments.

In the beginning of the 20th century, Americans were self-confident and optimistic. They felt that America had reached the epitome of Western Civilization. Daniel Burnham summed up the feelings of the times, by stating: "Make no little plans, they have no magic to stir men's blood, and probably themselves will not be realized. Make big plans; aim high in hope and work, remembering that a noble, logical diagram once recorded, will never die, but long after we are gone will be a living thing, asserting itself with ever growing insistency. Remember that our sons and grandsons are going to do things that would stagger us. Let your watchword be order and your beacon beauty."[1]

The McMillan Commission recommended the use of neoclassical-style architecture for new federal buildings, based on the principles taught at the École de Beaux Arts in Paris. Washington embraced the Beaux-Arts architectural style which, simply stated, is characterized by a French phrase, *horror vacui* (an abhorrence of undecorated surfaces). Stunning, temple-like structures had already been built along 17th Street, west of Lafayette Square and, classically styled buildings filled the financial district to the east, on 15th Street.

An optimistic, enthusiastic spirit energized Washington architects during the first quarter of the 20th century. However, the two World Wars and the Great Depression eventually sapped the essence from even the hardiest proponents of this new idealism. The architectural philosophy of "less is more" became the developers' credo and cheap buildings were designed to maximize the builder's profits. Parking spaces became more valuable than the irreplaceable, 19th century mansions, which were greedily and thoughtlessly demolished. In the late-20th century, after immeasurable damage had been done, preservationists finally began to successfully bring attention to the value of historical buildings.

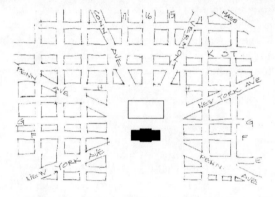

Lafayette Square — *the continuing history* —

The McMillan Commission focused part of its attention on Lafayette Park. In 1913, funds were appropriated to replace the old watchman's lodge with a modern lodge building that had two restrooms, a storage room, and a night watchman's locker room. The new lodge was designed to be inconspicuous and was covered with a decorative lattice over which vines were grown.

The buildings facing Lafayette Square were rapidly changing. In 1917, the U. S. Treasury Annex was built on the site of the razed Freedman's Bank (which earlier had replaced the Gunnell House). In 1922, the U.S. Chamber of Commerce building replaced the Slidell and Corcoran Houses. The Veterans Administration building replaced Arlington Hotel and the Sumner House. A new State Department Annex was planned, which would have replaced all of the Jackson Place Row Houses; however, the construction plans were delayed by the Great Depression. Meanwhile, several Jackson Place homes were privately purchased, razed, and replaced with three high-rise office buildings.

For two years, beginning in 1936, President Roosevelt's public works program, administered by the Works Progress Administration (WPA), provided funds for landscaping Lafayette Park. Trees and shrubs were relocated, flower gardens were planted, walkways were redesigned, and the park was made more accessible to the public.

During World War II Washington's population exploded, causing a shortage of government office space. The old plans to build monumental new federal buildings on Lafayette Square were revived. By the late 1940s, the government had purchased nearly all of the remaining Jackson and Madison Place row houses and buildings, in anticipation of clearing the site for construction. However, America's involvement in the Korean War delayed development again. No serious thought was given to the intrinsic worth of the historic structures across from the White House, facing Lafayette Square.

Early in the 20th century, the McMillan Commission Plan called for beautifying Lafayette Park with statuary, in anticipation of surrounding the park with neo-classical government buildings. Although the park already had two handsome statues (President Andrew Jackson and the Marquis de Lafayette), Congress approved plans for three more. By 1910, the new statues of Baron Von Steuben, General Kosciuszko, and Comte de Rochambeau were placed on the three remaining corner sites of Lafayette Square. The most important park in the city now honored one president and four heroes who came from Europe to help the Americans win their fight for freedom.

Comte De Rochambeau Statue — *a story* —
Lafayette Square — southwest corner

The Comte de Rochambeau was only a few years older than George Washington, but far more experienced in military training, when he and 7,000 French troops under his command were sent by France to aid the Americans. In 1781, Rochambeau, together with George Washington, marched the allied troops south from New York. They coordinated their plans with Comte de Grasse's fleet of thirty-seven war ships and 150 transport ships. Rochambeau, de Grasse, and Lafayette combined their efforts with the American troops, forcing the surrender of the British Lord Cornwallis in Yorktown, Virginia. Without the help of the French, who also supplied the Americans with as much as 90 percent of their gunpowder, the Americans might not have won their independence from Great Britain.

In 1902, a statue commissioned by Congress, of Comte Jean Baptiste Donatien de Vineur de Rochambeau, was dedicated by President Theodore Roosevelt. The families of Rochambeau and Lafayette were present at the dedication. The Comtesse de Rochambeau unveiled the statue (sculpted by J. Fernand Hamar), which is a replica of one at Rochambeau's birthplace in Vendome, France. The statue represents Rochambeau wearing the uniform of a major general in the Continental Army. He faces toward the White House, with his right arm extended and hand pointing, as if giving a command to his troops. In his left hand he clutches a battle plan.

Beneath Rochambeau's statue, on the south pedestal, stands an allegorical representation of *Liberty* as a proud, young woman. Her dress blows in the wind, while in her left hand she grasps two billowing flagpoles with a United States flag and a French flag. In her right hand she holds a drawn sword, pointed downward. *Liberty* stands ready to defend *America*, which is represented by an eagle whose right talons clamp onto a shield with thirteen stars and thirteen stripes. The eagle's left claw is poised and ready to attack. Waves break at *Liberty's* feet and a ship's prow is seen behind her.

The west face of the pedestal is dedicated to the Rochambeau family and the east face is dedicated to France. On the north face, a quote is inscribed: "We have been contemporaries and fellow laborers in the cause of liberty and we have lived together as brothers should do in harmonious friendship — Washington to Rochambeau, February 1, 1784."

General Kosciuszko Statue — a story —
Lafayette Square — northeast corner

General Tadeusz Andrzej Bonawentura Kosciuszko was a freedom fighter from Poland. In Paris, Benjamin Franklin met Kosciuszko and gave him a letter of recommendation, which Kosciuszko carried with him to America in 1776, when he came to help the Americans fight the Revolutionary War. Kosciuszko supervised the construction of the fort at West Point and helped found West Point Military Academy. He also supervised the building of the fort at Saratoga, New York. The ensuing Battle of Saratoga, in 1777, was an American victory, due, in part, to the design of this fort. This battle was also a turning point in the Revolutionary War. Kosciuszko was commissioned a brigadier general and, Congress awarded him $15,000 and 500 acres of land in Ohio.

In 1784, however, Kosciuszko returned to Poland and led Polish troops against the invading Russians. Ten years later, still fighting, he suffered a defeat when his troops were outnumbered at Raclawice, Poland. The wounded Kosciuszko was captured and imprisoned. Eventually liberated, Kosciuszko lived as a patriot without a country in Switzerland, where he continued his fight for Poland's freedom, until his death in 1817. He had requested that his land in Ohio should be sold and the proceeds used to establish a school in Newark, New Jersey, for people of African descent. He believed that education would help free those people who had been enslaved.

In 1910, President Taft dedicated a statue honoring Kosciuszko, which was a gift of the Polish-American Societies of America. The sculptor was Antoni Popiel. The Kosciuszko statue faces north. Kosciuszko is represented wearing the general's uniform of the Continental Army and, in his right hand, he holds his plans for the fort at Saratoga, New York.

On the east face of the pedestal is a statuary group showing Kosciuszko wearing an American military uniform and holding a flag and sword. He is freeing a young American soldier, symbolically liberating him from foreign domination. On the west face of the pedestal is a statuary group showing a wounded Kosciuszko in a Polish military uniform. He is directing a Polish peasant soldier to continue the fight for freedom.

On the north face of the pedestal, an eagle is sculpted with outstretched wings, defiantly guarding a portion of a globe showing America. Below the globe is inscribed, "Saratoga." The eagle clutches a sword, shield, and flag in its talons. On the south face of the pedestal, another eagle is struggling with a serpent, which represents despotism. That eagle is perched on a portion of a globe showing Poland. Below the globe is inscribed, "Raclawice," along with the phrase, "And Freedom shrieked as Kosciuszko fell."

Baron Von Steuben Statue — a story —
Lafayette Square — northwest corner

Frederick Wilhelm Augustus Henry Ferdinand Baron Von Steuben dedicated his life to military service. He had gained broad practical knowledge of military training techniques while serving in the Seven Years War under Frederick the Great. When Von Steuben arrived in Valley Forge in the winter of 1778 to offer his services to George Washington, he was immediately made an inspector general (drillmaster). Though he spoke no English, he was able to train the American troops into a disciplined force within a month. Von Steuben was highly praised for attaining "the most remarkable achievement in rapid military training in the history of the world."[2] After the war, Von Steuben stayed in America, became a citizen, and retired in New York, where he was given 16,000 acres and a pension of $2,500 a year. His former property is now known as Steubenville, New York. When he died, he left his estate to his two aides-de-camp, Colonel William North and Major Benjamin Walker.

In 1910, President William Howard Taft dedicated a statue honoring Von Steuben, seven months after he dedicated the Kosciuszko statue on a nearby corner of Lafayette Square. Von Steuben is represented wearing the uniform of a major general in the Continental Army. He is dressed for cold weather in a heavy cape and cocked hat. The sculptor of the statue was Albert Jaegers. Jaegers' daughter, Helen, unveiled the statue at the dedication ceremony. A replica of the Von Steuben statue was sent to the emperor of Germany, who had recently given a statue of Frederick the Great to America.

The statue faces northwest. An American eagle is carved on the front face of the pedestal, with an inscription in bronze lettering stating that the memorial was "Erected by the Congress of the United States to . . . Von Steuben in grateful recognition of his services to the American people in their struggle for liberty." On the southwest face of the pedestal is a bronze group of statues called *Commemoration*. The statues are of a seated woman and a kneeling boy holding laurels. They portray an allegorical representation of *America* telling heroic stories of Von Steuben and, welcoming his descendants to the United States. On the northeast pedestal facade, a bronze group of statues represent *Military Instruction*. The statues include a helmeted soldier portraying the allegorical figure of Mars, the god of war, seated next to a boy being taught to handle a sword. On the southeast, rear pedestal facade are two portrait panels, with the names of Colonel William North and Major Benjamin Walker, who were Von Steuben's aides-de-camp.

One controversy concerning the statue has still not been resolved. Von Steuben's date of birth is inscribed as November 15, 1730. The National

Council of the Steuben Society of America claimed that, indisputable church records declare he was baptized in the German Reform Church at Madgeburg, Prussia, on September 29, 1730 and was born on September 17, 1730. This information was "respectfully submitted" in 1932, to the Bicentennial of the Birth of George Washington Committee, with the request that a celebration for Von Steuben be held that year on September 17. The Steuben Society also requested that the date on the statue be changed. Lieutenant Colonel Ulysses S. Grant, III, who was director of public buildings and parks, explained that no action would be taken until he received official notification of an error.

Theodore Roosevelt, the 26th President, 1901-1909

Theodore Roosevelt was born into a wealthy New York family. He was well educated and well traveled as a child, although he suffered from asthma and other illnesses that left him weak and small. To overcome his disabilities, at age thirteen, he forced himself to participate in a rigorous physical exercise program that he followed throughout his life.

Roosevelt excelled at Harvard as an undergraduate student, but after one year in law school, he dropped out and entered politics. He was twenty-three years old when he was first elected to serve on the New York State legislature. Roosevelt was idealistic. He led a political reform group against corruption in the state legislature and, he was reelected. However, after both his mother and his wife, Alice, died within hours of each other on Valentine's Day 1884, he declined another reelection bid. Still grieving over his recent losses, Roosevelt moved to the Dakota Territory, where he managed a cattle ranch. In 1886, he decided to return to New York. He married his childhood sweetheart, Edith Carow, and began writing books on American history and life in the West.

In 1889, President Benjamin Harrison appointed Roosevelt to be U.S. civil service commissioner and, in that position, he fought the corruption of the spoils system. President Cleveland was impressed with his work and reappointed him. While serving as civil service commissioner, Roosevelt revised civil service exams, doubled the number of federal positions required to take the exams, and increased employment opportunities for women.

Roosevelt moved to Washington in 1897, when President McKinley appointed him as assistant secretary of the navy. During a temporary absence of Secretary of the Navy John Long, Roosevelt assumed the secretary's position. However, he stepped beyond his authority when he ordered Admiral George Dewey and the Pacific Fleet to Hong Kong, in anticipation of a war with Spain. In the event of a declaration of war, Admiral Dewey was under orders from Roosevelt to destroy the Spanish fleet in Manila Bay. On February 15, 1898, the *U.S. Battleship Maine* was sunk in Havana Harbor by an explosion. Two months later on April 24, Spain declared war on the U.S. Although outnumbered by the Spanish fleet at Manila Bay, Dewey's forces were prepared and proved victorious. Roosevelt was vindicated. He resigned from his navy appointment to join the fight in Cuba, where he was awarded the rank of lieutenant colonel and assembled a regiment that became known as the Rough Riders. Roosevelt's courage in the war with Spain became legendary. After the war, Roosevelt was a celebrity and, in November 1898, he received the Republican nomination for the vice presidency.

The power brokers of the Republican Party did not like Roosevelt because he was an independent thinker and refused to promote the interests of big business. However, the party leaders knew Roosevelt's popularity could secure the votes to win the election, even though they were unsure what he would do once he was in office. For the first few months after McKinley became president, Roosevelt had no vice presidential duties, so he traveled to Vermont to hunt and fish. While in Vermont, he learned of McKinley's mortal wounds inflicted by an assassin's bullet. With McKinley's death, Roosevelt was inaugurated and he declared that he would follow McKinley policies, but immediately instituted his own.

In trying to curb abuse by big business, Roosevelt asked Attorney General Philander Knox to prepare an antitrust suit against the Northern Securities Company, which was a railroad trust. The suit was settled several years later with favorable results for the U.S. government. Roosevelt then resolved a coal strike in Pennsylvania in 1902, by threatening to take over the mines unless the owners of the mines agreed to arbitration. The next year, in 1903, President Roosevelt supported a revolution in Panama against the Colombians controlling the land needed to build the Panama Canal. The U.S. Navy helped the Panamanians overthrow the Colombians. Panama then leased the Canal Zone to the United States for the construction and operation of the Panama Canal.

During the presidential election of 1904, Roosevelt ran against Alton B. Parker, a New York judge. Roosevelt's victory was overwhelming. This was the first time a successor president, who served the uncompleted term of his predecessor, won an election in his own right. Reform legislation was a top issue on Roosevelt's agenda during his second term. With his support, the Pure Food and Drug Act and the Meat Inspection Act were passed. Concerned about the ecology, Roosevelt designated 234 million acres of U.S. land for conservation. In 1905, he arranged a peace conference to settle the Russo-Japanese war and create a balance of power in the Far East between the two nations, preserving the Open Door Policy in China. For his efforts with the Russo-Japanese treaty, Roosevelt received a Nobel Peace Prize.

Alice Roosevelt was President Roosevelt's oldest daughter, by his first marriage. Alice's behavior was so ostentatious and flashy, that newspaper stories were published regularly about her. Alice and her friends, Maggie Cassini and Cissy Patterson, were known around town as the "Three Graces." They were often the invited guests of honor at Washington's most extravagant parties. In 1906, Alice married Speaker of the House Nicholas Longworth, III. She was very nonchalant about the White House wedding. Alice explained, "I wasn't excited, I wasn't nervous. It was another big party and I had been to big parties."[3] When asked to cut her wedding cake, however, Alice, with a touch of showmanship, grabbed the sword from Major Charles McCawley's sheath and wielded the weapon flamboyantly through the beautifully layered and iced confection, to the horror of her stepmother, Edith.

Roosevelt's second wife, Edith, was serious, intelligent, well read, and very organized. She ruled the White House with detachment and composure, which was necessary in handling her five children and, Alice, who was fiercely independent. Edith held weekly meetings with the wives of cabinet officials to orchestrate the official entertainment. She managed the curiosity of the press concerning the family by having posed photographs taken and distributed to the newspapers, along with managed stories. Edith's legacy to the White House is the permanent memorial of a portrait gallery of first ladies, which she established.

In 1908, Roosevelt supported his friend William Howard Taft to succeed him as president. After Taft won the election, Roosevelt left the country and traveled to Africa and Europe with one of his sons. However, Roosevelt became disillusioned with Taft and, in 1912, was persuaded to run against him by the Progressive Republican Party, which carried the moniker, Bull Moose Party, after Roosevelt declared that he felt "as fit as a bull moose." In October 1912, while Roosevelt was delivering campaign speech, a fanatic shot him in the chest, in an attempted assassination. Roosevelt insisted that he finish his prepared speech, which lasted an hour, before he was rushed to the hospital. Because of Roosevelt's popularity, the Republican Party vote was split between Roosevelt and Taft, so the Democrats won the election, with their candidate, Woodrow Wilson.

In 1916, the Republicans again asked Roosevelt to be the presidential candidate. Roosevelt, however, endorsed Charles Evans Hughs, who lost the election to Woodrow Wilson. Roosevelt had garnered so much support that he surely would have been a candidate in the 1920 presidential election, but, in January 1919, Roosevelt died in his sleep from an arterial blood clot. Theodore Roosevelt truly loved and believed in America. He gave his heart to his country. Roosevelt claimed that "ultimately no nation can be great unless its greatness is laid on foundations of righteousness and decency."[4]

Carbery House — the final story —
D.A.R. — a new story —
1776 D Street, NW

The Carbery House continued to be owned by the Carbery family for nearly eighty years. Ruth and Catherine Carbery were the younger maiden sisters of Thomas Carbery who built the house. They lived in the house until their deaths, at the end of the 19th century. A few fine residences and one office building (the Winder Building) had been built on lots north of the house before the Civil War. However, most of the land surrounding the Carbery House remained essentially open and undeveloped, except for a few shacks, several hot houses, and a fenced cattle yard.

By 1903, the Carbery House site was purchased by the Daughters of the

American Revolution (DAR). The DAR was founded in 1890, the same year the Sons of the American Revolution was founded and voted to exclude women. The aims of the DAR were stated as "patriotic, historical, and educational." The objective of the DAR was to fulfill the ideals of George Washington's decree in his farewell address, "to promote, as an object of primary importance, institutions for the general diffusion of knowledge."[5] At the first meeting, the DAR membership decided that a memorial building should be erected in Washington, to house historical relics.

In 1910, the DAR built a monumental, Beaux-Arts style, marble temple-like structure, which set the standard for neighboring buildings on either side. The DAR building was designed by Edward Pearce Casey, of the Army Corps of Engineers, who oversaw the construction of the Library of Congress, two decades before. Thirteen columns, representing the original thirteen states were placed on the building's south portico. Museum rooms were designed and created, for the display of historical home interiors from different states. A convention hall was constructed and named Memorial Continental Hall, where the DAR members were to meet each April, on the anniversary of the Battle of Lexington. The convention hall was eventually converted into a vast genealogical library, to assist potential members in tracing their ancestry.

Membership in the DAR is granted to a woman who is able to definitively trace her ancestry to a man or woman who served an active part in America's Revolutionary War. By 1920, the membership had grown to such an extent that the classical architect, John Russell Pope, was commissioned to design an addition to the building. The new structure, dedicated in 1929, included a new convention hall, named Constitution Hall. This is the largest auditorium space in Washington, accommodating nearly 4,000 people. The National Symphony Orchestra performed regularly, at Constitution Hall, before the John F. Kennedy

Center for the Performing Arts was opened in 1971. The DAR currently has nearly 200,000 members who continue to administer and maintain the largest group of buildings in the world, owned exclusively by women.

Van Ness House — the final story —

O.A.S. — the continuing story —

Constitution Avenue between 17th and 18th Streets, NW

©EDWARD F FOGLE EFF

Throughout the second half of the 19th century, the Van Ness House had many tenants. In the 1850s, Thomas Green, a newspaper editor who came to Washington from Richmond, lived in the house. At the beginning of the Civil War, the Van Ness House was converted and briefly used as a military hospital for wounded Union soldiers. The house became uninhabitable, however, when the Washington Canal, located in front of the house, was put to use as an open sewer. Across the canal (Constitution Avenue, NW), the land around the Washington Monument had been fenced and was utilized as a cattle yard. The cattle were slaughtered in a nearby slaughterhouse to feed the Union troops camped in Washington and, the refuse was thrown into the canal.

After the Civil War, an optimistic entrepreneur leased the Van Ness House for a restaurant and beer garden. The grounds were later used as a florist's nursery. George Fields, the White House gardener, cared for his flowers in the hothouses near the Van Ness House. For a few years, the city government used the house and surrounding lot as a headquarters for the street cleaners.

In 1903, the president of Columbian University purchased the Van Ness property, which was in desperate need of repair. At the same time, a group of ladies had formed the George Washington Memorial Association to increase opportunities for women in higher education. The ladies offered to build an administration building with offices, a lecture hall, and research facilities for Columbian University on the Van Ness property. In keeping with the spirit of the original wishes of George Washington for a national university, the ladies asked the university to change its name to: The George Washington University. The new name was approved in 1904 and grand plans were submitted for constructing a group of monumental buildings. However, the five-acre site and the funding soon proved inadequate for the expanding university's needs.

In 1907, Elihu Root, President Roosevelt's secretary of state, and Charles C. Glover, Sr., president of Riggs National Bank, offered to purchase the Van Ness property for $200,000 from the university. A year later, the Van Ness House was demolished. In its place a new building was erected for the International Bureau of the American Republics, which for nearly two decades had been located in two Jackson Place row houses on Lafayette Square. The Bureau was later called the Pan American Union and renamed again, as the Organization of American States (OAS). Andrew Carnegie contributed $850,000 toward the building's construction.

The OAS building, designed by Albert Kelsey and Paul Cret, is a beautiful example of Beaux Arts-style architecture with a Spanish and Latin American flair. Around the outside of this temple-like structure are carvings depicting Aztec, Inca, Toltec, and Mayan motifs. Gutzon Borglum sculpted the representation of *North America* to the north of the entry. Isador Konti sculpted the representation of the *South American* to the south of the entry. The interior center courtyard was filled with tropical plants and a fountain, designed by Gertrude Vanderbilt Whitney. Originally, the glass roof of the atrium could be opened, but it was sealed shut when air conditioning was installed.

Andrew Carnegie also financed the construction of a small building behind the OAS that served as the residence for the secretary of the Pan American Union for many years. In 1976, the residence became the Art Museum of the Americas. The only remaining vestige of the Van Ness House and Latrobe's architectural genius can be seen in the rear of the parking lot behind the main building. All alone, surrounded by a field of asphalt, is the original wood frame stable, now covered with pebble-dash stucco and topped with a red metal roof.

William Howard Taft, the 27th President, 1909-1913

William Howard Taft was born in Cincinnati, Ohio. He attended Yale University and graduated in 1878, second in his class. Taft then returned to

Ohio to practice law with his father, Alphonso Taft, who was a prominent Cincinnati lawyer. Alphonso Taft had served as President Grant's secretary of war, attorney general, and was the ambassador to Austria-Hungary and Russia.

In 1887, William H. Taft was appointed judge of the Cincinnati Superior Court. A few years later, President Harrison appointed Taft judge of the U.S. Circuit Court, a position he held until 1900. President McKinley promised Taft an eventual appointment to the Supreme Court if he accepted the position of president of the U.S. Philippines Commission. Taft was then appointed governor-general of the islands. He was responsible for establishing a civil government and reorganizing the Philippines' court system. Taft dearly wanted to serve on the Supreme Court, but refused two Court appointments while in the Philippines because he felt duty-bound to finish his work in the islands.

When Theodore Roosevelt asked Taft to serve as secretary of war in 1904, Taft agreed on the condition that he could continue supervising the work in the Philippines. Taft also supervised the preparations for the construction of the Panama Canal project. He traveled to Japan and negotiated a secret agreement with Japan concerning U.S. noninterference with Japan's affairs in Korea in exchange for Japan's recognition of U.S. influence in the Philippines. He sailed to Cuba where he served as acting provisional governor, in 1906. That same year, Taft made the journey to California to oversee the relief efforts on behalf of the victims of the San Francisco earthquake.

In 1908, Taft did not want to be chosen as the Republican candidate for the presidency, but Roosevelt pushed him, as did Taft's wife, Helen, who especially wanted to be first lady. Williams Jennings Bryant was the Democratic candidate in the 1908 election campaign. Taft easily defeated him. During his four years in office, Taft actively pursued antitrust cases. He brought ninety antitrust suits against big businesses, including Standard Oil and American Tobacco. Taft also promoted the passage of the Sixteenth Amendment to the Constitution that instituted federal income tax.

Taft's wife, Helen, was a compelling force behind her husband's successes. She was unquestionably ambitious and wished for her husband to be in the national limelight. When Taft was elected president, Helen went against precedence when she rode at his side in the inaugural parade. She served as her husband's advisor and was involved in many of his political decisions. Helen readily admitted that she did not enjoy social events, finding them frivolous. She much preferred being involved in serious political discussions.

When Helen Taft visited Japan with her husband, she saw the beautiful Japanese cherry blossom trees in bloom in the spring. In 1907, a Washington travel writer named Eliza Skidmore, wrote to Mrs. Taft suggesting that the heavenly cherry blossom trees would look magnificent standing near the Potomac River shore. Eliza first saw the Japanese cherry blossom trees in 1885. For years she tried, unsuccessfully, to have them transplanted in Washington. Helen Taft realized that planting the beautiful trees in the Nation's Capital was one way to help clean up the city. She viewed Washington as "a mosquito-infested swamp, rendez-vous of tramps, and a hiding place for criminals."[6]

In 1910, Mrs. Taft officially received 2,000 Sakura (Japanese cherry blossom trees), a gift from the Japanese people and a Japanese chemist named Jokichi Takamine. Unfortunately, the trees were infested with scale, insects, and larva, and they had to be destroyed. Two years later, 3,000 new trees arrived. On March 27, 1912, Mrs. Taft and the Viscountess Chinda planted the first of the famous cherry blossom trees around the Tidal Basin in Washington.

In 1912, Taft was again pushed into the presidential campaign. Theodore Roosevelt wanted the nomination and decided to run against Taft, splitting the Republican vote and giving the victory to the Democratic candidate, Woodrow Wilson. In 1913, Taft gladly accepted a professorship at his alma mater, Yale University, even though he still dreamed of serving on the Supreme Court. In 1921, President Warren G. Harding appointed Taft to fill the vacancy on the Supreme Court left by Chief Justice Edward White. Taft was a moderate and his opinions and decisions were conservative. While Taft served as chief justice, the Supreme Court Chamber was still located in the Capitol, where the Court had met since 1801. Taft saw the need and gained approval for construction of a new Supreme Court building, though he did not live to see it completed in 1935.

Taft resigned his position as Supreme Court chief justice in February 1930, because of a weak heart. He died a few weeks later and was buried in Arlington Cemetery. His wife, Helen, who died in 1943, was buried beside him. For thirty-three years, Taft was the only president buried in Arlington Cemetery, even though, according to the cemetery's military regulations, all presidents qualify to be buried there.

Red Cross — a story —

17th between D and E Streets, NW

The American Red Cross building on 17th Street, NW, serves as the national headquarters for the largest volunteer organization in the United States. In 1881, Congress chartered the Red Cross. Congress also dictates many of the duties of the Red Cross, such as support of the armed forces and disaster relief.

Funding for the Red Cross relief work, however, comes totally from private contributions and, the workforce is comprised primarily of volunteers.

In 1912, Miss Mabel Boardman, who was serving as the executive head of the organization, personally requested the Senate to pass a bill allocating funds for the construction of a headquarters building for the Red Cross in Washington. In 1913, Congress appropriated $400,000 to purchase land and assist with the construction of the new building, with the provision that not less than $300,000 should be raised by general contribution.

In 1917, Breck Trowbridge and Goodhue Livingston designed a three-story temple-like building of Vermont marble for the Red Cross. The building, which was set back from 17th Street, has an expansive lawn and sweeping driveway. The entry portico is ornamented with beautifully carved Corinthian columns supporting a pediment to which an enormous, electrified Red Cross was added, years later. The building was dedicated to the heroic women of the Civil War.

Inside, by the main sweeping staircase, two phrases are inscribed: "To the women of the North" and, directly below it, "To the women of the South." Hiram Powers sculpted the busts of Faith, Hope, and Charity that look down from the windows' ledges of the stair landing. Three fabulous stained glass windows, designed and manufactured by Louis Comfort Tiffany, are in the Assembly Room on the second floor. Women of the North and women of the South paid separately for two of the windows. Together they paid for the third. The Honorable Elihu Root chose the windows' representational themes. The scenes are of "St. Filomena" (patron saint of the sick), the "Red Cross King" (armored knights ministering to a fallen comrade), and "Una" (a graceful figure who personifies truth and fortitude from Spenser's *Faerie Queene*).

In 1930, a second Red Cross building was built behind the first one, facing onto E Street, NW. The second building was also constructed of marble, with a facade of columns and was dedicated as a memorial to the women of World War I. In 1932, a third building facing 18th Street was added and, a lovely garden was created in the courtyard formed by the three surrounding buildings. In the garden is a sculpture by Felix de Welden, dedicated in 1959, entitled *The Red Cross Men and Women Killed in Service*. Another sculpture in the garden, by Robert Tait McKenzie, is a memorial to Jane Delano, the founder of Red Cross Nursing Services. The 7-foot-tall bronze female statue represents the *Spirit of Nursing*. On the base of the sculpture is a quote from the Ninety-first Psalm, "Thou shalt not be afraid for the terror by night; not for the arrow that flieth by day; nor for the pestilence that walketh in darkness; nor for the destruction that wasteth at noonday." Delano was one of 296 Red Cross nurses who died in service in World War I.

New Corcoran Gallery of Art — *the continuing story* —
17th Street and New York Avenue, NW — southwest corner

In 1891, land was purchased by the trustees of the Corcoran Gallery of Art in anticipation of erecting a new gallery building for the growing Corcoran art collection. The property was two blocks south of the original Corcoran Gallery, on 17th Street, NW. Ground was broken in 1893 for a palatial marble structure designed by Earnest Flagg of New York. Flagg had just graduated from the École of Beaux-Arts in Paris where he had studied the grand architecture of European museums. White Georgian marble was used on the new Corcoran Gallery's exterior and decorative wrought iron work covered the windows. The building was topped with a green copper roof and an ornamental cornice. Built on a trapezoidal site with a broad, acute angle on one edge, the gallery building gracefully wraps around the corner, creating a beautiful, semicircular gallery inside. The main floor has double atrium galleries and a grand central stairway flanked by platforms for sculptural displays.

At the beginning of the 20th century, the gallery received a gift of an eclectic collection of European art by Senator William A. Clark, who was born and raised on a farm in Pennsylvania. Clark taught school in Missouri before moving to Montana where he became a multi-millionaire copper magnate. He was also a one-term senator from Montana. Among the items in Clark's collection were paintings, sculpture, bronze statuettes, tapestries, carpets, laces and needlepoint, stained glass, Majorca ceramics, and other objects d'art. Clark's bequest to the Corcoran Gallery carried a stipulation that the art collection should be kept together and displayed together in perpetuity.

W. W. Corcoran was one of the first art patrons to consider photography as an art form and recognize the talent of American artists by dedicating his gallery to the "American Genius." The art school associated with the Corcoran has been responsible for bringing recognition to talented American artists. As early as 1875, the Corcoran trustees allowed students to set up their easels in the gallery and copy great works of art. E. F. Andrews, a local painter who rented studio space in the Corcoran Office Building on 15th Street, NW, often came to the gallery to offer free advice and criticism to the students. Andrews' critiques were so sought after that the gallery began to overflow with aspiring artists. In 1887, the trustees appointed Andrews as the art director of the Corcoran School.

In 1889, a building called the "Annex" was erected as a studio and art school behind the Corcoran Gallery, on 17th Street. The Annex was designed by one of the members of the board of trustees, Edward Clark who was the Architect of the Capitol. It was the first Beaux Arts-style structure in the city and looked like an elegant, brick carriage house, with classical decorations.

When the new Corcoran Gallery of Art was opened in 1898, both the old gallery building and the Art School Annex were sold to the government and used by the U. S. Circuit Courts. The Annex was used for the storage of records, until it was torn down in 1966 to make way for the New Executive Office Building. The Corcoran School of Art was transferred to the new gallery building, where instruction is still provided for talented, young artists.

The "new" Corcoran Gallery of Art, now over a hundred years old, is an architectural treasure that has been designated as a historic structure in Washington. The lions at the main entrance are copies of Antonia Canova's marble originals from St. Peter's Cathedral in Rome. A phrase is inscribed above the entry door, proclaiming the gallery's purpose and, perhaps, describing the gallery's founder, Corcoran, as well. It simply reads "Dedicated to Art."

Octagon House — the continuing story —
18th Street and New York Avenue, NW — northeast corner

In 1899, the American Institute of Architects (AIA) signed a five-year-lease on the Octagon House. When the lease expired, Charles McKim and

Glenn Brown, who were AIA trustees, authorized the purchase of the Octagon House for $30,000, even though the AIA had only $500 in its treasury. Sufficient loans from optimistic members and friends were secured, allowing the AIA to also purchase the smokehouse, stable, and 22,322 square feet of surrounding land. Within a year, an interested buyer offered the AIA $50,000 for the Octagon House and property. However, AIA members were early pioneers in the work of historic preservation. They were not interested in selling their architectural gem. Perhaps never before or since has a historic building been given so much attention by so many professionals. The rescue of the Octagon House set a precedent as the second major architectural preservation effort of an American building, following the 1858 effort to save Mt. Vernon.

The AIA leased some of the rooms in the Octagon House as offices. The tenants included the American Federation of Arts, the Archaeological Institute of America, the Washington Archaeological Society, and the Washington Society of Fine Arts. By 1912, the AIA was able to purchase the two lots adjoining the Octagon House property.

In the late-1930s, the AIA needed more office space, so a new administration building was constructed on the property behind the garden. At the beginning of World War II, however, the government leased the new building as emergency office space for the State Department's Inter-American Defense Board. The AIA was forced to move back into crowded quarters at the Octagon House. Finally in 1949, the AIA returned to its office building and, the repair and restoration of the Octagon House became a primary concern.

A few rooms in the Octagon House continued to be leased in the 1950s, as offices to select tenants, including the National Trust for Historic Preservation. From 1949 until 1956, the Octagon House underwent a major structural renovation. The stable building in the rear was converted into the AIA library. In 1961, the Octagon House was designated a National Historic Landmark. Nine years later, in 1970, the house was officially opened to the public, both as a museum and exhibition space for architectural displays.

In the same year the house was opened, the old administration building behind the garden was demolished. In 1973, a seven-story, $7 million, modern concrete and tinted ribbon-glass, office building was constructed in its place. The new AIA headquarters was designed as a wrap-around, backdrop building for the historic old home. The new building was criticized by some for being cold and monotonous. Others praised it for not overpowering and competing with the Octagon House, but for standing on its own while deferring to its historic partner. The AIA described their new headquarters building as "a buffer, shielding the venerable brick house from the modern development going on to the north and east."[7]

Winder Building — a story —
604 17th Street, NW

In 1848, William Winder built an office building called the Winder Building and rented it to the government. The Winder Building was well ahead of its time, serving as Washington's first high-rise speculative office building. Incorporated into the building were several modern innovations. A central heating system was installed and, structural cast iron beams were used for framing and fireproofing. Two years earlier, James Renwick had introduced the use of cast iron in the Smithsonian Castle building as a fireproof technique, but the Winder Building was the first to use structural cast iron throughout. Four years after it was built, the government purchased the Winder Building for the use of the War Department, which had its main office across 17th Street, NW.

William Winder was the nephew of the distinguished General William H. Winder, for whom the building was named. General Winder had commanded the military districts that included the District of Columbia, Maryland, and part of northern Virginia in the early part of the 19th century. Winder had fought in the northwest territory and had been a prisoner of war in Canada. In late spring 1814, Winder strongly advised that troops should be called into active duty and made ready to defend Washington in case of an invasion. His pleas went unheeded. In August 1814, the city of Washington had no defenses when Admiral Cockburn and General Ross led the British troops into the Nation's Capitol to burn the federal buildings. General Winder had hastily gathered his troops when he heard of the British advance, but he had only 900 regulars (against Ross' 4,500 veteran soldiers) and no chance of stopping the invaders.

Dolley Madison mentioned General Winder in a letter to her sister, dated Tuesday, August 23, 1814, the day before the British entered Washington. She wrote, "Dear Sister, --My husband left me yesterday morning to join General Winder. He [Madison] inquired anxiously whether I had courage to remain in the Presidential house till his return, and on my assurance that I had no fear but for him and the success of our army, he left me, beseeching me to take care of myself and of the Cabinet papers, public and private."[8]

During the Civil War, the Winder building was a gathering place for military officers to hear and share the latest news of the war. In 1885, the building housed the Ordinance Museum of the War Department, which displayed a large collection of arms and relics of different wars with an emphasis on artifacts associated with the Civil War.

The Winder Building's exterior was renovated in 1979, when the Federal Home Loan Bank building was erected on the same block to the north. To make way for the new building, an early-20th century, classical little structure, used by a branch of the Riggs Bank, was razed. However, the carved column capitals, featuring squirrels and owls that once decorated the bank building were saved and placed on odd, iron pedestals near the waterfall fountain in the lower level plaza between the Federal Home Loan Bank building and the Winder Building.

Grant Building — a story —
17th and F Streets, NW — southwest corner

An attractive old house, known as the Grant Building, was located on the southwest corner of 17th and F Streets, NW. In the early years of the 19th century, Nathan Towson built the old home, which later was converted for office use. The house had 14-foot high ceilings on the main floor, fifteen rooms, and a full basement. Towson was the paymaster general of the armies and lived in the house from 1827 until his death just a few years before the Civil War. General Winfield Scott utilized the building as his office until his retirement in 1861. General Halleck, the army's chief of staff, was stationed in the building when he received Grant's famous proclamation that he wired from Richmond: "I propose to fight it out on this ground, if it takes all summer."[9]

The house received its name because, during the Civil War when General Grant was in Washington, he used it as his headquarters. The government purchased the building during the war and, for years, the War Department occupied it. In 1937, the Public Buildings Administration leased the Grant Building. From 1942 until 1947, the Department of State leased the Grant Building for its Division of Cultural Relations, which arranged for different nations to exchange professors, teachers, and students in order to share with other countries their national art, music, and literature.

In 1945, a proposal was made to construct an apartment building or a hotel where the Grant Building stood, but the plans were never realized. The next year, the United Steelworkers of America purchased the house in anticipation of erecting a new headquarters building on the property. The United Steelworkers were being forced to vacate their offices at 718 Jackson Place, because the government had bought their Lafayette Square building and planned to raze it. In 1947, the United Steelworkers replaced the Grant Building with a parking lot. A few years later, a modern office building was erected on the site.

Seven Buildings — *the continuing story* —
Pennsylvania Avenue near 19th Street, NW — north side

The distinguished row of Seven Buildings survived into the 20th century and, like most downtown residences, was adapted for commercial use. By 1905, the most famous of the Seven Buildings, the corner house, which was once called the "House of a Thousand Candles," was converted into the first location for Peoples Drug Store, a local pharmacy. Within twenty years, Peoples Drug

Store boasted that it was "one of the largest drug store organizations in the country," with twenty-four locations in Washington and forty-six throughout Maryland, Virginia, West Virginia, and Pennsylvania. An advertisement of the time mentioned the "sanitary soda fountains where thousands daily enjoy tempting, wholesome foods and refreshing beverages at moderate prices." The advertisement also referred to Peoples' slogan, *"Fair Prices - Efficient Service* and a whole-hearted desire to be *Helpful* to all."[10]

In 1959, five of the Seven Buildings, including the corner house, were razed and replaced with a black-glass and steel, multi-story office building. Peoples Drug Store continued to lease space on the first floor of the new building until the mid-1990s, when the drug store chain was bought by CVS Pharmacy. Two of the original Seven Buildings survived the wrecking ball and were occupied by a liquor store and a restaurant, for many years. Eventually, a compromise between local preservationists and a developer saved the facades of the two old houses. However, they were significantly altered when a high-rise structure was built beside, behind, and above them. The beautiful, original, entryway keystones, carved to resemble angelic female faces, had disappeared years before. The remnants of the two house facades were combined and incorporated into the new building for use by the Embassy of Mexico.

Metropolitan Club — a story —
17th and H Street, NW — southwest corner

Six officials of the U.S. Treasury met in 1863 to discuss the possibility of forming Washington's first literary and social club. In 1872, the club was officially chartered and named the Metropolitan Club. Securing a prominent location in the city to hold club meetings was of utmost importance to the club's founders. For several years, they met in three different leased properties on H Street, near Lafayette Square. Finally, in 1883, a site at the southwest corner of 17th and H Streets, NW was selected for the erection of a permanent clubhouse.

The membership of the Metropolitan Club included the most important men of the day: congressmen, cabinet officials, Supreme Court justices, bankers, businessmen, American and foreign diplomats, military men, literary men, journalists, scientists, and professionals in law and medicine. Many of the early club members lived in the neighboring houses on Lafayette Square, such as: W. W. Corcoran, George W. Riggs, Montgomery Blair, James G. Blaine, Admiral Charles Wilkes, General William T. Sherman, General Philip Sheridan, Henry Adams, John Hay, John Nicolay, Charles Glover, Sr., Alexander Robey Shepherd, Senator Charles Sumner, Senator Reverdy Johnson, Senator Ira Harris, and Major Henry Rathbone.

The Metropolitan Club encountered some problems as its membership grew. In 1882, the following resolution was passed: "Whereas the use of Apollinaris Water has become so general that the practice of serving it without extra charge has resulted in a serious loss to the Club, RESOLVED that Apollinaris Water shall hereafter be served at a charge of *fifteen* (15) cents for a *small* bottle and *twenty* (20) cents for a *large* bottle."[11] Rule XVI set out a new prohibition against sleeping on "any sofa or lounge."[12] The complaint book was filled with comments about members using abusive language and playing cards on Sunday. Several comments were specifically about members making disparaging remarks in a loud voice about the executive committee. Gambling bets on any card games, roulette, dice, and all mechanical gaming devices had to be limited to two dollars, because the losses incurred by some members caused bad feelings. It was resolved, in 1891, that "the complaint book is not a proper vehicle for making complaints of the conduct of members of the Club. . . a box for the reception of such communications"[13] was the replacement.

In 1892, members of the Metropolitan Club established the Chevy Chase Club for the purpose of reviving the sport of riding the Dublane Hunt in Montgomery County. Clarence Moore was Master of Hounds at the Chevy Chase Club, until he traveled to England to purchase new hounds and ponies. He booked his return passage on the *Titanic* and, unfortunately, Moore was not among the survivors. Some members were also interested in the game of golf, so the club established the Washington Golf Club. This nine-hole course was laid out in Arlington County on the property that later became Colonial Village, the residential apartment complex built in the community of Rosslyn, during the late-1930s. (Colonial Village, located between Lee Highway and Wilson Boulevard, was designated a historic property in the mid-1980s.)

In 1904, the Metropolitan Club building was severely damaged by fire and the club moved to a temporary residence in the Arlington Hotel Annex. An architectural competition was held for the design of a new clubhouse and, a design submitted by George Heins and George LaFarge was chosen. (Heins and LaFarge had recently designed the new St. Matthew's Catholic Church on Rhode Island Avenue, a few blocks north of Lafayette Square.) The new Metropolitan Club, completed in 1908, was built in a Renaissance Revival architectural style, fronting on H Street with symmetrical bays of buff colored brick trimmed with limestone. The clubhouse stands, somewhat defiantly, on the corner of 17th and H Streets, NW, coupled to a post-modern office addition facing 17th Street, designed by the architectural firm of Keyes Condon Florance.

Woodrow Wilson, the 28th President, 1913-1921

Thomas Woodrow Wilson was the son of Joseph Wilson, a Presbyterian minister who served as a chaplain to Confederate troops when the Wilson family lived in Georgia during the Civil War. In 1873, Wilson enrolled in college in North Carolina, but was forced to leave because of illness. A few years later, while attending Princeton University, he pursued his studies in government. After graduating from Princeton, he attended the University of Virginia to study law. Again, illness forced him to leave school, but Wilson continued his studies independently and, he was admitted to the bar in 1882. The next year, Wilson attended Johns Hopkins University as a graduate student, where he studied history and continued his studies of government.

Woodrow Wilson dropped his first name, Thomas, before he published his first book, *Congressional Government,* in 1885. That same year he became an associate professor at Bryn Mawr College and was awarded a doctorate degree. In 1890, Wilson's alma mater, Princeton University, offered him a professorship. Twelve years later, he was elected Princeton's president. He advocated democratic principles in education and attempted to focus college life on academics rather than the social and sports activities of the privileged.

When Wilson was nominated as a candidate for governor of New Jersey in 1910, he accepted on the condition that he would not be obligated to fulfill any patronage promises. Wilson won the election because he was an eloquent speaker and, he was highly regarded as the president of Princeton. As New Jersey's governor, Wilson sponsored antitrust acts, reform legislation for workers' compensation, the regulation of utilities, and the reorganization of public school education.

Two years later, in 1912, Wilson won the election for the presidency of the United States. He was an independent, innovative, and open president, who instituted weekly press conferences. Wilson permitted the first income tax to be imposed, when he signed the Underwood Tariff Act. He also signed the Clayton Anti-Trust Act, which assisted the government's efforts to break up monopolies. Wilson urged Congress to pass the Federal Reserve Act of 1913, which created regional banks to regulate currency. He also established the Federal Trade Commission, which supported the regulation of businesses.

Wilson and his wife, Ellen, who was also the child of a Presbyterian minister, had been married twenty-seven years when Wilson was elected president. Ellen was compassionate, intelligent, and artistically talented. Although rumors abounded about possible affairs between the president and other ladies, the Wilsons' 1,400 surviving personal correspondences serve to reinforce their strong devotion to each other. Two of the Wilsons' three daughters were married in the White House, which added to the busy schedule Ellen Wilson carried out while serving as first lady.

Ellen brought attention to the underprivileged by touring Washington's decrepit neighborhoods and, she urged legislation to improve housing for the poor, which resulted in the passage of "Ellen Wilson's Bill" in 1914. Ellen suffered from Brights' disease (a kidney ailment) and died in August 1914, a few days after the passage of the housing legislation named for her. Several years later, however, the bill was declared unconstitutional by the Supreme Court.

Soon after Ellen's death, World War I began in Europe. President Wilson wanted the United States to remain neutral. When German submarines sank the passenger ship *Lusitania* in 1915, with more than 100 Americans aboard, Wilson issued only a diplomatic protest.

Eight months after Ellen's death, Wilson was introduced to Edith Bolling Galt, the widow of Norman Galt, a well-known Washington jeweler. Edith and Woodrow were immediately attracted to each other and, in December 1915, they were married in a quiet ceremony at Edith's home. Edith enjoyed entertaining and brought new life to the White House parties.

The 1916 presidential campaign was one of the closest in history. Wilson narrowly won a victory over Supreme Court Justice Charles Evans Hughs. In

January 1917, Wilson called for "peace without victory" when tried to end World War I by establishing a League of Nations that would mediate disputes between neighboring countries. The Germans responded by aggressively attacking U.S. ships in the Atlantic. On April 2, 1917, Wilson asked Congress to declare war, which it did four days later, allowing Wilson to immediately institute many emergency war measures. The support given the to Allies by the American troops brought World War I to an end on November 11, 1918.

During the war, Edith had curtailed White House entertainments. She sewed items for the Red Cross and economized on living expenses by bringing sheep to trim the grass on the White House lawn.

In December 1918, Wilson attended the Treaty of Versailles Peace Conference. He promoted his Fourteen Points for a just and lasting peace and, his idea for the League of Nations. The European Allied powers insisted on imposing harsh penalties on Germany in return for accepting the League of Nations plan. When the final version of the Versailles treaty was presented to the Senate for approval, Senator Henry Cabot Lodge fought vehemently against it. He insisted on adding provisions to the treaty that Wilson felt would nullify the establishment of the League of Nations.

Wilson embarked on a speaking tour across the United States to rally support for his proposal of the League of Nations, but he became ill and stopped his tour. Upon his return to Washington, Wilson suffered a stroke on October 2, 1919, which left him incapacitated for several months. Edith Wilson, who was very self-assured, protected her husband after his stroke. She carefully scrutinized all correspondences and limited the number of his visitors. Many people felt Edith wielded too much power and made too many important decisions for her husband, though she claimed that her control lasted only a few weeks while Wilson recuperated from his stroke. The Senate took advantage of the president's condition to rally support against the Treaty of Versailles. When Wilson recovered his strength, he was unable to gain the two-thirds Senate majority vote needed for the passage of the treaty.

In the 1920 presidential election, Wilson backed the Democratic Party candidates, James M. Cox and Franklin D. Roosevelt. However, they lost to the Republicans, Warren G. Harding and Calvin Coolidge. Wilson's hopes of the United States entering into the League of Nations were destroyed with Harding's victory. Nonetheless, in November 1920, Wilson was awarded the Nobel Peace Prize for his efforts to promote world peace. On Inauguration Day, 1921, the Wilsons moved into a home in the Kalorama neighborhood of Washington, which ten friends helped the Wilsons to purchase. In 1924, only three years after leaving the presidency, Wilson died and was entombed in the Washington National Cathedral. Wilson was the only president to retire and remain in the Nation's Capital and, the only president buried in Washington.

Edith Wilson outlived her husband by almost four decades and she remained active in Democratic politics, while traveling and writing her memoirs. Edith continued to live in the house in Washington, which she generously donated to the National Trust for Historic Preservation. She died on Wilson's birthday, December 28, 1961, the same day she had planned to dedicate a Potomac River bridge named to honor Woodrow Wilson. Edith was buried with her husband in the Washington National Cathedral.

Tracy House — *the final story* —
1624 I Street, NW

The Tracy House was destroyed by fire in 1891 and, the next year, it was rebuilt by Augustus Tyler. From 1898 until 1911, the new house served as the first Imperial Russian Embassy. One of the ambassadors to reside in this Embassy was Count Arturo Cassini. Because he was a bachelor, his official hostess was sixteen-year-old Marguerite Cassini. He introduced Marguerite to society as his "niece," but he later adopted her as his daughter.

The count was labeled as a bore when he arrived in Washington, but Marguerite ("Maggie") was described as romantic, exotic, and flirtatious. She made her Washington debut in 1899 with Del Hay, son of John Hay, as her escort. The newspapers predicted that she was "likely to shine conspicuously" among the social butterflies of the day. Maggie's best friend was Alice Roosevelt, Theodore Roosevelt's willful and unconstrained teenage daughter. Maggie later described her friendship with Alice as having the "violence of a bomb . . . a combination of two heedless girls who used their position thoughtlessly to impose their fads, their caprices on everyone –[creating] a veritable reign of terror."[14]

Maggie Cassini was not accepted to be of equal rank among the diplomatic wives, because she was the count's "niece." Count Cassini wanted equal status for Maggie, so he returned to Russia and appealed to the Czar, who allowed him to officially adopt her. The count had been married three times, but was divorced when he arrived in Washington. His third marriage had been in defiance of the Czar. It was rumored that Cassini was sending huge blackmail payments to his third wife. Many years later, Maggie wrote her autobiography explaining that her governess, Madame Stephanie Scheele who accompanied her to Washington, was actually her mother and the count's fourth wife, by a secret marriage. Mme. Scheele had been a well-known vaudeville performer.

When Maggie returned to Washington from Russia for the next social season, she was introduced to society as not only the count's daughter, but as a countess who could now preside over official receptions. Maggie owned and drove one of the first automobiles in the city. She wore clothes that were flamboyant and excessive, powdered her nose in public, and smoked cigarettes.

Maggie told her friend, Alice Roosevelt, that Nicholas Longworth had asked her to marry him. Alice jealously decided that she wanted to marry Nick. A year later, Alice and Nick were married with pomp and pageantry at the White House. Maggie later confessed to really being in love with Del Hay, who was killed in an accident at Yale. Maggie returned to Russia and married someone she described as "hopelessly Russian." During the years of the Russian Revolution, Maggie traveled with her two sons through Europe and eventually returned to Washington. She rented a small house in Georgetown where she opened a dressmaker's atelier. Maggie's two sons, Oleg and Igor, worked with her and both later became famous fashion designers.

The Tracy House, where the count and Maggie had been residing, was a two-story structure of an undistinguished style, topped with a mansard roof. The dining room accommodated only twenty-four people. Maggie Cassini soon found a finer house in Washington for their ambassadorial residence. In 1903, Count Cassini leased Levi Morton's grand home on Rhode Island Avenue, NW, facing Scott Circle, just a few blocks north of Lafayette Square. However, the Russo-Japanese War forced Count Cassini to leave Washington in 1905. When the new Russian ambassador, Baron Rosen, arrived in the city, the Tracy House, once again, served as the official Russian Embassy.

In 1913, the Tracy House was sold to the Men's City Club, which in turn sold it in 1922 to the American Association of University Women (AAUW). The AAUW kept the house until 1959. The property, located at the southeast corner of Connecticut Avenue and I Street, NW, across from Farragut Square, was sold for $500,000 in 1960. The Tracy House was razed and a thirteen-story, modern office building was erected on the site. Several years later, the Farragut West Metro subway station opened beneath the building.

Riggs House — *the final story* —

1617 I Street, NW

Miss Jane and Miss Alice Riggs inherited their father's house (the Riggs House) in 1881 and, they continued to live there for the rest of their lives. Neither sister ever married. In their later years, the two sisters became rather reclusive. In 1919, the Prince of Wales (later the Duke of Windsor) came to Washington. It was decided that the prince should pay a visit to the Riggs sisters. They were among the last surviving "belles" in the city who had been present at the visit of the former Prince of Wales (later Edward VII), in 1860. The prince's visit to the Riggs House was unplanned. No advance notice was given to the Riggs sisters that the prince intended to call upon them. The butler who answered the door at the Riggs' home did not recognize the prince, so he was not admitted.

Later, during the prince's visit to Washington, the Riggs sisters did have the opportunity to entertain him. They both served as regents at Mount Vernon. Their father, George Washington Riggs, had assisted Miss Ann Pamela Cunningham in the original purchase of that property for the Mount Vernon Ladies' Association. The sisters greeted the Prince of Wales when he toured the first president's home and, they escorted him to see the tomb of George Washington, where he laid a memorial wreath. This visit with the prince was the last public appearance the Riggs sisters ever made.

Miss Jane and Miss Alice refused to adapt to the modern customs of the day and, they resolutely refused to sell their home. Miss Jane died in 1927. Miss Alice died in 1930. The beautiful Victorian home was purchased and razed in 1935. The site became a parking lot, which was a sad irony, since the sisters abhorred the intrusion of cars in their lives. An office building, erected by Morris Cafritz, now stands on the site of the old Riggs House.

Myer House — *the final story* —
Army Navy Club — *a new story* —

17th and I Street, NW — northeast corner

The huge, gothic-style Myer House was situated in an enviable central location between Lafayette Square and Farragut Square, near government offices and Washington's downtown business district. In 1911, the Army Navy Club purchased the Myer House, with the intention of using the site for a clubhouse. Before the Army Navy Club was officially established, several local hotels near Lafayette Square had been referred to as "army-navy hotels" because so many military officers were listed as residents.

Sixty military officers stationed in Washington in 1860, a year before the Civil War began, established the United Service Club (later called the Army Navy Club). They leased the rooms above Klutz' Restaurant, at 1706 G Street, west of the White House. Several clubhouses were located nearby, including the Metropolitan Club, Cosmos Club, Men's City Club, Women's City Club, and Racquet Club (the University Club). Chartered clubs with clubhouses were very popular by the end of the 19th century, because they helped to create a sense of community among people with similar interests.

The Army Navy Club razed the Myer House to make way for a larger facility. The new clubhouse building, which was designed by Joseph Hornblower and J. Rush Marshall, stood six stories tall, with a two-story rusticated stone base, similar in style to many Washington apartment buildings of the day. The clubhouse was the tallest structure in the area. On the top floor was an observation porch, which afforded a clear view across the Potomac River to Virginia. The neighborhood surrounding the new clubhouse was still predominately residential: the Riggs House was next door and the Tuckerman House stood across the street. In 1950, the clubhouse was expanded. An extra side bay was attached to the building and a top-floor ballroom was added.

In the 1980s, the Army Navy Club required additional space for offices and parking. The architectural firm of Shalom Baranes Associates was hired to save the old facade, raze the structure, and significantly enlarge the facility. Four stories were dug out below street level to accommodate a parking garage and a health club. The top floor of the building was raised up four stories and the clubhouse was also expanded to the side and the rear. Office space fills the new additions. In the core of the building where the old clubhouse once stood, some of the original light fixtures, wood paneling, and murals have been reinstalled.

Tuckerman House — *the final story* —
1600 I Street, NW — southwest corner

Lucius Tuckerman lived in the magnificent Washington residence he built for only four years before died in 1890. His wife, Elizabeth, continued to reside there until her death in 1906. The next year, Congressman Henry Kirke Porter purchased the house. Porter, like Tuckerman, was a wealthy Pittsburgh businessman and it is likely that the two families were acquainted with one another. Porter manufactured light locomotives and iron rails for the railroads.

Though the exterior appearance of the Tuckerman House was massive and masculine, the interior decorations of the home, by contrast, were delicate and classical. A theme of floral and geometric details decorated the rooms, complimented by the beautiful brass doorknobs and heating grates. The ceilings were high and ornamented with intricate, plaster moldings. The drawing room featured an elegant, 18th century English, Carrara marble mantle with caryatid columns. The mantle had been removed from a grand mansion in New York. The quality and craftsmanship of this marble mantle matched the mantle in the dining room at Mt. Vernon, which had been a gift to George Washington from an English friend.

The Porters filled their new home with a fabulous collection of rare textiles. Annie-May (de Camp) Hedgeman Porter, Henry's wife, was an artist and she donated many items from their collection to the Smithsonian Institution. Annie's daughter, Annie-May Hedgeman, donated the balance of the textile collection to the Smithsonian Institution, after her mother's death. The Porters' also collected rare books, furnishings, and art that Annie-May donated to the Library of Congress and the Corcoran Gallery of Art, in 1936. The donations were valued at $1 million, which was the largest donation ever given to the government. In 1938, Annie-May wrote a bequest deeding the Tuckerman House to the Library of Congress, with a proviso that, when it was rented or sold, the proceeds should be divided equally between the Library of Congress and the Smithsonian Institution.

The Cosmos Club expressed interest in leasing the Tuckerman House, but decided against it. The Office of the President leased the property, in 1941, for use by the Division of Defense Housing. In 1948, when Miss Hedgeman died, the Motion Picture Association of America purchased the Tuckerman House for $600,000, from the Library of Congress. A two-story private movie theater was built in the rear garden. In 1964, the house was designated as a landmark of cultural heritage. The National Capital Park and Planning Commission and Joint Committee on Landmarks recommended that the building be preserved. However, the Motion Picture Association was able to destroy the home in 1967, despite the recommendations and public outcry against its destruction. A few of the interior decorations were auctioned, including the Carrara marble mantle and a few items were donated to the Smithsonian Institution. A plain, modern office building was built in its place.

Warren G. Harding, the 29th President, 1921-1923

Warren Gamaliel Harding, the oldest of eight children, was raised on a farm in Caledonia, Ohio. Upon graduating from college, he moved to Marion, Ohio, where he and two friends purchased a small newspaper, the *Marion Star*, at a bankruptcy auction. Within a few years, Harding bought his friends' interest in the newspaper and made it a financial success. Harding was attracted to the Republican Party and served in the Ohio State senate from 1899-1903.

After returning to Marion, Ohio to manage his newspaper, Harding continued to be actively involved in the Republican Party. In 1912, he gave the nominating speech for the presidential candidate, William Howard Taft, at the Republican National Convention. Two years later, Harding was elected to the U.S. Senate. While serving in the Senate, Harding developed a reputation of missing the roll call for Senate votes. He spent much of his time drinking, gambling, and cultivating a group of political friends. In Congress, Harding was a proponent of women's rights and, oddly enough, he supported Prohibition.

In 1920, Harding entered the presidential campaign, but was not among the top four Republican contenders. However, none of the four favorites received a majority vote and, by compromise, Harding was chosen. He was congenial, good looking, and known to be a Republican Party leader. People across the country were tired of the sacrifices of war and feared any further involvement in world affairs. Harding easily won the election by promising a "return to normalcy." He was especially appealing to the women, who, in 1920, for the first time in the history of the country, were allowed to vote for a president.

Harding was strongly opposed to Wilson's concept of a League of Nations. The Senate had never ratified the Versailles Treaty to formally end World War I, so immediately upon becoming president, Harding arranged separate peace treaties with Germany, Austria, and Hungary. These separate treaties ended any prospect of the United States entering into the League. Harding also advocated a disarmament conference. His Secretary of State, Charles Evans Hughes, drafted a treaty that successfully reduced the size of the navies of France, Germany, Japan, Italy, Great Britain, and the U.S.

Warren Harding had married Florence King DeWolfe in 1891. She was an independently wealthy divorcee with one daughter. Florence was domineering and demanding, in direct contrast to her husband whom she considered to be submissive and manageable. After they were married, Florence took control of the *Marion Star* so that Harding could pursue his interest in politics. Florence enjoyed meeting people and, when she became first lady, she spent a good deal of time entertaining. However, she neglected many other responsibilities of her position. Despite her outward strength, Florence suffered from a kidney ailment and nearly died from a serious kidney infection in 1922.

Florence and Warren Harding had a deteriorating marital relationship by the time they moved into the White House. Her shrill voice, her lack of beauty, and her tenacious personality prompted Harding to label her the "Duchess." Harding's affair with Nan Britton, who was thirty years his junior, was not a very well kept secret. Nan and Harding had a daughter who was born in 1919. Three years after Harding's death, Nan published a book documenting their long love affair, which was entitled, *The President's Daughter*.

Scandals permeated Harding's presidency, though many were not made public until after his death. Like most presidents before him, Harding's "spoils system" policy permitted his friends to secure high government appointments and, to use their newly acquired power to increase their personal wealth. The most famous scandal of Harding's administration was the 1922 Teapot Dome Affair, involving oil rights on government-owned land (in Teapot Dome, Wyoming and elsewhere). The oil-rich land was to have been reserved for the use of the navy. However, it was secretly leased to the Mammoth Oil Company, which was controlled by Harry F. Sinclair. Several government officials and the oil company presidents were eventually indicted by a grand jury, on charges of bribery and conspiracy to defraud the United States. A number of Harding's acquaintances were convicted, included Secretary of Interior Albert Fall, Secretary of the Navy Edwin Denby, Attorney General Harry Daugherty, and Charles Forbes, head of the Veterans Bureau.

In 1923, Harding traveled across the United States on a speaking tour to gain support for the Republican Party, which had lost a number of seats in the recent congressional election. When Harding was in Seattle, he suffered severe abdominal pains that were not properly diagnosed. While visiting San Francisco a few days later, Harding died. Florence refused to allow an autopsy and rumors circulated that Harding had committed suicide over the scandals or, that he had been poisoned, although no evidence was ever found to support the claims.

J. Calvin Coolidge, the 30th President, 1923-1929

John Calvin Coolidge was raised on a farm in Vermont. As a teenager, he attended a private preparatory school. Although, he failed the entrance exam at Amherst College, he reapplied, was admitted and graduated with honors in 1895. Two years later, Coolidge was admitted to the bar and started a law firm in Northampton, Massachusetts. He was a supporter of the Republican Party and became involved in Massachusetts State politics. Coolidge served first on the city council, next as state representative, then as mayor of Northampton, and finally as state senator. In 1918, Coolidge was elected governor of Massachusetts. During his first year as governor, the Boston police went on strike resulting in a crime spree that spread throughout the city. Coolidge called on the state militia to maintain order. The leader of the American Federation of Labor (AFL), Sam Gompers, claimed Coolidge's actions were unfair. Coolidge responded with a statement that made him famous, "There is no right to strike against the public safety by anybody, anywhere, any time."[15]

In 1920, Coolidge was the surprise choice as the vice presidential running mate with Warren Harding, the compromise Republican presidential candidate. Coolidge was popular and he and Harding easily won the election over the Democratic contenders, James Cox and Franklin Roosevelt. On August 3, 1923, while Coolidge was vacationing with his family in Vermont, he received the unfortunate and unexpected news that President Harding had suddenly died. Coolidge's father, John Coolidge was a justice of the peace and notary public. He administered the oath of office to his son in the sitting room of their home.

President Coolidge was a practical, honest leader, who proved to be a successful administrator. In 1924, he was nominated for reelection in the first national party convention to be broadcast on radio. His image as a simple, small-town boy who quietly got things done, coupled with a strong national economy won him the election. The economy was further strengthened when Coolidge decreased personal income tax and lowered the national debt. Consumers had more money, which encouraged spending and stimulated investments. However, over-speculation in the stock market eventually led to its crash in October 1929, which, in turn, led to the Great Economic Depression.

Calvin Coolidge had married Grace Goodhue in 1905. She was the first first lady to have received a college education at a coeducational college, the University of Vermont. Grace was a teacher for the deaf and she remained interested and active all her life in assisting those who were hearing impaired. She was charming, outgoing, and had an enviable memory for faces and names. Grace was a great complement to her rather dour husband. Her love of baseball made her popular with the men. Her cheerfulness, vivaciousness, and fondness for music and theater made her equally popular with the women. She and Calvin had two sons. Sadly, one son tragically died of blood poisoning from a blister, while the Coolidges were in residence at the White House.

Grace's skills as a hostess were legendary. Her fashion sense was simple and elegant and, she entertained in a dignified and unpretentious style. She was tactful, diplomatic, and possessed great *joie de vivre*. In 1931, Grace Coolidge was voted to be one of America's top twelve living women and, the National Institute of Social Sciences awarded her a gold medal for her "fine personal influence exerted as First Lady of the Land."[16]

The Coolidges retired from the White House to Northhampton, Massachusetts, where they purchased a nine-acre estate, called Beeches. Calvin lived only four more years and died in 1933. Grace lived until 1957, never losing her delightful sense of gaiety and fun. In Calvin Coolidge's autobiography, he wrote of his wife, saying, "For almost a quarter of a century she has borne my infirmities, and I have rejoiced in her graces."[17]

McLean House — the final story —

Lafayette Building — a new story —
1500 I Street, NW

John R. McLean wanted a house with which he could dazzle the "provincial capital." In 1907, McLean hired architect John Russell Pope to redesign his home near Lafayette Square. The house was enlarged to measure 133-feet wide by 133-feet deep, covering a significant part of the block. Within the walls of the new home, Pope incorporated the original 1860 house built by Jonah Hoover, along with the many extra rooms McLean had added in the 1890s. New walls, built over the existing ones, were extended to create new spaces. The third story of the original house was removed, making the newly redesigned home horizontal and palatial. The style of the opulent and unorthodox McLean House was described as neo-Renaissance.

John Russell Pope was a talented architect, but fairly inexperienced when McLean hired him at the turn of the century. Pope later created many famous residences in Washington including the George Hewitt Myer House (the Textile Museum) next to the Woodrow Wilson home and, the two homes on Crescent Place, NW, of Irwin Laughlin and Henry White. Pope also designed such monumental structures as the Jefferson Memorial, National Gallery of Art, National Archives, Scottish Rite Temple, and National City Christian Church.

The McLean House was never meant to be a full-time residence, because the McLeans also owned a country estate located above Georgetown, named Friendship. Rather, the renovated house near Lafayette Square was to be used for entertaining crowds of people. On the first floor of the house were three major reception galleries, a library, a large dining room, and a courtyard. Two of the reception rooms had glass ceilings and the third was designed to display huge tapestries, over-stuffed furniture, marble statues, gurgling fountains, and massive imported mantles and chimneys. Family bedrooms were on the second floor and, the living quarters for thirty servants were on the third floor.

In the summer of 1912, McLean's wife, Emily, died unexpectedly of pneumonia, despite McLean's desperate efforts to hire a private railroad train to take her personal physician from North Carolina to Bar Harbor, Maine, where she was spending the summer when she became ill. McLean never completely recovered from the loss of his wife. Four years later he died. He left the McLean House, the country estate, the *Cincinnati Enquirer*, the *Washington Post*, and $7 million to his only son, Ned, who had been a spoiled child. In 1908, when Ned was twenty-two years old, he married Evelyn Walsh, the daughter of Thomas Walsh who had made his fortune in Colorado gold mining. Years later, Evelyn wrote about her family's wealth saying that, every morning her family woke up richer than they had been the night before when they had gone to sleep.

Ned McLean took over the management of the *Cincinnati Enquirer* and the *Washington Post*, but he was not a successful manager. He had joined the Republican Party, using these newspapers to present biased Republican viewpoints. Among the Republicans Ned supported was Warren G. Harding. Like many of Harding's friends, Ned became entangled in the Teapot Dome Affair, involving improper leasing of the naval oil reserves by Secretary of Interior Albert Fall. Ned's careless lifestyle eventually caused him to lose the *Washington Post*, which was sold at a bankruptcy auction to Eugene Meyers. In 1930, Ned was declared mentally unstable and spent the rest of his life in the Shephard and Enoch Pratt Hospital in Towson, Maryland. Ned died in 1941.

In the early years of their marriage, Ned and Evelyn entertained fabulously at the two McLean residences and the Walsh House, at 2020 Massachusetts Avenue, NW, built by Evelyn's father in 1903. These parties afforded Evelyn the opportunity to show off her dazzling jewelry collection. She was the last private owner of the Hope Diamond, the largest blue diamond in the world. Unimpressed by the solitary, blue, 45.5-carat diamond, Evelyn frame-mounted it in an oval platinum setting, encircling it with sixteen large, brilliant diamonds.

Dangling beneath it was a huge, pear-shaped diamond. The magnificently displayed gem was then attached to a long, diamond-studded, platinum chain.

Evelyn and Ned had four children. One young son, Vinson, was tragically killed, after being struck by a car. Ned's erratic behavior was difficult for Evelyn to endure, and she sued Ned for separate maintenance in 1930, on the grounds of desertion. She lived at Friendship, their country estate, until 1942, when it was sold to the government, razed, and replaced with war housing. The property was renamed McLean Gardens and converted into apartments.

In 1942, Evelyn moved into a roomy house on the corner of Wisconsin Avenue and R Street in Georgetown. She continued to entertain during World War II and, among her guests were many soldiers stationed in Washington. Throughout the war, she offered the use of her house at 2020 Massachusetts Avenue, NW, to the Red Cross.

During their lifetimes, Evelyn and Ned managed to spend approximately $100 million on entertaining and traveling, nearly the entire combined wealth of the Walsh and McLean families. After Evelyn's death in 1947, her estate was auctioned and, Harry Winston, a famous New York jeweler, purchased the Hope Diamond necklace at the auction. Winston donated the Hope Diamond, along with the diamond-chain necklace, to the Smithsonian Institution where it is on display in the National Museum of Natural History.

In 1935, the McLean House had been leased to the government and converted into office space for three New Deal agencies: The Federal Emergency Relief Administration, the National Bituminous Coal Commission, and the Works Progress Administration. In 1939, the house was purchased for $2 million and demolished. Two years later, the Lafayette Building was erected, which was one of the only privately funded office construction projects in the city during World War II. The Lafayette was designed by A. R. Clas (assisted by Holabird and Root of Chicago), and cost $5.5 million to construct. Clas later designed the State Department addition in Foggy Bottom and the Washington Hilton Hotel on Connecticut Avenue. The Lafayette Building, faced with unadorned limestone over brick, is businesslike, somber, and functional. The building housed the Federal Loan Agency, along with the Reconstruction Finance Corporation and other government lending organizations, in the 1940s. For years, the Export-Import Bank has occupied the Lafayette Building.

Chamberlain Club — the final story —

Bowen Building — a new story —
819-825 15th Street, NW

The Chamberlain Club hotel was located across 15th Street, NW, from the McLean House 1892. It was John Chamberlain's charisma and charm that captivated his patrons and, after Chamberlain's death, the hotel closed. For a while, the hotel building served as an actors club. In 1919, the Chamberlain Club hotel, which was comprised of a series of connected older row houses, was sold and demolished.

On the northern corner of the former hotel site, at 825 15th Street, NW, a small bank building was designed for the Liberty National Bank, by Harvey L. Winslow, a New York architect who specialized in bank design. The impressive bank building was just two stories tall with a mezzanine. In 1956, when the Liberty National Bank building was renovated, two stories were added and the lower front facade was faced with marble. A year later, Liberty National Bank merged with the National Bank of Washington, which was sold in 1990, by the Federal Deposit Insurance Corporation. The Riggs National Bank purchased and occupied the handsome little building.

On the southern part of the former Chamberlain Club hotel site, at 819 15th Street, NW, the Smith Building was erected in 1921. Jules Henri de Sibour, a French-trained architect, designed this speculative office building for the F. H. Smith Company. De Sibour also designed the Hibbs Building on 15th Street and, many buildings and homes near Dupont Circle, including the McCormick Apartment Building (currently owned by the National Trust for Historic Preservation) and the home for Clarence Moore of the Chevy Chase Club, who died with the sinking of the *Titanic*.

F. H. Smith Company was a real estate and investment business that was forced into bankruptcy during the Great Depression. In 1932, the Bricklayers, Masons, and Plasterers International Union of America purchased the Smith Building at a foreclosure sale. Many trade associations and unions had begun purchasing buildings with enviable and fashionable addresses near the White House, in order that their organizations might have a notable presence in the Nation's Capital.

The Smith Building was renamed the Bowen Building to honor William J. Bowen, a past president of the Bricklayers Union. The union's need for additional space resulted in two respectful additions to the Bowen Building. In 1935, the New York architectural firm of Voorhees, Gemlin, and Walker added a section on the building to the north. In 1939, architect Philip M. Jullien added a second section onto the first. The additions were sensitive to Jules Henri de Sibour's splendid Renaissance Revival style and allowed the original de Sibour-designed building to predominate.

Shoreham Hotel — *a continuing story* —

Shoreham Office Building — *a new story* —

15th and H Streets, NW — northwest corner

Competition was stiff among Washington hotel owners. Levi Morton spent a considerable sum of money to renovate the Shoreham Hotel in 1902, a year after a rival luxury hotel, the New Willard, was built nearby to replace the old Willard. The newly renovated Shoreham Hotel became an extremely popular place to reside. Woodrow Wilson and his family stayed at the

Shoreham before his first inaugural and, it became a favorite hotel with some of Wilson's closest advisors, including William McAdoo and Bernard Baruch. Baruch was an unofficial advisor to seven presidents and was affectionately called, "Mr. Facts." During World War I, Baruch was known as the "Park Bench Statesman" because he often walked out of his 16th Street office in order to conduct his business in Lafayette Square, saying he "could always get more done on a park bench than at a desk."[18] The Boy Scouts of America honored Baruch's contributions to the United States by placing a plaque next to his favorite Lafayette Square park bench.

In 1925, Washington developer Harry Wardman purchased the Shoreham Hotel, with plans to raze and replace it. Wardman was the first developer to acknowledge the demand for apartment buildings in Washington and, he built 400 of them. Eight of the apartment buildings were luxury properties called apartment-hotels. Altogether, he built 4,000 residences, two clubs, two hospital annexes, one large parking garage, and twelve office buildings. Wardman called himself a "junk dealer . . . I buy old buildings, rags of buildings, bones and bottles of discarded houses, and turn them into habitable homelike dwellings and apartments."[19] Before the Great Depression in the 1930s, Wardman had amassed a fortune of $30 million.

Wardman viewed the Shoreham Hotel property, however, not as a site for another residence hotel, but as a prime location for a new office building. Wardman's main architect was Mihran Mesrobian, who was trained at the Académie des Beaux Arts in Istanbul, Turkey. He had immigrated to America in 1921. While working for Wardman, Mesrobian designed the Shoreham Office Building, which was erected on the site of the old Shoreham Hotel. The twelve-story tall office building's façade featured limited but interesting decoration and detail. Mesrobian also designed two hotels for Wardman: the Carlton at 16th and K Streets and the Hay Adams on Lafayette Square.

In the late-1920s, a new Shoreham Hotel, designed by Joseph Abel, was erected several miles away on property overlooking Rock Creek Park. The new Shoreham was built as a spacious, sprawling, expansive structure. Across Calvert Street from the new Shoreham Hotel is the Wardman Park Hotel, which Harry Wardman and Mihran Mesrobian had built a few years earlier.

Herbert Hoover, the 31st President, 1929-1933

Herbert Clark Hoover was born in Iowa and sent to live with Quaker relatives in Oregon, after he was orphaned at the age of eight. Hoover's strong math skills helped him gain acceptance to Stanford University's first freshman class of engineering in 1891. A few years after graduating, Hoover was hired as an engineer for an international mining company. He traveled all over the world managing mines and was one of the most respected and highest paid mining engineers in the world. Hoover became a multimillionaire while he was still a young man.

Herbert Hoover met Lou Henry at Stanford University, when he was a senior and she was a freshman. Lou was the first woman to pursue geology as a major field of study at Stanford. When she graduated in 1898, Herbert Hoover sent her a telegram from Australia, where he was managing a mine and he asked her would marry him. In 1899, they were married in California and immediately left for China, where Herbert had accepted a position with a mining firm. Lou traveled with her husband throughout his career, visiting Europe, Siberia, Australia, Egypt, Burma, Ceylon, and Japan.

During the beginning years of World War I, the Hoovers were in Europe. As chairman of a committee of Americans for relief work, Hoover aided stranded American tourists throughout Europe and raised funds to help people in the war-torn countries. After America's entry into the war in 1917, Herbert and Lou Hoover returned to the United States. Woodrow Wilson then appointed Hoover to the position of U.S. Food Administrator and later, as chairman of the Allied Food Council, making him responsible for distributing food to millions of Europeans impoverished by the war. At the war's end, Hoover attended the Versailles Peace Conference as President Wilson's economic advisor.

The Hoovers, especially Lou, became famous through their successfully organized relief efforts. In grateful acknowledgement of her work, Lou Hoover was awarded the Cross of Chevalier by Belgium's King Leopold, one of Belgium's highest honors. Lou gave generously to many charities in the U.S. and she was active in helping the Girl Scouts. After her death in 1944, Herbert Hoover called her "a symbol of everything wholesome in American life."[20]

Though Hoover had supported great men of both the Democratic and Republican Parties, he declared himself a Republican in 1920 in order to enter the presidential race. However, Warren G. Harding received the presidential nomination instead. When Harding was elected, he appointed Hoover secretary of commerce and, in 1920, the Hoovers moved to Washington. Hoover continued to serve as secretary of commerce for eight years.

In 1928, Hoover was nominated as the Republican presidential candidate.

The Republicans claimed responsibility for the economic prosperity of the 1920s and Hoover easily won the election against the Democratic candidate, Al Smith. When the Hoovers moved into the White House, they entertained elegantly but on a small scale, always using their own money to pay for the social events. Seven months after Hoover was elected president, the stock market crashed and one quarter of the nation's workforce was unemployed. The economic conditions worsened dramatically during Hoover's administration. Although Hoover inherited the conditions that led to the Great Depression, he was blamed for being the cause of it.

The economic depression grew worse despite Hoover's efforts to increase government loans, reduce income tax, and establish some public works programs. Hoover believed that Americans should be self-reliant, so he refused to support federal relief and benefit programs to help the poor and unemployed. In 1932, Hoover was nominated as the Republican presidential candidate, but lost the election by a huge majority to the Democrat, Franklin D. Roosevelt. When Hoover left Washington, he returned to his home in Palo Alto, California, where he outwardly criticized Roosevelt's New Deal programs.

During Truman's administration, Hoover was appointed to chair the Famine Emergency Commission, which was responsible for aiding those Europeans who were left destitute after World War II. In 1947, Truman asked Hoover to investigate and recommend organizational changes for the executive branch of the government, in order to make it more efficient. Many of the "Hoover Commission" recommendations were implemented and proved to be so effective, that President Eisenhower appointed Hoover to head a second commission to evaluate government organization. Hoover finally retired from public service in 1955, but stayed active in Republican politics until his death, at age ninety, in 1964. The only other president to outlive Hoover was John Adams, who lived 136 days longer.

St. Matthew's Church — *a continuing story* —

Southern Building — *a new story* —

15th and H Streets, NW — northeast corner

At the turn of the century, the congregation of St. Matthew's Catholic Church abandoned its location across from the Shoreham Hotel near Lafayette Square and moved to its new copper-domed, Byzantine-style church near Dupont Circle. The old church building at 15th and H Streets, NW, was offered for sale.

The Southern Commercial Congress, whose purpose was to "boost the South" in Washington, bought the old St. Matthew's church in 1910 and razed it to make way for their new office building. The new building was named the Southern Building. The designer of the Southern Building was the Beaux-Arts architect Daniel Burnham, from Chicago. Burnham had been a member of the McMillan Commission and, he designed Washington's Union Station in 1907 as well as the adjacent Main Post Office Building in 1912.

© EDWARD F POGUE EFT

Burnham's design for the Southern Building was an exuberant, U-shaped, terra-cotta-trimmed office structure that reflected his love of Italian Renaissance ornamentation and symmetry. The Southern Building's fanciful new style was widely imitated in Washington. The U-shaped design was practical and efficient in the early-20th century before the invention of central air-conditioning, because it allowed light and fresh air into all of the offices. The delightful, white terra-cotta embellishments, including the lion's head decorations that poke out between the windows, were described as "confectionery allusions."

The Southern Building was designed to be nine stories tall, even though zoning allowed for an eleven-story building on the site. Two more stories were added in 1988, when the building was restored by the architectural partnership of Shalom Baranes Associates.

Wormley's Hotel — the final story —

Union Trust Building — a new story —

15th and H Streets, NW — southwest corner

Wormley's Hotel closed after James Wormley's death in 1884. However, it soon reopened under a new name, the Colonial Hotel, and the new manager was Charles E. Gibbs who had previously managed the Ebbitt House. In 1904, the Union Trust and Storage Company (later, First American Bank) purchased the old Victorian hotel and demolished it.

The Union Trust and Storage Company had been incorporated in 1899. When the Wormley Hotel site was chosen for the location of the company's office building in 1904, a decision was made to emphasize the banking and trust business rather than the company's storage services. The bank's name was shortened Union Trust Company.

Waddy Wood and his partners, Edward Donn and William Deming, designed the Union Trust Company's six-story building, with an impressive façade on the 15th Street side. Four-story tall Corinthian columns, rising up from above the first story, overpower the façade and imitate the architectural style of Treasury Department two blocks away. A 1909 article in *Architectural Record* called it "typical of the best class of banks which have recently been built"[21] in Washington. The American Bar Association bought the building in the 1990s.

Columbian University — the final story —

Woodward Building — a new story —

15th and H Street, NW — southeast corner

©EDWARD F FOGLE EFF

The fabulous, five-story, molded brick Columbian University building, which was erected in 1883, stood at the corner of 15th and H Streets until 1910. The beautiful multipurpose structure, with huge arched windows and terra-cotta trim, was built in the old-fashioned, Victorian- style. By the turn of the century, Columbian University suffered financial difficulties and was forced to sell the building. S. Walter Woodward purchased the structure, razed and replaced it.

The new handsome Woodward Building was constructed as a Renaissance Revival-style, U-shaped office building. The first floors were faced in stone, the middle stories were of unadorned brick, and the top two stories were faced with glazed terra-cotta. The Washington architects, Harding and Upman, designed the building for S. Walter Woodward who kept his offices there. Woodward also financed Harding and Upman's design for the new YMCA building at 18th and G Streets, NW, and the Woodward Apartment Building on Connecticut

Avenue, NW, at the edge of Rock Creek, south of the Taft Bridge.

S. Walter Woodward and Alvin M. Lothrop started a department store in Washington that operated for 115 years before it closed in 1995. Woodward was the son of a ship builder from Maine and Lothrop was from northern Massachusetts. Both traced their ancestry back to the Mayflower pioneers. Woodward and Lothrop had met as young clerks in a dry goods store. They disagreed with the store's sales policy of leaving merchandise unpriced, which encouraged clerks to engage in unfair bargaining. Consequently, the two men lost their jobs, so they decided to go into business for themselves. In 1870, they arrived in Washington and opened a store where they gave their merchandise a fixed price. They also instituted a return policy that was almost unheard of at the time. The Woodward and Lothrop Department Store, located a few blocks east of the Woodward Building, had become one of the largest department stores in the United States by the time the Woodward Building was erected in 1911.

S. Walter Woodward was highly regarded and known as one of the city's great philanthropists. His obituary in 1917, noted that he had "little opportunity for his own personal recreations. He loved the science of trade . . . and was happiest when employed in that undertaking . . . he was warm in his affections, cordial in his friendships, heartily appreciative of the feelings of others."[22]

National Savings & Trust Bank — a story —

15th Street and New York Avenue, NW — northeast corner

Toward the end of the 19th century, Washington's Financial District was beginning to expand along 15th Street, NW, near Lafayette Square, forever changing the residential character of the neighborhood. Financial institutions in the Nation's Capital began to invest a significant percentage of their assets in the construction of grand, imposing, new banking houses. One of the first new bank buildings, on 15th Street, was a commanding, impressive, five-story, red brick structure, designed for the National Savings and Trust Company (NS&T). The bank was erected on a highly visible, triangular corner property, diagonally northeast of the Treasury Department. James Windrim designed the bold, new Victorian-style building in 1888. It stretched for 130-feet along 15th Street and 65-feet along New York Avenue. Small stores leased the ground-floor space facing 15th Street and the upper-floors offices were rented to various tenants.

The NS&T bank was originally called the National Safe Deposit Company and was formed in 1867, by a special act of Congress, for the purpose of storing securities and valuables. Wealthy Washingtonians stored their boxes of jewelry and trunks of silverware with the National Safe Deposit Company, which shared space with the National Savings Bank in the Plant Building, located on the corner lot at 15th Street at New York Avenue. In 1875, George H. Plant sold the three-story Plant Building to the National Safe Deposit Company. Thirteen years later, the building was razed. In 1890, the National Safe Deposit Company and National Savings Bank merged into the National Savings and Trust Company (which, a century later, was purchased by Crestar Bank).

In 1911, the NS&T bank building was enlarged. A 50-foot addition was attached to the New York Avenue-side of the bank, with 42-inch thick masonry walls on the first three floors. In 1925, a second matching addition was attached to the first one, extending that side of the building to a length of 165 feet. Both additions blend in so beautifully that it is difficult to distinguish them from the original structure. In the 1980s, a third addition was added that is remarkably sympathetic with the older structure, in style, scale, and color.

The grand and inviting corner entry, with attractive double doors, was designed for the original building. Rising above the second story of the entryway is a beautiful, three-story, bronze corner bay, topped with a huge round clock. Above the clock is an eye-catching, two-story, gilded cupola, crested with a decorative finial. The building's brick ornamentation becomes more detailed as it rises toward elaborately decorated uppermost fifth story. This Victorian-style bank building holds a prominent position in Washington's financial district and, provides a wonderful, sharp contrast to the classical lightness and whiteness of the marble, Beaux Arts-style neighboring structures.

Welcker's Hotel — the final story —

Hibbs, SRH, & Securities Buildings — a new story —

723-729 15th Street, NW

In the 1880s, the old Welcker's Hotel (renamed the Barton Hotel) stood on 15th Street, at the north end of the block from the NS&T Bank. Located between the hotel and the bank, was a small lot on which the elegant, tall, slender Hibbs Office Building was erected in 1889. The building was a visual delight of white marble and granite, designed by Jules H. de Sibour. It was ten-stories high, topped with a fancy, copper and slate Mansard-style roof, and ornamented with small balconies, carved garlands, swags, urns, and bas relief panels. The new Hibbs Building was built and occupied by the William B. Hibbs brokerage firm.

Jules Henri de Sibour designed the Hibbs Building early in his architectural career, while he was still in partnership with Bruce Price of New York. This gem of an office building, housed a bank on its first three floors. The upper-floor offices were leased to prominent professionals. In 1907, de Sibour moved to Washington to start his own architectural firm. He remained in Washington until his death in 1938 and was responsible for designing some of the most beautiful, Beaux Arts-style commercial and residential structures in the city. From 1910 until 1922, de Sibour's architectural firm occupied the top-floor offices in the Hibbs Building.

William B. Hibbs was a popular investment banker in Washington. He was described in a *Saturday Evening Post* article, as "being an old timer, a good mixer, and what is technically known as a straight shooter, having no political leanings except toward sanity and honesty in government . . . the names of his prominent friends and regular visitors, if placed end to end, would make the

Hall of Fame look like a packing case. Presidents, cabinet officers, commission heads, financiers, bureau chiefs, editors, admirals, generals, senators, newspaper correspondents, ambassadors, consuls, authors, representatives, governors, railroad presidents, labor leaders, manufacturers and what not have sat in his big front room, ten stories above Fifteenth Street."[23]

For many years, W. B. Hibbs & Company was the only Washington brokerage firm to be a member of the New York Stock Exchange. The Hibbs firm was also a member of the Boston, Philadelphia, and Washington Stock Exchanges, the New York Cotton Exchange, and the Chicago Board of Trade. In 1953, the Hibbs Building was renamed the Folger Building, when W. B. Hibbs & Company joined with Folger, Nolan, Fleming & Company.

In 1906, the old Welcker's Hotel building was razed and replaced with several new commercial structures, of various sizes. In 1907, Paul Pelz designed a tiny, one-story, ornate, marble *petit palais*, to sit next to the Hibbs Building and, it was often mistaken as being a part of the Hibbs Building. The "palace's" entrance was flanked by a pair of Corinthian columns with statuary groupings of allegorical, angelic, female figures holding a monogrammed cartouche with the initials SRH, for Swartzell, Rheem, Hensey & Company.

Swartzell, Rheem, Hensey & Company was a leading mortgage banking firm, started in 1869 by B. H. Warner. By 1902, Warner sold his interest to his long-time partners, Clarence B. Rheem and George W. F. Swartzell. When Clarence Rheem died in 1913, his son Edmund took his place in the business. Edmund was married to the daughter of developer, Harry Wardman (who built many Washington residences, hotels, apartment houses, and office buildings). When Wardman built the Shoreham Office Building, at 15th and H Streets, SRH provided the financing. In 1931, Edmund Rheem lost $162,000 of the firm's money in stock market speculation. The firm declared bankruptcy, causing the 1,200 creditors to lose more than $3 million. Edmund was sentenced to five-to-seven years in jail at Lorton Reformatory. In 1935, he was paroled, with the understanding that he would never enter the District of Columbia again. Between 1933 and 1940, the SRH Building served as the office for Laidlaw and Company, stockbrokers. For the next eight years, it was the Del Rio Restaurant. In 1948, Simon B. Zelnik converted the building into a movie theater and, for many years, the SRH Building was known as the Playhouse Theater.

In 1988, the First Washington Development Group financed a new, twelve-story office building to be placed around the little structure. The architectural partnership of Mariani & Associates designed the building, encumbering the original *petit palais* with a disconcerting and incongruous addition. Above the Beaux Arts-style marble palace looms a modern, ten-story bay harshly sheathed in contrasting black glass with white marble-banding, featuring protruding, boxy, marble balconies, which mercifully step back on the upper levels.

In 1925, the Securities Building was erected between the SRH Building and the Woodward Building, at 729 15th Street, NW. Harry Wardman, the flamboyant Washington developer, designed and built the curious, tall, narrow, gray Securities Building. It's architectural style was called "Jacobean Revival," and featured a two-story arched entry, faced in granite and marble. Above the entry, two narrow, carved, granite columns stretch upward seven stories to the roof. Three long, linear panels of window bays parallel the columns. The surrounding Beaux-Arts style office buildings caused the Securities Building to stand out, looking odd and eccentric, perhaps, reflecting the character of the builder, Harry Wardman, whose business offices were located there.

Evans & The Washington Buildings —a story—
1420 New York Avenue and 1435 G Street, NW

In 1908, when the nine-story Evans Building was erected at 1435 G Street, many of the old row houses still stood on the triangular block formed by 15th and G Streets, and New York Avenue. The houses had been converted into fashionable clothing shops, railroad and steamboat ticketing agencies, and professional offices. The Evans building awkwardly towered above its neighbors, dominating the southeast corner of the block. The first floor of the Evans Building was filled with street-level shops and named, the Evans Arcade. The upper-floor offices were leased by various financial and professional firms. The building's architect, Frederick Pyle, kept his office was on the seventh floor, from 1912 until 1933. Pyle also designed many fine Washington homes, including S. Walter Woodward's residence in the neighborhood of Kalorama and several homes in the Mt. Pleasant neighborhood.

Terra-cotta ornamentation on the upper stories added exuberance of the Renaissance Revival-style Evans Building. Two years after its construction, Daniel Burnham extensively employed similar decorations on the Southern Building nearby. The *Washington Post* called the Evans "the latest addition to Washington's recent acquisition of modern office structures, standing out strongly as the highest rung of architectural skill and development."[24]

In 1926, the Washington Building was erected next to the Evans Building. It wrapped around the corner from New York Avenue to 15th Street and back to G Street, NW. The building was distinguished from its neighbors because it incorporated the smooth, slick surfaces and stylized details of the Art Moderne-style. Chocolate-brown colored granite, used sparingly at the street-level, enticed passers-by into the arched openings of the shops and businesses. Investment bankers, insurance companies, trade associations, and lobbyists were the early tenants of the upper-floor offices. From 1935 until 1948, the Washington Stock Exchange was located in Washington Building.

The architectural firm of Coolidge, Shepley, Bullfinch and Abbott designed the Washington Building. Harry Shepley was H. H. Richardson's grandson and, the firm was the successor to Richardson's firm that designed the Hay and Adams Houses. The architectural firm later specialized in designing hospitals and college buildings, including many at Yale University.

In 1987, a top story was added to the Washington Building, during its renovation, by the architectural partnership of Keyes Condon Florance. The same chocolate-brown colored granite was utilized on the upper-level addition. A whimsical, oversized, limestone decoration was added on each top-floor corner, creating a stylized acroteria that resembles an opened fan.

Rhodes Tavern — *the final history* —

Metropolitan Square — *a new story* —

15th and F Streets, NW — northeast corner

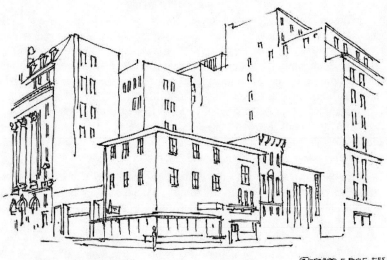

© EDWARD F FOGLE EFF

Against overwhelming odds, Rhodes Tavern survived for almost two centuries in a prestigious location across from the Treasury Department. Over the years, however, the three-story tavern lost its classical proportions as the building was enlarged with several additions. Before the Civil War, claims agents leased offices in Rhodes Tavern and, in 1852, Charles S. J. Chubb & Brothers bought the building and operated a private bank there. During the Civil War, the government occupied the offices in the building, although a few bankers and shopkeepers continued to lease space on the first-floor. Toward the end of the 19th century, private offices again moved in.

In 1881, Washington's first Stock Exchange was located in the Rhodes Tavern building. In 1909, the National Press Club rented space on the second and third floors of the building, until their new office building was constructed nearby. The ground-floor space continued to be leased to a variety of shopkeepers and entrepreneurs, including a cigar store, bootblack, news agency, restaurant, candy shop, souvenir shop, record shop, and fruit market.

In 1977, preservationists brought attention to the old Rhodes Tavern building, which had witnessed every inaugural parade in Washington, since President Jefferson's inaugural in 1801. The fight to save Rhodes Tavern continued for seven years. Washingtonians overwhelmingly approved a ballot initiative to preserve the building. In 1970, the National Capital Planning Commission's publication noted, "Restoration of Rhodes' Tavern could create an attractive and useful visual link with the city's difficult formative years and the present. If properly restored, it would be of great tourist interest and a fine example of civic responsibility on the part of the developers."[25]

In 1984, despite the referendum to save Rhodes Tavern and years of struggling by determined preservationists and concerned residents, the building was suddenly razed by the property site developer, Oliver T. Carr, Jr., to make way for a new office structure named Metropolitan Square. The protestors had angered him to such an extent, that he even refused to allow a plaque dedicated to the old tavern, to be placed on the exterior wall of the new building.

In 1998, the Metropolitan Square building was sold to Morton Zuckerman. In June 1999, the new owner agreed to allow a plaque to be placed, identifying the site of Rhodes Tavern, on the southwest corner of the building at 15th and F Street, where the Galt & Sons Jewelers retail store (established 1801) is located. Morton Zuckerman also generously paid for the installation of the 18-inch by 18-inch historical, commemorative bronze plaque.

The Riggs House was a fine, small hotel, located north of Rhodes Tavern on 15th Street, near G Street. James Garfield played billiards regularly at the Riggs House, before he was elected president. In 1911, the old Riggs House was razed. Jules Henri de Sibour designed a new building for the site and named it, the Riggs Building. The Beaux Arts-style marble building, located across from the Treasury Department, was a stunningly handsome structure. Incorporated into the Riggs Building (later renamed the Albee Building) was the new Chase Theater, which later was known as Keith's Theater.

Between old Rhodes Tavern and the Riggs/Albee Building was the small building built for the Metropolitan Bank in 1905. B. Stanley Simmons and the architectural firm of Gordon, Tracy & Swartout designed the splendid little marble-faced, Beaux-Arts bank building. From the time the Metropolitan Bank was founded in 1814, it had occupied only three different locations in Washington, all within the same block on 15th Street.

The Metropolitan Bank and the Riggs/Albee Building were threatened with destruction along with Rhodes Tavern in 1984. The architects of the huge Metropolitan Square project, Skidmore, Owings and Merrill, agreed to incorporate some of the façade of the Albee and the Metropolitan Bank buildings into the new building complex. The elegant arched, marble entryway to Chase/Keith's Theater became the entrance of a restaurant, called the Old Ebbitt Grill, that was relocated from a F Street row house. The restaurant's interior decorations and paneling, which originally were in the Ebbitt House hotel and later in the F Street row house, were incorporated into the new restaurant.

Corcoran Office Building — the final story —

Hotel Washington — a new story —

15th Street between Pennsylvania Avenue and F Street, NW — east side

©EDWARD F FOGLE ℮ℱℱ

The handsome Corcoran Office Building, built in 1875, remained on the prominent piece of property, across from the Treasury Department, until 1911, when it was demolished in to make way for a new hotel. By 1917, the Hotel Washington, designed by John Merven Carrère and Thomas Hastings, was erected on the site. Carrère and Hastings also designed the first Senate and House Office Buildings, as well as the Townsend Mansion (the Cosmos Club) on Massachusetts Avenue.

The dignified Hotel Washington was designed to occupy half of a city block on a highly visible site near the White House. Three of the hotel's four sides faced important streets (F and 15th Streets, and Pennsylvania Avenue). The hotel was built of brown brick and stone, and decorated with wonderful Sgraffito carvings between the upper floor windows. Sgraffito carving is a near-extinct Italian technique of sculpting decorative pictures into an outer coating of colored plaster to reveal the plaster of a different color beneath. This type extraordinary architectural embellishment is found nowhere else in Washington. The designs represent various themes, including Masonic signs from the ancient Coptic religion, portraits, and symbols for such concepts as "life after death."

No documentation seems to exist to explain the choice of symbols or the names of the Sgraffito artisans who created the original designs. In the 1980s, the Pennsylvania Avenue Development Corporation's (PADC) preservation advisors identified the Sgraffito on the Hotel Washington as unique, valuable, and worthy of restoration. A New York sculptor and art restorer, Ivan Valtchev, was hired to revive the designs that, over time, had disappeared into dull, red blocks of color. Among the symbols he uncovered were Aladdin's lamp, representing *Illumination,* and bats beside an urn, representing *Night and Death.* Portraits of Thomas Jefferson, Abraham Lincoln, George Washington, along with Rafael and Shakespeare were also identified. One crest on the wall depicted a swan for *Beauty and Nobility* and, two stripes and three stars for *Influence.* This crest on the Hotel Washington is very similar to the family crest on the coat of arms of the Washington family from Sulgrave, England, from which George Washington is descended.

F Street Row Houses — the final story —
F between 9th and 15th Streets, NW

©EDWARD F FOXLE EFF

The end of the Civil War brought the beginning of the drastic changes to the residential character of F Street, NW. New office and commercial space was in demand. Many of the old row houses were either adapted for commercial use or demolished and replaced with towering commercial buildings. By the late-1860s, the neoclassical styled Treasury Department, and the Patent Office and Post Office (six blocks east on F Street), were nearing completion after thirty years of construction. The Masonic Lodge building was erected on F Street, across from the Patent Office in 1870.

Three new "skyscrapers" (eight- and nine-stories tall) made their debut, in the late-1880's, across F Street from the Masonic Lodge building: the new Riggs Bank, the National Union Building, and the Atlantic Building.

The very first skyscraper built in the city was the Baltimore Sun Newspaper Building, at 1315 F Street near John Quincy Adams' house. (Some argue that it was the first in America.) The Sun Building was designed in 1885 by Alfred Mullett, supervisory architect of the Treasury, who had designed the State, War and Navy Building next to the White House, a dozen years earlier. By the end of the century, F Street had been revitalized. Corcoran rebuilt his office building, Caleb Willard rebuilt the Ebbitt House, and Joseph Willard, Jr. rebuilt the Willard Hotel.

Turn-of-the-century, office buildings on F Street, included the Westory (1906), the Interstate Building (1912), and the Homer Building (1913). The area also attracted many sophisticated, new shops. The fanciful, new Woodward and Lothrop Department Store, near F and 11th Streets, replaced the old store in 1901. The Garfinckel's Department Store building, with its attractive limestone façade, was erected on the corner of F and 14th Streets in the late-1920s.

Franklin Delano Roosevelt, the 32nd President, 1933-1945

Franklin Roosevelt lived a sheltered life as a child. Franklin's father, James Roosevelt, was a lawyer and railroad executive who had inherited great wealth. James Roosevelt had a son by his first marriage that was twenty-eight years older than Franklin and the same age as Franklin's mother, Sara, (who was thirty years younger than her husband).

Roosevelt attended Harvard University in 1900, where he studied history, economics, and law. A year before he graduated from Harvard in 1902, he met Anna Eleanor Roosevelt, a distant cousin. They fell in love and, in 1905, they were married. Since she had been orphaned at the age of ten, Eleanor's uncle, President Theodore Roosevelt, gave her away at the wedding. Franklin Roosevelt's career in politics began in 1910, when he won the election to the New York state senate as a Democrat in a predominately Republican district.

The first years of marriage were terribly difficult for Eleanor because she was so shy and self-conscious and, because her mother-in-law, Sara, ruled the household. When President Wilson appointed Roosevelt as assistant secretary of the navy in 1913, Eleanor and Franklin moved to Washington, leaving Sara behind in New York. However, soon after moving to Washington, Eleanor discovered her husband was involved in an extra-marital love affair. She was devastated and she redirected her thoughts and energies toward teaching English, history, and drama. She earned an income by lecturing and writing. She also opened a furniture factory with two other women. Eventually, Eleanor realized that her husband's political success depended partly upon her involvement and she felt duty-bound to become active in Democratic politics.

In 1920, Roosevelt was nominated as the Democratic candidate for vice president along with presidential candidate James M. Cox. Although Cox and Roosevelt had Wilson's support, they lost the election to Warren G. Harding.

The next year, Franklin contracted poliomyelitis. He was thirty-nine years old. Although the disease left him crippled, he was determined to continue his life of public service. In 1924, Roosevelt delivered the presidential nominating speech for the Democratic candidate, Al Smith. Roosevelt's courageous appearance on crutches overshadowed the fact that Smith did not receive the nomination. Four years later, Al Smith won the 1928 presidential nomination and he resigned as governor of New York. Smith then urged Roosevelt to campaign for the New York governorship that he was vacating, against the Republican candidate, Herbert Hoover. Roosevelt won the governorship, despite the tremendous odds against him. Two years later in 1930, he was reelected.

By 1932, Roosevelt's popularity made him a leading Democratic candidate for the presidency. He won the nomination. John Nance Garner of Texas, who was Speaker of the House, was nominated as vice president. An assassination attempt was made on Roosevelt's life while he was campaigning in Florida. An unemployed bricklayer, Giuseppe Zangara, fired six shots at Roosevelt while he sat in an open car. Miraculously, Roosevelt was not hit, but five others were shot, including the mayor of Chicago, Anton Cermak, who was killed.

After Roosevelt won the presidential election, he tackled the severe problems of the country's economic depression with his "New Deal" solutions. Working with Congress, Roosevelt created the Federal Emergency Relief Act, which provided government aid for many of the 15 million unemployed citizens. He also created the Civilian Conservation Corps, which employed thousands of young people on conservation projects. Roosevelt abandoned the gold standard, increased bank loans, created federal bank deposit insurance, and successfully infused the economy with federal money to ease the depression.

Roosevelt's self-confidence and determination gave confidence to the impoverished citizens of America. His weekly "fireside chats" kept people abreast of his policies to help the nation. He worked for unemployment insurance, Social Security, and federal aid to dependent children. His popularity increased and he easily defeated Republican Alfred Landon in the 1936 presidential election. In 1937, Roosevelt tried to increase the number of Supreme Court justices from nine to fifteen, because he felt the Court was too conservative. His "court-packing" idea backfired and Roosevelt was pelted with severe criticism by both the press and the public.

An unwritten and unenforceable premise had guided past presidents from serving no more than two consecutive terms. However, when Roosevelt was nominated for a third presidential term in 1940, the majority of people did not object or complain. He easily won a victory over Wendell Willkie.

A year before the 1940 election, Hitler's Germany invaded Poland and World War II began in Europe. Roosevelt vowed to remain neutral but fought for aid to Great Britain and other allied countries. In 1941, the Lend-Lease Act was passed, which gave Roosevelt the authority to supply weapons and equipment to the Allies. The supply convoys headed for Britain were accompanied by Warships. These warships were under orders to attack German vessels on sight, thus involving the United States in war activities months before Congress declared war. On December 7, 1941, Japan attacked Pearl Harbor, Hawaii and Congress declared war against Japan the next day. Two days later, Germany and Italy declared war against the U.S. and, on December 11, 1941, Congress adopted a resolution recognizing a state of war in Europe.

In late November 1943, Roosevelt met with Winston Churchill and Joseph Stalin in Tehran to discuss war strategy. A little more than a year later, in January 1945, Roosevelt was inaugurated as president for the fourth time. The next month Roosevelt, Churchill, and Stalin secretly met in the Ukraine, at Yalta, to discuss the postwar reorganization of Europe. The three leaders discussed chartering an international peace-keeping organization that would meet in April at a United Nations Conference. However, Roosevelt did not live to attend the conference. On April 12, at age sixty-three, Roosevelt died from a cerebral hemorrhage in Warm Springs, Georgia.

Eleanor Roosevelt was the most active first lady to serve in the White House, often traveling in place of her husband to meet with people across the United States. During the war, Eleanor visited Europe to meet with the troops, and she was the first first lady to travel by airplane, doing so when most people were afraid of air travel. She was called the "first lady of the world." Through writing, she earned her own income but donated most of the money to charity. Eleanor resolutely criticized racial discrimination, advocated women's rights, and influenced the choice of the first female cabinet official, Frances Perkins, as secretary of labor. She gave radio speeches and public lectures and, she personally answered her correspondence, often working eighteen hours a day. For many years after Franklin died, Eleanor continued her active public service. As a delegate to the United Nations, she assisted in writing the Universal Declaration of Human Rights. Her last public appointment was in 1961, as the chair of President Kennedy's Committee on the Status of Women. Eleanor suffered from bone marrow tuberculosis and in November 1962, she died.

Harry S Truman, the 33rd President, 1945-1953

Harry S (no period) Truman's middle initial stands for nothing, since his parents could not agree on which grandfather to name him after, Anderson Shippe Truman or Solomon Young. He was the son of a Missouri mule trader. Truman's poor eyesight limited his involvement in sports, so he concentrated on reading and playing the piano. He showed an early interest in politics and, when he was sixteen years old, he worked as a page during the 1900 Democratic presidential convention in which William Jennings Bryant was nominated.

Because Truman could not afford college, he accepted the opportunity to manage his grandmother's farm and turned it into a successful business. During World War I, he fought with distinction and attained the rank of major before leaving the service. After the war, Truman opened a haberdashery in Kansas City. However, he never lost interest in local politics. In 1926, he was elected to an administrative judgeship and held several similar positions for eight years. Truman gained a reputation in Kansas City for his honesty and, in 1934, he was elected to the U.S. Senate. He was reelected in 1940. During both terms, he heartily supported Franklin Roosevelt's "New Deal" legislation. In 1944, Truman was nominated as the vice presidential candidate for Roosevelt's successful fourth-term election.

Truman served as vice president for only eighty-two days and assumed the presidency on April 12, 1945, upon Roosevelt's death. As president, Truman put all his efforts toward ending World War II. On May 7, 1945, Germany surrendered. Truman traveled to Potsdam, Germany, to meet with Churchill and Stalin to discuss dividing Germany into occupied zones. While in Potsdam, Truman was informed that the United States had successfully tested the atomic bomb. In an agonizing decision, he authorized dropping the atomic bomb on Hiroshima on August 6 and on Nagasaki three days later to hasten the end of the war. On September 2, 1945, Japan surrendered.

By 1947, the unreconcilable differences between the political policies of the United States and the Soviet Union had developed into a "cold war." President Truman requested that Congress authorize $400 million in aid to Greece and Turkey to prevent their governments from being taken over by Communist insurgents. Truman defended his request by saying, "I believe that it must be the policy of the United States to support free peoples who are resisting attempted subjugation by armed minorities or by outside pressures."[26] This proposition became known as the Truman Doctrine. Working with Secretary of State George C. Marshall, Truman radically increased foreign aid to help rebuild Western European economies after the war. In 1948, the Marshall Plan was instituted and has lasted as one of the great successes of the Truman administration. However, many of Truman's domestic policies, such as his progressive civil rights legislation, failed due to congressional opposition.

In the 1948 presidential election campaign, the Democratic Party was divided three ways: the Truman supporters, the ultra liberals championing Henry Wallace, and the southern Democrats ("Dixiecrats") who were against Truman's civil rights policies and who promoted Senator Strom Thurman of South Carolina. Truman was reelected in 1948 by so slim a majority that, in an early release, the newspapers incorrectly announced that his Republican opponent, Thomas E. Dewey, had won.

Truman's wife, Elizabeth Virginia (Bess) Wallace, grew up in Independence, Missouri, and had known Harry since he was a child. However, their romantic relationship developed gradually and they were not married until after he returned from World War I. Bess was calm and practical, loved sports, and shunned publicity. She edited nearly all of Truman's speeches, papers, and correspondences. Truman claimed that his wife's judgment was immeasurably important to him and her calming effect was a blessing against his hot temper. Truman's anger was as legendary among his staff as his wife's admonishment: "You didn't have to say that." Bess guarded her privacy so much that she rarely granted interviews and the press called her a "riddle." Nonetheless, the Trumans were wonderfully close as a family. Their daughter, Margaret, attended George Washington University and, for a while, had a singing career.

From November 1948 until March 1952, President Truman, Bess, and

Margaret lived in the Blair House while the White House interior was completely dismantled and rebuilt. On November 1, 1950, an assassination attempt was made on Truman's life by two Puerto Rican nationalists, Griselio Torresola and Oscar Callazo, who tried to force their way into the Blair house, shooting at the house with automatic weapons. Truman was in residence at the time, but luckily, was not injured. A Secret Service agent, Leslie Coffelt, however, was killed while attempting to protect the president.

The Korean War eclipsed most of Truman's policies in the 1950s, as the Communist troops from North Korea invaded South Korea. Truman sent U.S. troops as a part of the United Nations forces, to push back the North Korean invaders while advancing into North Korea. The goal was to unite the country. Communist China joined with North Korea and pushed the UN troops back into South Korea, deadlocking the war. When General MacArthur, commander of the U.N. troops, publicly advocated invading China, against Truman's diplomatic policies, Truman fired him for insubordination. Public sentiment was with MacArthur and Truman's popularity declined.

Harry and Bess Truman retired to Independence, Missouri, where Harry lectured and oversaw the construction of the Truman library. By the time he died in 1972, Truman had gained the reputation of a folk hero. Bess continued her quiet lifestyle and died at age ninety-seven. Margaret Truman became an author and wrote several best-selling mystery novels set in Washington.

Ebbitt House & Newspaper Row — the final story —

National Press Club — a new story —

F and 14th Streets — southeast corner

Long after the turn of the century, the Ebbitt House remained a popular Washington hotel for visitors and temporary residents. In 1927, the Ebbitt House was razed to make way for the National Press Club building. The splendid interior of the old Ebbitt House restaurant bar and grill was dismantled, moved across the street, and reassembled in a row house at 1427 F Street, NW. The Old Ebbitt Grill occupied the F Street Row House until the 1980s, when the row house was torn down and replaced by a modern office building, called Metropolitan Square. The interior of the Old Ebbitt Grill was salvaged and moved around the corner into its new location in Metropolitan Square.

The National Press Club was an outgrowth of the old Newspaper Row. The new Press Club building was built beside the row of houses that were once used as newspaper offices and, it stretched between 13th and 14th Streets on F Street. The $10 million building was hailed as a "monument to the American press." Major Ernest Graves of the U.S. Army supervised the construction of the fourteen-story building. The largest movie theater ever built in Washington, the Fox Theater, was incorporated into the east end of the National Press Club building and could accommodate 3,500 patrons. Twenty-four marble columns stood inside the theater's lobby and the interior decoration resembled a palatial

Hollywood movie set. George Rapp of Chicago was the architect of both the Fox Theater and the National Press Club building. Rapp and his brother, C.W. Rapp, designed many major movie houses in Chicago. George Rapp later served as a consulting architect for New York's Radio City Music Hall.

LEONARD F FOGLE EFF

When movies were shown at the Fox Theater, they were preceded by a number of entertainments and shows. Sing-alongs kept the audience amused as a bouncing ball of light danced across the projected words on the movie screen. The musical accompaniment for the sing-alongs came from an organist playing a Wurlitzer organ that was raised up from the orchestra pit. After the sing-alongs, several vaudeville acts were performed on the stage while a fifty-piece orchestra played. These engaging shows were followed by the movie.

When the Great Depression of the 1930s caused the financial ruin of the Fox film empire, the theater was sold to Loew's, Inc. In 1939, a contest was held for renaming the theater and, the name, "Capitol," was the winning choice. By 1953, the orchestra pit was covered over and the vaudeville acts were discontinued. Ten years later, the National Press Club closed the theater; removed the seats, marble columns, and decorations; and converted the palatial movie theater into mundane office space.

Between 1978 and 1982, the National Press Club building was gutted and rebuilt. The only remnant of the former grandeur of the theater is the F Street marble entrance façade, which rises seven stories in a neoclassical-style. The

Press Club entrance was planned at the west end of the new building with shops and restaurants located at the east entry level. Connected to the Press Club building, facing south onto Pennsylvania Avenue, is the J. W. Marriott Hotel, which was built in 1984 and sheathed in a utilitarian, gray/brown brick.

The National Press Club Building/Marriott Hotel complex surrounds the renovated National Theater, which was nearly demolished in 1978. The original National Theater was financed by banker W. W. Corcoran and erected in 1835 on the same spot where the current theater is located. The original building was the scene of President Polk's inaugural ball in 1845. A few years later, the theater burned to the ground and was rebuilt in 1852. Fires were common in theaters because theater buildings were tall, open spaces filled with flammable materials, such as curtains, props, costumes, and flats. The National Theater burned again in 1857 and was rebuilt in 1862. It burned again in 1873 and was rebuilt the same year. In 1885, the National Theater again burned and was rebuilt, and that building remained until 1922. A few months after the disastrous collapse of Washington's Knickerbocker Theater on January 27, 1922, in which ninety-three theater patrons were killed, the National Theater was rebuilt with steel beams to satisfy the city's new building code. The National Theater was renovated in the early 1980s and continues to serve as a popular Washington theater.

Willard Hotel — *the continuing story* —
Pennsylvania Avenue at 14th Street, NW — northwest corner

Throughout the 19th century, Joseph Willard managed the Willard Hotel, which his brother Henry had established in 1847. Joseph dedicated all his energy to managing the hotel, becoming progressively more reclusive and frugal after the death of his wife, Antonia, in 1871. When Joseph Willard died in 1897, he was said to be worth $7 million.

Joseph's son, Joe, Jr., was a lawyer in Fairfax County, Virginia. When his father died, he inherited a fortune. His inheritance included the Willard Hotel, which he considered architecturally old fashioned and outdated. Joe hired the New York architect Henry Hardenberg to design a new hotel to take the place of the old one. The new Willard Hotel had the city's largest ballroom on the top floor and became the premier hotel in Washington for the first half of the 20th century.

Gradually, the Willard Hotel fell out of favor and into disrepair. Washington's newer hotels, such as the new Shoreham, Wardman Park, Carlton, Statler Hilton, Mayflower, and Hotel Washington provided plenty of competition. After World War II, the Willard family sold the hotel to the Abbell Hotel Company for $2.8 million. In 1954, the hotel was completely redecorated and modernized. A new kitchen and air conditioning was added. The grand ballroom, which had been closed for many years, was reopened, with a seating capacity of 1,000. Even so, the Willard's popularity did not revive and seven years later, it was sold again.

GEORGE F POLE EFT

In 1961, when newly elected President Kennedy and his wife, Jacqueline, drove along Pennsylvania Avenue after the inauguration, they commented on how neglected "America's Main Street" looked. An advisory council, called the Pennsylvania Avenue Development Corporation (PADC), was established at the request of the president to develop a Master Plan for improving Pennsylvania Avenue. The plan proposed razing the Willard Hotel to make way for a National Square and, the hotel closed in 1968.

Washingtonians became sentimental about the Willard Hotel once it was closed. A group of local preservationists, calling themselves "Don't Tear It Down" (later renamed the D.C. Preservation League), organized concerned citizens to save both the Willard and, the Old Post Office building on Pennsylvania Avenue at 12th Street. The public supported the preservation efforts. A number of proposals for readapting the Willard Hotel building were suggested, including refacing it and converting it into an office building. In 1974, the Willard Hotel's owners obtained a demolition permit, but they were unable to immediately proceed with the building's destruction.

The PADC advisory council reversed its stand, on the fate of the Willard in 1976. They no longer felt it was necessary to tear down the once-elegant, old hotel. Senator Daniel Patrick Moynihan, who worked with the advisory council, was a strong voice for preservation. PADC was able to secure funding for preserving the Willard Hotel. In 1978, the negotiations for its purchase were completed and bids were accepted for the hotel's restoration. Ten years later, in 1986, the hotel reopened and immediately became one of the most poplar and prestigious places to stay while visiting the Nation's Capital. This grand dame of Washington hotels was once again called the "Crown Jewel of Pennsylvania Avenue."

Riggs & American Security Banks — *the continuing story* —

American Security & Walker Buildings — *a story* —

Pennsylvania Avenue and 15th Street, NW — northwest corner

ⓒEDWARD F FOGLE EFF

Riggs and Company used the stuccoed bank building and cashier's house (designed for the Bank of the United States by George Hadfield in 1824) throughout much of the 19th century. However, the bank trustees wanted a new look for the new century. Charles Glover, the president of Riggs for many years, first changed the bank's name from Riggs and Company to the Riggs National Bank and, in 1898, razed the cashier's house located in the center of the block, on Pennsylvania Avenue. With Glover's guidance, a new, marble, neoclassical-style structure replaced the cashier's house and, set the precedent for the Beaux Arts-style marble and granite buildings that would fill the financial district during the first third of the 19th century.

The architectural partnership of York and Sawyer designed the 1891 Riggs Bank Building, which was later extended on the west, by Appleton P. Clark in 1922. The addition replaced the old Arlington Insurance building. Riggs' old main bank building was sold to American Security and Trust Company, which was organized in 1889 and had its first offices at 15th and G Streets. The old Riggs building was razed in 1904. In its place, a neo-classical structure, also by York and Sawyer, was built to complement the new Riggs Bank building. The

American Security and Trust Building has been described as looking "like a little granite cash box, where piles of money and mortgages sit, seemingly secure behind rusticated walls and iron bars."[27]

Rising up behind the American Security and Trust Company building, on 15th Street, is a ten-story building named the American Securities Building. York and Sawyer designed this complementary office building in 1930, with the first three floors made to match the style of both bank buildings (Riggs and American Security and Trust Company). The American Securities Building towers seven stories above the two bank buildings, but the plainness of the upper facade tends not to draw attention to its height.

In 1937, a twelve-story in-fill office building was erected on 15th Street between the American Securities Building (1930) and the Union Trust Building (1906), which completed the block of high-rise buildings. The new Walker Building replaced the Hendricks house, an old, residential structure that had been used, briefly, by the German Embassy. The architectural firm of Porter and Lockie built the Walker Building for William H. Walker, a residential real estate developer. Designed as a tall, sleek, cream-colored stone structure, the Walker Building features decorative bronze work and unusual stylized details. The most prominent decorations on the building are the brightly-colored, Egyptian-inspired, mosaic tile patterns, inlaid above the first floor windows.

In 1905, more than thirty years earlier, William H. Walker had erected the building across the street at 729 15th Street, NW and named it the Walker Building. The first Walker Building housed the real estate firm that was started by Walker's father, R. W. Walker, who died in 1907. William H. Walker became the sole heir to his father's business, which included a loan and insurance company. The original Walker Building was sold and razed in 1925, by Harry Wardman, who replaced it with the Securities Building.

U.S. Treasury Annex — a story —
Pennsylvania Avenue at Madison Place, NW

The property, on which the U.S. Treasury Annex was constructed in 1917, was once occupied by the Gunnell House and later, by the Victorian-style Freedman's Savings Bank. The Freedman's Bank was demolished in 1899, when the Department of Justice, which had been housed in the elegant bank building since the late 1870s, anticipated replacing it with a new office building. However, the appropriated funds proved insufficient to construct a building that adequately suited the needs of the Justice Department, so the lot stood vacant for eighteen years. The Department of Justice moved from Lafayette Square to a building on Vermont Avenue at K Street, NW.

In 1915, the Treasury Department's new Annex building was designed, by the architect Cass Gilbert, for the Freedman's Bank site. Gilbert was a member of the Commission of Fine Arts and had established an admirable reputation for designing public buildings in the Beaux Arts-style. As an advocate of the Senate Park Commission Plan (McMillan Plan), Gilbert embraced the idea of erecting handsome, neo-classical structures facing onto Lafayette Square.

Gilbert's design for the new Treasury Annex was inspired by the monumental style of Robert Mill's main Treasury Department across the street, built between 1835 and 1865. Originally, the new Annex was to have extended the full length of Madison Place, from Pennsylvania Avenue to H Street, NW. In 1917, the plan for the size of the building was reduced to only one third of the Madison Place block. The Annex building and the Treasury's main building were connected by a tunnel under Pennsylvania Avenue and, the Income Tax Division was the first occupant of the new Treasury Annex.

Many employers experience problems with their employees upon moving into a new office building. The Treasury Annex employees proved to be no exception. In 1924, a number of letters were exchanged within the department concerning a delicate situation. One letter dated August 12, 1924 states, "It is reported to me by the supervisor of our laboring forces that great quantities of toilet paper are being used in Treasury Annex #2 for drying hands, instead of employees taking their towels with them to the toilet room. It appears that the situation is equally bad in both the men's and the women's toilet rooms."[28] The final solution to the problem was not documented in the department files.

Arlington Hotel — the final story —

Veterans Administration — a new story —
Vermont Avenue between H and I Streets, NW — west side

During the last quarter of the 19th century, the Arlington Hotel and the Ebbitt House were considered to be among the best places to reside in the city. By the turn of the century, the Arlington Hotel's business suffered due to strong competition from the nearby Shoreham Hotel that had been recently renovated, and the Willard Hotel that had been rebuilt. Plans were made to tear down the older Arlington Hotel and to build an elegant, new, eight-story hotel on the site. J. Pierpont Morgan was a regular patron who always stayed at the Arlington Hotel when he was in Washington and, he maintained a permanent suite of rooms there. Morgan agreed to be the financial backer for the new hotel on one condition: that his suite of rooms be perfectly duplicated in the new building, with the exact furnishings, paintings, and decoration. In 1911, the Arlington Hotel was razed to make way for the new structure and the hotel's furnishings, antiques, and paintings (except those in the Morgan suite) were auctioned off. When Morgan died suddenly before the new construction began, the funding arrangements were invalidated and the new hotel was never built.

After America's entry into World War I, the government purchased the Arlington Hotel site in 1918 and erected a new building, costing $4.2 million, designed by James A. Wetmore (of the Office of the Supervising Architect of the Treasury Department) along James B. Wyatt and William G. Nolting. The Veterans Administration was the second building erected under the auspices of the McMillan Plan. The ten-story structure was taller than any neighboring building, although the new Arlington Hotel originally had been designed to be only eight-stories-tall. The Veterans Administration building was rushed to completion by 1919 and, initially was named the Arlington Building.

The office of the War Risk Insurance Corporation moved into the Arlington Building from the office space it had borrowed in the Smithsonian Institution. The corporation was immediately responsible for administrating the estates of four million servicemen during the war and, after the war, for distributing cash bonuses and handling veterans' benefits. In 1921, the War Risk Insurance Corporation was renamed and designated the Veterans Bureau, by an Act of Congress.

The style of the Arlington Building (the Veterans Administration building) was not popular, partly due to the somber façade of gray Indiana limestone. Only minimal architectural details break the long face of the Vermont Avenue front of the building, such as the decorative pediments over the second-floor windows and ten, two-story tall Ionic columns centered over the entry. Similarly placed columns break the short façade on the building's H Street side. A critic complained, "St. John's [Church] is framed against the hideous walls of the Veterans Bureau, which tower above it like the overhanging sides of some sinister mountain cañon (sic). Here in the days of early World War hysteria, was committed an atrocious crime against the beauty of Washington."[29]

Corcoran & The Slidell Houses — *the final story* —

U. S. Chamber of Commerce — *a new story* —

H Street and Connecticut Avenue, NW — northeast corner

The Corcoran House was continually used as a private residence before it was razed in 1922. W. W. Corcoran lived in the house until his death in 1888. Corcoran's grandson, William Corcoran Eustis, next occupied the house for a few years after his grandfather died.

In 1892, Senator Calvin Steward Brice leased the Corcoran House for six years. Brice had served in the Civil War and later, became a corporate lawyer. He was involved in the planning, development, and management of railroads. Brice successfully developed railroads in Ohio, the Mid-west, and the South and received a commission from the Chinese government to develop a railroad in China between Canton and Hankow. As a civic leader in his hometown of Lima, Ohio, Brice became involved in Democratic politics. In 1890, he was elected to the Senate but, after one term, he decided not to run for reelection. Collecting fine art was one of Brice's passions. His collection included watercolor paintings, pencil drawings, Chinese porcelain, and rare books. The Corcoran House, which Brice filled with his collections, was the scene of many grand parties noteworthy enough to be regularly reported on in the newspapers. Brice died in 1898 before finishing his Chinese Railroad project.

Senator Chauncey Mitchell Depew was the next occupant of the Corcoran House. Like Brice, Depew was a lawyer who had made his fortune from the railroads. While serving as Cornelius Vanderbilt's attorney, Depew consolidated several independent railroads, creating the New York Central Railroad. Politics interested Depew and, he resigned his position as president of the New York Central Railroad in 1899 when he was elected to the Senate.

Depew was popular and witty. He was also a skillful orator who had been a principal speaker at the opening of the Chicago World Fair, at the unveiling of the Statue of Liberty, and during the commemorative ceremonies at the Tomb of Lafayette in Paris. The Corcoran House served as Depew's residence during his first of his two Senate terms. The house's spacious proportions and ideal location were used to advantage by Depew when he entertained friends and fellow members of Congress. Depew died in New York in 1828.

William Corcoran Eustis, Corcoran's grandson, returned to the Corcoran House in 1908 and was its last resident. Eustis was born in France while his father was secretary of the Confederate legation. Both of Eustis' parents died not long after the Civil War ended, while he and his siblings were young. They were brought to Washington to live with their grandfather in his house on Lafayette Square. In 1900, Eustis married the daughter of Levi P. Morton. Eustis and his wife purchased and restored Oatlands Plantation in Loudoun County, Virginia (which now belongs to the National Trust for Historic Preservation). Like his grandfather, Eustis was extensively involved with philanthropic endeavors and was interested in public service. In 1917, Eustis accompanied General Pershing overseas to serve as his French interpreter and later, became his private secretary. In 1921, Eustis sold the Corcoran House to the United States Chamber of Commerce. Eustis died of pneumonia in 1921.

Next door to the Corcoran House, the Slidell House had become a fashionable school for girls, called the Hamilton Institute. The school occupied the house from 1903 until 1912. From 1914 until 1917, Thomas Ewing leased the Slidell House while he was serving as President Wilson's commissioner of patents. Ewing's grandfather was the first secretary of the interior and had lived in the Blair House in 1849. From 1919 until 1921, the Slidell House was leased to the Association of Collegiate Alumnae (which merged with the Southern Association of College Women and formed the American Association of University Women). Like the Corcoran House, the Slidell House was sold in 1921 to the United States Chamber of Commerce.

In 1922, both the Corcoran and the Slidell Houses were demolished. In their place, a monumental, neo-classical structure for the U.S. Chamber of Commerce was built. The McMillan Commission proposals for Lafayette Square were slowly being realized as the grand old homes were razed, one by one, and replaced with Beaux Arts-style structures. Cass Gilbert, architect of the newly completed U.S. Treasury Annex, also designed the matching U.S. Chamber of Commerce building. Both buildings occupy corner sites and have colonnades rising three stories from the second floor to the roofline and stretching across the full width of two sides of the buildings. The two buildings have been described as "polite and dignified," though the U.S. Chamber of Commerce building is the more handsome of the two. After completing the Chamber of Commerce building, Gilbert designed the U. S. Supreme Court building on Capitol Hill in 1929.

The Chamber building is faced with Indiana limestone and its prominent site overlooking Lafayette Square gives it a powerful presence. In 1957, two floors were added to Cass Gilbert's original building. The addition is set back behind the roof balustrade and is not visible from Lafayette Square. Originally, Cass Gilbert provided an inner court to the building, preserving the garden area so cherished by both Daniel Webster and W. W. Corcoran when they lived in the house that was once occupied the site. In 1980, the open-air courtyard was enclosed to serve as the Briefing Center for the Chamber of Commerce. The Briefing Room's ceiling was painted sky blue and the carpet was patterned to represent a central fountain and to give an illusion of the original courtyard.

The United States Chamber of Commerce was founded in 1912. President Taft felt that the business community of the nation should be represented in Washington: "The Chamber's mission is to advance human progress through an economic, political and social system based on individual freedom, incentive, initiative, opportunity and responsibility. The Chamber develops consensus business positions on vital issues, represents business interests before legislative, executive and judicial branches of government, and informs its members about important developments."[30]

Hay & Adams Houses — the final story —

Hay Adams Hotel — a new story —

16th and H Streets, NW — northwest corner

When John Hay died in 1905, he deeded his Lafayette Square house to his daughter, Alice Hay Wadsworth. She and her husband, James Wolcott Wadsworth, lived in the Hay House until 1925. Alice bought the Adams House next door, after Henry Adams died in 1917. She leased it to the government of Brazil for their embassy. After the neo-classical U. S. Chamber of Commerce building was built next to the Adams House, Alice agreed to lease the property, on which the houses were built, to developer Harry Wardman in 1925. Alice's agreement with Wardman stated that within four years Wardman must raze the two houses and erect a new building valued at not less than $500,000. The property would be on a ninety-nine year lease and, Wardman would have an option to purchase the property within twenty years for $600,000.

Wardman demolished the Hay and Adams Houses in 1927. Only a few architectural remnants were saved; they were sold at auction and incorporated into other homes in the area. At first, it was thought that Wardman's new hotel would be an annex to the Carlton Hotel, which he had recently erected nearby. Instead, Wardman created a luxury residence hotel and named it the Hay Adams Hotel to honor John Hay and Henry Adams. In 1934, the hotel dining room was fitted for air conditioning, making it one of the first air-conditioned dining rooms in the city. Julius Garfinkel, who owned Washington's premier department store at 14th and F Streets, NW, was listed as an occupant of one of the new Hay Adams Hotel apartment suites. Among the famous guests who stayed in the Hay Adams Hotel, in the 1930s, were Charles Lindberg, Amelia Earhart, Sinclair Lewis, and Ethel Barrymore.

The Depression years financially ruined Harry Wardman, who lost all of his properties, including the Hay Adams Hotel. The hotel management stayed on in the Hay Adams after it became the property of the Washington Loan and Trust Company. In 1936, the hotel was sold to the Manger Hotel chain and, despite the transitions, the Hay Adams Hotel retained its first-class reputation, with one employee for every two guests. The hotel's location was the best in town, overlooking the White House and Lafayette Square. Between 1973 and 1979, the Hay Adams Hotel was sold twice for between $10 and $15 million, the most ever paid for a hotel in Washington. Only minor changes were made before the hotel was sold again in 1983 to David H. Murdock whose wife, Gabrielle, completely and lavishly redecorated it. Interior designer, Rose Narva, supervised the renovation that included the addition of a carriage porch to the front and a new dining room off the lobby facing Lafayette Square.

The Hay Adams Hotel was built with incomparable views from the south, east, and north windows. The view to the south was across Lafayette Square to the White House. Until 1955, a delightful view of St. John's Church could be seen from the east windows, before the AFL-CIO building dominated the scene. Until 1967, the north view overlooked the lovely Tuckerman House and gardens, before the house was razed and replaced with an office building.

Harry Wardman's head architect, Mihran Mesrobian, designed the Hay Adams Hotel to be eight stories high, faced in limestone, and decorated with classical details. Mesrobian had recently completed his work on the Carlton Hotel when Wardman asked him to design the Hay Adams. In the few years that he worked for Harry Wardman, Mesrobian designed several luxury apartment complexes and residential subdivisions, as well as Wardman Towers on Connecticut Avenue and the Shoreham Office Building at 15th and H Streets. Mesrobian's work for Wardman stopped in 1930, after Wardman declared bankruptcy. Mesrobian later formed his own successful private practice in Washington. When Mihran Mesrobian died in 1975, he chose to be buried in Rock Creek Cemetery, not far from the graves of Henry and Clover Adams.

Ashburton House & St. John's Church
— *the continuing story* —
1525 H Street / 16th and H Streets — northeast corner

The Ashburton House, which stood next to the Arlington Hotel, was owned by two sisters, Mrs. Margaret Buckingham and Miss Isabel Freeman. The sisters zealously guarded their home against commercial encroachment. At the beginning of the 20th century, the proprietors of the Arlington Hotel were considering expansion. They approached Mrs. Buckingham to inquire about purchasing the property behind her home. "The representative [of the hotel] was said to have asked the price of part of the property which she devoted to a garden. Mrs. Buckingham was said to have replied that she was thinking of expanding her garden and what would be the price of the hotel."[31]

Miss Isabel Freeman died in 1929 and her sister, Mrs. Margaret Freeman Buckingham, stayed alone in the house until her death in 1947. Ashburton House and its L-shaped property, which surrounded St. John's Church and fronted both on H Street and 16th Street, NW, were sold to the American Federation of Labor (AFL) after Mrs. Buckingham's death.

For more than thirty years, the AFL had occupied a building located at 901 Massachusetts Avenue. In the late-1940s, the AFL needed additional office space. George Meany, the AFL's secretary-treasurer, searched for a more prominent and prestigious location for a new headquarters building. Many powerful labor organizations and unions were moving to the Lafayette Square neighborhood and, the AFL followed the trend. The Ashburton House property, which the AFL purchased, was located across Lafayette Square from the Jackson Place headquarters of the Congress of Industrial Organizations (CIO) headed by Phil Murray. The United Auto Workers and the United Steelworkers also leased space in Jackson Place Row Houses. The United Mine Workers, headed by John Lewis, owned the University Club on the northwest corner of 15th and I Streets and, the Bricklayers, Masons, and Plasterers International Union owned the Bowen Building at 815 15th Street.

The members of St. John's Church immediately approached George Meany about purchasing the Ashburton House for the church. Meany seemed to feel that it would be bad luck to build a new headquarters building that completely engulfed and surrounded a church and, he was open to negotiations. St. John's owned two buildings north of the church property, 819 and 821 16th Street, which they offered to trade for the Ashburton House, along with a balance of cash. By coupling this additional 16th Street frontage with the 16th Street property behind the Ashburton House, Meany reasoned that he could have an imposing headquarters building opening onto 16th Street. He agreed to the trade.

The balance of the cash payment presented a problem for St. John's congregation. However, just a few months after the negotiations for the Ashburton House were finalized in 1947, Captain John Rufus Edie, USN, died, leaving his estate, worth $250,000, to St. John's. The estate included a house at 1628 16th Street, NW. His niece and two nephews contested Edie's will in court, claiming their uncle was insane. The case was settled in favor of the church, which then agreed to pay $7,000 each to the relatives. The house was sold to the D.C. Baptist Convention and the proceeds helped purchase the Ashburton House, which has served as St. John's Parish House ever since. Horace Peaslee, a Washington architect, dedicated preservationist, and parishioner of St. John's, remodeled the Ashburton House and connected it to the church. The Ashburton House was partly furnished with some of the antiques Captain Edie donated to St. John's from his estate.

The architect for the new AFL building was Ralph Walker of Voorhes, Walker, Foley and Smith. In 1954, Walker worked together with a committee from St. John's to create a backdrop building intended to preserve the dignity of the Latrobe-designed church. However, the final result overshadowed and enveloped the little, bright yellow, stuccoed building. In 1955, the AFL merged with the CIO resulting in an organized labor force in the U.S. totaling 15 million members. The two organizations together occupied the new building. In 1999, the AFL-CIO began renovation of its headquarters building.

Dolley Madison & Tayloe Houses — the continuing story —
1520 H Street and 21 Madison Place, NW

The Cosmos Club's membership had notably increased by the beginning of the 20th century. The Dolley Madison House and adjoining properties proved inadequate to accommodate the large membership, and the club sought to build a larger clubhouse. In 1909, the two houses owned by the club to the south of the Dolley Madison House on Lafayette Square (the Ingersoll and Windom houses) were razed and replaced with a new five-story clubhouse addition, designed by Thomas J. D. Fuller. In 1917, the Cosmos Club was able to purchase the Tayloe House from the Cameron estate, and converted it into the women's annex for the wives and daughters of club members. The Cameron stable house, behind the Tayloe House, was remodeled as an assembly hall.

By 1922, the Cosmos Club was forty-two years old and had increased the size of its clubhouse facilities nine times. In 1928, the club purchased the house at 1516 H Street, west of the Dolley Madison House. Half of the Madison Place block now belonged to the club, and their Lafayette Square property was considered one of the most valuable real estate investments in Washington. In the 1930s, the executive branch of the government had begun to occupy offices in some of the Jackson Place Row Houses, with the intent of purchasing, razing, and replacing all the Lafayette Square homes with federal office buildings. In 1939, the government offered the Cosmos Club $1 million for their land and buildings, forcing the club members to begin searching for another clubhouse site. The club members felt that the government's offer was unreasonably low. However, knowing that the property could be taken by eminent domain if the club refused to sell, the offer was accepted.

When World War II began, the government leased the Lafayette Square clubhouse buildings back to the Cosmos Club, indefinitely. However, discussions concerning a new location for the clubhouse continued for years. Finally, in 1950, the Cosmos Club purchased the Townsend House on Massachusetts Avenue $364,635 from Sumner Wells. Wells was President Roosevelt's under secretary of state, and Mathilda Townsend's second husband. Mathilda Townsend, who died in 1949, had lived in a Jackson Place Row House with her parents in the 1890s, while this elegant Massachusetts Avenue mansion was being built for them (designed by a former member of the Cosmos Club, John Carrère). By 1952, the Townsend House had been renovated and the Cosmos Club moved to their new Massachusetts Avenue clubhouse.

The Dolley Madison House on Lafayette Square was leased from 1952 until 1958 by the National Science Foundation. From 1958 until 1964, it was leased to the Office of the Administrator of the National Aeronautics and Space Administration (NASA). Visitors to the house, when it was leased by NASA, included the first American astronauts in space: Navy Lt. Commander Walter N. Schirra; Navy Lt. Commander Alan B. Shepard, Jr.; Navy Lt. Malcolm Scott Carpenter; Marine Lt. Colonel John H. Glenn; and Air Force Captain Leroy Gordon Cooper, Jr.

Belasco Theater — a story —
17 Madison Place, NW

In 1895, the Rodgers House was razed and replaced with the Lafayette Square Opera House, an imposing, six-story, tan brick structure built to accommodate 1,800 people. Uriah B. Painter, a civil engineer and lobbyist, commissioned the architectural partnership of Wood and Lovell of Chicago to design the Opera House. Painter claimed the building was "absolutely fireproof," which was an impressive statement because the nearby National Theater had burned and been rebuilt four times in thirty-three years. There were 1,800 Edison incandescent lamps to light the stage, three balconies, thirty-one private boxes, and "superior acoustics." Elevators were installed to take guests to the roof garden or to the Turkish Baths in the basement.

Painter hired John W. Albaugh, a theater manager from Baltimore, to oversee the management of the Opera House. Albaugh engaged Lillian Russell, one of the most popular actresses of the day, as the opening performer. When Painter became dissatisfied with Albaugh's work, he fired him and attempted to manage the Opera House by himself. Painter's inexperience caused him to lose his investment and eventually he was forced to sell the Opera House in 1904 to a group of New York entrepreneurs, the Shubert Brothers and David Belasco. In 1905, Helen Hayes, a Washingtonian, made her theater debut at age five on the stage of the Lafayette Square Opera House, which, in 1906, was renamed the Belasco Theater.

Among the performers who came to the Belasco Theater were Enrico Caruso, Sarah Bernhardt, Ethel Barrymore, Will Rogers, Geraldine Farrar, and Washingtonian, Al Jolson. Plays, ballet, opera, and theatrical shows continued to be produced and performed for thirty years at the Belasco Theater. The success was due in part to the manager, L. Stoddard Taylor, who was a showman in his own right. Taylor enjoyed personally greeting his patrons and making them feel at home. The Depression years, however, forced the transformation of the Belasco from a live theater to a movie house by 1935. Two years later, however, it reopened as a legitimate theater.

In 1940, the government paid $1.4 million to purchase the Belasco Theater along with the Cosmos Club buildings. In 1941, the seats in the theater were removed and, the building was converted into office space and a records warehouse for the Department of the Treasury. In October 1942, the theater was reopened as the Stage Door Canteen for servicemen. Six thousand volunteers came to entertain millions of servicemen between 1942 and 1946. When the building was closed in 1946, both General Eisenhower and Admiral Nimitz made a special appearance on stage. In 1950, during the War in Korea, the theater was reopened again, as the Lafayette Square USO Club. The old Lafayette Square Opera House/Belasco Theater was demolished in 1962 to make way for the new U.S. Court of Claims (National Courts) Building.

Dwight D. Eisenhower, the 34th President, 1953-1961

Dwight David Eisenhower grew up in Kansas. At the age of fourteen, he developed such a severe case of blood poisoning that the doctors insisted on amputating his leg to save his life, but Eisenhower refused the operation and recovered. Because Eisenhower had no money for college, he applied to West Point Military Academy and was accepted, but proved to be an average student. In 1915, while serving as an army officer assigned to San Antonio, he met Marie (Mamie) Geneva Doud, whose family's winter home was located there. They fell in love and married in 1916. During the next thirty-five years, Mamie and Dwight moved twenty-eight times with his military career.

During World War I, Eisenhower served as a troop instructor. In 1925, he attended the Army General Staff School and graduated first in his class. After serving on the staff of the assistant secretary of war in 1932, he was appointed to be an aide to General MacArthur. When the United States entered into World War II, Eisenhower was a brigadier general. He was called to Washington to plan the war strategy, and his reputation as a skilled tactician and diplomatic military leader prompted his appointment as commanding general of the European Theater of Operations.

Eisenhower became one of America's most prominent war heroes. In 1942, he directed the successful invasion of Allied troops in North Africa. The next year, he was made a full general in command of the Italian and Sicilian invasions, and then was named supreme commander of all Allied Forces in Europe. President Roosevelt directed Eisenhower to develop a plan to invade France. On June 6, 1944, Eisenhower commanded the invasion at Normandy, and eleven months later, on May 7, 1945, Eisenhower accepted the surrender of the German army. He was appointed chief of staff in 1945 and retired from the military three years later to become president of Columbia University. In 1950, at President Truman's request, Eisenhower returned to active military service as supreme commander of the forces of the North Atlantic Treaty Organization (NATO) in Europe.

Both Democrats and Republicans approached Eisenhower as a possible presidential candidate as early as 1948. He maintained his neutrality and refused any political offers until 1953, when he accepted the Republican nomination for president. Because of his popularity as a war hero, he won easily over the Democratic candidate, Adlai E. Stevenson II. Soon after Eisenhower was elected president, an armistice was signed ending the Korean War. Although Eisenhower supported the Truman Doctrine of attempting to contain Communism, in 1954 he refused to send troops to Vietnam to aid the French who were forced out by Vietnamese nationalists. In 1956, however, Eisenhower committed the U.S. to use force against Communist aggression in the Middle East, and troops were sent to aid Lebanon.

Toward the end of his first term in office, Eisenhower suffered a heart attack and was incapacitated for several months in 1955. At first, the Republican Party felt he would not be the favored candidate for the 1956 election, but he recovered, campaigned against Adlai Stevenson again, and won. Economic growth in the country was strong during Eisenhower's administrations. He supported limiting defense spending, enforced the new civil rights legislation, and initiated the national interstate highway system.

Mamie Eisenhower brought a return to femininity to the White House, introducing ruffles and frills in her decorating style. She enjoyed entertaining and she worked diligently to fulfill her social obligations. Her style of dress and even her recipes were imitated. Mamie was cheerful, outgoing, and popular, but suffered from a weak heart all her life. She also had a chronic inner ear condition that caused her to lose her balance, giving rise to false rumors that she was an alcoholic. After eight years of living in the White House, the longest she had ever lived in one place in her married life, she and Dwight (Ike) retired to a farm near Gettysburg, Pennsylvania. In 1968, Ike suffered several heart attacks and died the next year. Ten years later, Mamie suffered a stroke and died in 1979. Her birthplace in Boone, Iowa, is now a national museum. The only other first lady thus honored is Abigail Adams.

National Grange Building — a story —
740-744 Jackson Place, NW

The property directly south of Decatur House was a walled garden for over a century. In 1929, a new eight-story, limestone-faced building was constructed on the garden property. When this high-rise office building was erected, local historian John Clagett Proctor noted that "it obscures from view the window on the south side of the second floor [of Decatur House] which was cut there in 1834 by direction of Martin Van Buren in order that he might see and respond to the signals displayed from the White House by his most confidential friend, Andrew Jackson,"[32] (when Van Buren served as Jackson's secretary of state).

The offices in the new high-rise building were leased to several organizations, including the Institute for Government Research, the Institute of Economics, the American Council for Education, the American Association of University Professors, and the American Engineering Council. Later tenants were the Lutheran Board, the Christian Education Board, and the Civilian Conservation Corps Study (the American Youth Commission).

One of the early tenants of the new Jackson Place building was the Institute for Government Research, the brainchild of Robert S. Brookings. Brookings had made his fortune in St. Louis in the wholesale hardware business. In 1896 at age forty-six, he retired as a multimillionaire and devoted himself to public service. When Brookings was appointed to President Taft's Commission of Economy and Efficiency, he was appalled at the laxity in government finances and the lack of a federal budget. When adequate appropriations for Taft's commission were not forthcoming, Brookings used his own money to establish the Institute for Government Research, in 1916. The institute examined fiscal problems on both national and state levels and studied the budgetary systems of European nations for comparison. The details of the studies were published in reports. The reports were also issued to the press and published in the newspapers, resulting in Congress authorizing the federal budget system in 1921.

Expanding beyond budgetary matters, the Institute for Government Research investigated other problems of the national government, and published a series of reports on the findings. Brookings then secured a Carnegie Corporation grant in order to fund a new research project, called the Institute of Economics. In 1923, with his own financing, he established the Robert Brookings Graduate School of Economics and Government, in Washington. In 1927, the three foundations – the Institute for Government Research, the Institute of Economics, and the Brookings Graduate School – were combined into a single organization called the Brookings Institute. The Institute continued to lease space in the office building at 740-44 Jackson Place until 1932, when a new Brookings Institute building was erected on the site of the Ewell House, at 722 Jackson Place, NW.

———————

In 1947, the National Grange of Patrons of Husbandry purchased the office building at 740-44 Jackson Place, NW, and the building took on the name of that organization until it was razed in the early 1960s. The Grange was started as a fraternal organization in 1867 to help desperate and destitute Southern and Western farmers after the Civil War. Most farmers, at the time, did not understand the new commercial and mechanized methods of farming. The majority of citizens in the United States were living in rural areas, and the new western pioneer families were struggling to make a living. The National Grange of Patrons of Husbandry began as a social and educational organization to aid farm families, but it evolved into an organization that provides community service and promotes legislative action.

The Grange fought hard to save their building on Lafayette Square, and the government consented to trading the Jackson Place site for a property lot on H Street, NW, behind Decatur House. The Grange was also given $360,000 toward the construction of a new building. The new Grange building is the only non-government structure on the west side of Lafayette Square, and the only one not built of brick.

Marcy House & Glover House — the continuing story —
730—736 Jackson Place, NW

After the turn of the century, the Marcy House, at 736 Jackson Place, NW, was no longer used as a private residence. The house was occupied by the Netherlands Legation until 1920, when the Women's City Club purchased the house and converted it into their clubhouse. For the next twenty-three years, the

Marcy House was known as "the Home of the Women's City Club." In 1943, the house was sold for $75,000 to the National Lutheran Council, which occupied it until the government purchased the Marcy House in the mid-1950s.

The Glover House, at 734 Jackson Place, NW, continued to be used as a residence until the mid-1920s when the house was purchased and converted into an office building by the Research University. In the 1940s, the American Peace Society occupied the Glover House until just after World War II when the International Labor Office moved in. In the early-1950s, the Brookings Institute leased the Glover House as an annex to the other properties it owned and occupied on Lafayette Square.

The house south of the Glover House, at 730 Jackson Place, NW, remained a residence through the mid-1930s. Like many other Jackson Place homes, the house was purchased and used as an office building by the late-1930s when the U.S. Conference of Mayors moved in and remained there through the 1950s. The National Institute of Municipal Law Offices and the American Association of Junior Colleges also leased offices in the Glover House. By 1962, the Treasury Office of Defense Lending was occupying the house.

Ewell House & Its Neighbor — the final story—

Brookings Institute — a new story —

722 & 726 Jackson Place, NW

@EDWARD F FOGLE EFF

John R. McLean was living in his home at 1500 I Street, NW, when he purchased the Ewell House, at 722 Jackson Place, NW, from his mother in 1895. He later sold it to his sister, Mrs. Mary McLean Ludlow, who lived there with her husband, Rear Admiral Ludlow, until 1903.

The Honorable Elihu Root, secretary of state under President Theodore Roosevelt, leased the Ewell House for two years, from 1903 until 1905. The Honorable William Randolph Hearst of New York City next leased the house until 1908, while he served as a member of Congress.

The Ambassador of the Republic of Brazil, Joaquim Nabuco, and his family, leased the Ewell House in 1908. Nabuco and his wife hosted a grand affair in honor of the justices of the Supreme Court, which, the newspapers noted, was one of the most celebrated entertainments to have ever occurred in the Ewell House. Eighty people were invited to the sit-down dinner. The entire banquet room was decorated to resemble a Brazilian rainforest, and the room was subtly lit by electric light bulbs hidden among the potted palm trees.

In 1909, Mrs. Ludlow returned to live in the house for five years. She then leased it to the Home Club in 1914, whose members were employees of the Department of Interior. The Home Club was "organized for the purpose of mutual benefit, social improvement, and educational advancement of its members."[33] Women were also members of the club, although it was not clear whether the women members were the wives of the members, or if women employees of the Interior Department, unrelated to male members, could also join. The name, "Home Club," was selected "in the first place because of the relation of the work of the Department [of Interior] to the home, and secondly on account of the historic fact that the Department of Interior was originally known as 'The Home Department,' the title which it bears in England today."[34]

Between 1918 and 1921, the Ewell House was rented by Alice Paul and the National Women's Party (NWP). Alice Paul authored the Equal Rights Amendment in 1923. She founded the NWP, which was a militant group of women working to achieve women's suffrage. The NWP members brought attention to their cause by staging a suffrage parade in Washington on the day before Woodrow Wilson's first inaugural. They wanted to have an amendment added to the Constitution giving women the right to vote, rather than trying to work through the individual states.

Before moving to the Ewell House, the NWP rented the Tayloe House on Madison Place, NW, from mid-1916 until November of 1917. The women held the first "Silent Sentinels" in front of the White House in January 1917. Five months later, the police began arresting these women. Newspaper stories written about the arrests revealed how inhumanely the women were treated in jail. When the Cosmos Club purchased the Tayloe House in November 1917, the women found a new home across Lafayette Square. They moved into the Ewell House. The location across from the White House was crucial to their cause. The NWP members again faced jail when they held protests in front of the Lafayette statue, just across Pennsylvania Avenue from the White House.

The NWP members started a "watchfire of freedom" on New Year's Day, 1919, lighting an urn and burning copies of the president's speeches. A bell, which hung in the balcony of the Ewell House, rang hourly. Finally, the Wilson administration reluctantly agreed to support the women's right to vote, but many members of Congress would not commit themselves on the controversial issue. The demonstrations and arrests continued until Congress called for a special session. On May 19, 1919, the Susan B. Anthony Amendment (the 19th Amendment, which was first introduced in Congress in 1878) passed by a majority vote in the House of Representatives. Three weeks later, the 19th amendment passed in the Senate, and Wisconsin was the first state to ratify it.

Two bulletin boards were placed in front of the Ewell House to keep count of the states as they ratified the suffrage amendment. Ratification by three-fourths of the states (thirty-six states) was needed. Tennessee was the thirty-sixth state to ratify the amendment on August 26, 1920, and the right to vote for women became law. A flag had been sewn with stars for each state that ratified the nineteenth amendment. When Tennessee ratified the amendment, Alice Paul unfurled the thirty-six-star flag from the balcony of the Ewell House. By 1922, the NWP moved to Capitol Hill, directly across the street from the Capitol. In 1929 they purchased the Sewell-Belmont House at 144 Maryland Avenue, NE, which continues to serve as the headquarters for the National Women's Party.

The historic Ewell House was razed in 1932, and a nine-story, limestone-faced, high-rise building was erected on the site, for the expanded Brookings Institute. The building, which cost $700,000, was paid for by Mrs. Isabel Valle Brookings, as a memorial to her mother. Unfortunately, Robert Brookings died before it was completed. The architectural partnership of Porter and Lockie designed the building to be used as both a research and an educational facility. This new headquarters building housed the administrative offices of the Brookings Institute that were formerly located in leased office space in the high-rise building south of Decatur House. The new Brookings Institute building also contained several libraries, lecture rooms, dining rooms, recreation rooms, a lounge, accommodations for resident fellows of the institute and for visiting scholars, and five floors of offices for research.

Robert Brookings was a self-made man who started working when he was seventeen years old for twenty-five dollars a week. He was a millionaire by the time he was thirty. At age forty-six, he retired and devoted his time and his money to research and education in the fields of government and economics. He was seventy-seven years old when he married Isabel Vale January, who was independently wealthy. When Brookings died in 1932, at age eighty-two, he generously left an endowment fund of $3 million to the Brookings Institute.

The house north of the Ewell House across the alley, at 726 Jackson Place, NW, was occupied by the American Red Cross, in the 1920s. In the mid-1930s, the house was demolished and replaced with an eight-story, limestone-faced building owned by the International Bank. The offices in the International Bank building were rented to the Christian Science Reading Room, the Indian Rights Association, the National League of Women Voters, and the National Anti-Tuberculosis Foundation. Among the other tenants were several lawyers, engineers, and architects, including Waddy Wood, who designed the Union Trust Building at 15th and H Street, NW, and Philip Hubert Frohman, the architect of the Washington National Cathedral. By the late-1940s and early-1950s, real estate offices were leasing space in the building along with the Apple Association, Philco Radio Company, and MacDonald Aircraft Corporation. By the mid-1950s, the Brookings Institute purchased the International Bank building. The building was razed in the 1960s by the government.

Mr. Brookings felt that "there was no other real estate like Jackson Place real estate."[35] He began investing in property on Lafayette Square when he bought the Ewell House and the Glover House, at 734 Jackson Place, NW. After buying the International Bank building, the Brookings Institute sold the Glover House, at 734 Jackson Place, NW, to private investors who already owned the two homes on either side of it, at 730 and 736 Jackson Place, NW. In 1957, the investors announced their intentions to raze all three homes and erect one large office building on the three lots. The government opposed the construction of such a large commercial structure, so close to the White House. The speculative commercial building was never constructed and the government eventually purchased the three homes.

Mary Jessup Blair Houses — a story —
716 and 718 Jackson Place, NW

Mary Jessup Blair owned two adjacent houses on Lafayette Square and lived in the larger one, at 718 Jackson Place, NW. At the beginning of the 20th century, her daughter and son-in-law, Violet Blair Janin and Albert Janin, occupied the house. The house was sold in 1937 to the Congress of Industrial Organizations (CIO), which razed it and replaced it with an office building. The CIO leased part of the building to the United Steelworkers of America. In 1955, the CIO merged with the American Federation of Labor and moved into the AFL's new building behind St. John's Church. The Union Building Corporation then bought the CIO's office building. It was razed in the 1960s.

Mary Jessup Blair's smaller house, at 716 Jackson Place, NW, was used as an investment property. Her daughter, Violet, inherited it and continued to rent it. During President Woodrow Wilson's second administration, his committee to popularize World War I leased the Blair investment property. The William Corcoran Hill Real Estate Company also leased space in the building. In 1937, the Andrew W. Mellon Trust purchased the house at 716 Jackson Place, and used it during the construction of the Mellon Gallery (The National Gallery of Art). Mellon renovated the house with federal-style details. After the construction of the Mellon Gallery was completed, the property continued to be used for office space. Lawyers kept offices there through the 1940s. The Mellon Trust also purchased the two adjacent houses on the south, 712 and 708 Jackson Place, NW. Those three houses were sold to the government in the 1950s.

Jackson Place Row Houses — the continuing story —
700 - 712 Jackson Place, NW

The Department of Justice briefly leased the house at 712 Jackson Place, in the early 1900s. Several lawyers became tenants and continued to lease offices there for years. By 1925, the Wayfarer's Bookshop leased space in the house, along with the William Corcoran Hill Real Estate Company, which had moved from next door. By 1948, the National Candy Wholesalers' were tenants. In the 1950s, the International Federation of Agricultural Producers shared space in the house with the National Trust for Historic Preservation.

The home at 704 Jackson Place was occupied for nearly twenty years by the Bureau of American Republics (the Pan American Union, later called the Organization of American States). The French Institute of Washington also shared space there. In 1910, Andrew Carnegie purchased 704 Jackson Place and the adjoining home on the north, 708 Jackson Place, for use by the Carnegie Endowment and Foundation for International Peace. Carnegie wrote to the foundation trustees, in 1910, that he was transferring "to the trustees of the Carnegie Peace Fund, $10,000,000 of 5% first mortgage bonds–the revenue of which is to be administered by you to hasten the abolition of war, the foulest blot upon our civilization."[36] By 1938, the Peace Fund boasted of having distributed 17,000 books to libraries in fifty-seven nations, and the Peace Foundation had sponsored numerous scholarships, special lecture tours, and research projects.

By the early-1950s, 708 Jackson Place, formerly occupied by the Carnegie Peace Foundation, was leased by the Virginia State Travel Bureau. The American Society of International Law also occupied some of the offices in the house, along with the National Security Council.

In 1957, the government began to institute its plan for redevelopment, forcing a mass exodus from the buildings on Jackson Place. The National Trust for Historic Preservation left Jackson Place for temporary offices, then moved to the historic McCormick Apartment Building at 1785 Massachusetts Avenue, NW; and the Brookings Institute built their new building next door. The United Auto Workers moved from Jackson Place to 1126 16th Street, NW. The National Grange, however, refused to move, and filed a lawsuit contesting the condemnation of their Jackson Place building.

While awaiting the government's final decision on the fate of the Lafayette Square homes, office space in the homes and buildings were leased to government-affiliated organizations. The National Aeronautics and Space Administration (NASA) became a tenant at 708 Jackson Place, along with the Fine Arts Commission. The National Science Foundation was moved into three floors of the former International Bank building, and the Atomic Energy Commission moved into the vacated Brookings Institute building.

Blair House — *the continuing story* —
1651 Pennsylvania Avenue, NW

At the turn of the century, Montgomery Blair's youngest son, Gist Blair, returned to Washington from St. Louis, where he had been practicing law. He took up residence in the Blair House and, continuing a tradition started two generations before, he was often an invited guest at the White House.

Gist Blair inherited the archives of Andrew Jackson, which had been given to his grandfather, Francis Preston Blair. F. P. Blair had intended to write a

Jackson biography, but he never found the leisure time to complete the project. Gist Blair donated these unpublished papers to the Library of Congress, along with a vast and valuable assortment of the Blair family's personal papers.

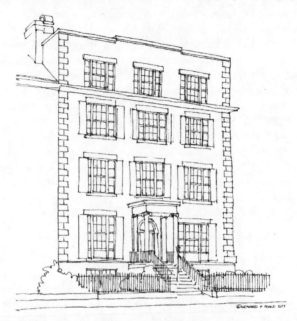

Gist Blair was considered the most eligible bachelor in Washington. As a young man, he had fallen in love with Laura Lawson Ellis, but she chose to marry another man. Her marriage was not happy, however, and it finally ended when she was fifty-two years old. Gist, who was the same age and still in love with her, seized the opportunity to propose marriage. By his own account, he invited her to dinner at the Blair House one rainy evening. When she was about to depart, he stooped to help her with her overshoes, then carefully stole the evening slipper from her foot and teasingly resisted returning it until she agreed to marry him. They married and adopted Laura's niece and namesake, who grew up in the Blair House and attended the National Cathedral School.

In the 1930s, Gist Blair's affection for his ancestral home led him to pursue a plan to protect it, along with the family furnishings that had been kept in the house through three generations. In 1940, Gist Blair died and in his will, he expressed his strong desire to preserve the house as a residence. His widow, Laura, remained in the house, and lived for two more years. Twenty-one days after Laura's death, on October 29, 1942, the Department of State purchased the Blair House, designating it as a guesthouse for the president's official visitors.

The previous year, in 1941, the government had purchased the neighboring Lee House for office use. Elizabeth Blair Lee and her husband, Samuel Phillips Lee, had lived in the Lee House until 1876. In 1893, their only son, Blair Lee, returned to live in Lee House with his wife, Anne Clymer Brooke, for ten years. Anne died suddenly on Christmas Eve 1903, and Blair Lee moved to the Silver

Spring estate to raise his two sons, Edward Brooke Lee and Phillips Blair Lee. Both sons served with distinction in World War I, and Edward Brooke Lee became involved in Maryland politics, as did his descendants. Blair Lee died on Christmas Day 1942. In 1943, the government combined the Lee House and the Blair House into one residence.

Following the death of President Franklin Roosevelt in April 1945, Harry S Truman resided in the Blair House with his family, while they waited for Mrs. Roosevelt to move from the White House. Again, from November 1948 until March of 1952, the Blair House became the official presidential residence for the Trumans, while the White House was being extensively renovated.

Only foreign dignitaries who come to Washington on "official" or "state" visits may stay in the president's guesthouse. President Kennedy's Office of Protocol defined a "State Visit" as a full-scale visit by a chief of state (president, king, queen, or emperor) at the official invitation of the president of the United States; the visit is to last three days and the guests are to stay at Blair House. An "Official Visit" was defined as a full-scale visit by a head of government (prime minister, premier, or chancellor) at the official invitation of the president; this visit is also to last three days and the guests are to stay at the Blair House. An "Informal Working Visit" was defined as one in which the foreign visitors stay in their government's quarters, and a "Private Visit" was defined as one in which the foreign visitors stay at their country's embassy.

Some of the official foreign visitors have literally filled the rooms of the Blair House. Nikita Khrushchev of the Soviet Union stayed in the Blair House in 1959, and brought 824 trunks and suitcases with his entourage. In 1960, Queen Kirikit of Thailand brought eighty pieces of luggage to the house, with three large and six medium trunks, and her retinue. King Hassan II of Morocco visited in 1967, escorted by 137 people and 500 pieces of baggage.

Decatur House — the continuing story —
748 Jackson Place, NW

Truxton Beale, the son of General Edward Beale, inherited Decatur House upon the death of his father in 1893. As a young man, Truxton studied diplomacy, law, and engineering. He received military training as well. Truxton Beale was a career diplomat who served as minister to Prussia, Greece, Rumania, and Serbia. Beale returned to Washington from his overseas duties in 1893, just two months before his father died. In 1894, Beale married Harriett S. Blaine, the daughter of James G. Blaine. The couple had one son, Walker Blaine Beale, but the marriage was not happy and ended in divorce. Beale left Washington and traveled to Siberia, Turkestan, and Kashgar in China, sometimes living among the nomads in their tents. When he returned to the United States, he visited the California ranch his father had established but decided to return to his home in Washington. In California, he had fallen in love with Marie Chase Ogle. They were married at Decatur House in 1903.

The members Washington society delighted in welcoming the new couple with parties and receptions. In turn, the Beales entertained often. Truxton and

Marie started a Washington tradition of hosting an annual supper for the entire diplomatic corps after the President's Official Reception. The Beales often traveled between Washington, California, and Europe, but they called Washington their home. By the 1920s, the Beales were among the only residents still living on Lafayette Square, and they were the last Lafayette Square residents to regularly and graciously entertain. During the Prohibition years, Decatur House had a fully stocked wine cellar that outlasted the prohibition era, thus making receptions at Decatur House all the more inviting.

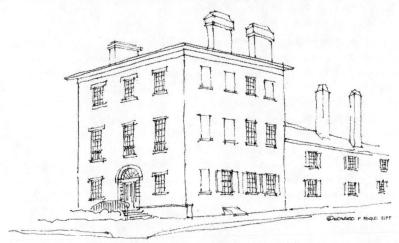

Truxton's older sister, Mary, married a secretary of the Russian Embassy, Georgi Petrovich Bakhmeteff. In 1911, after thirty years of living abroad, they returned to Washington, and the Bakhmeteff's were frequent visitors to Decatur House. The Bakhmeteffs lived at the Imperial Russian Embassy at 1125 16th Street, NW. He was the last Imperial Russian envoy and held the position until 1917. The Truxton's other sister, Emily, was the wife of John R. McLean, who built his opulent house two blocks away, at 1500 I Street.

Marie Beale was strong supporter of Franklin Roosevelt's "Good Neighbor Policy" with Latin America. At the request of the State Department, she hosted dinners at Decatur House, with a carefully selected guest list. Truxton Beale died in the mid-1930s. Marie, however, continued to entertain her wide variety of friends. She invited the young bachelor senator from Massachusetts, John F. Kennedy, to dinner in 1952. When Kennedy did not arrive with the rest of her dinner guests, Mrs. Beale's butler telephone him. Kennedy had mistakenly thought the dinner was on another Tuesday. He immediately hailed a taxi and rushed to Decatur House. Marie Beale greeted Kennedy with a good-natured scolding for his tardiness, and noting that he wore a brown suit and red tie to a black tie dinner, she asked, "You come to my house dressed like that?"

Decatur House was constantly being threatened with destruction in the name of progress. Marie Beale fought the trend, by beginning a restoration effort on the house in 1944. She continued to entertain, carrying on the tradition started 125 years before, by Commodore Stephen Decatur and his wife Susan. In 1956, Marie Beale generously bequeathed Decatur House to the National Trust for Historic Preservation, guaranteeing its safekeeping and assuring its survival, by having it held "in Trust for the Nation."

John F. Kennedy, the 35th President, 1960-1963

John Fitzgerald Kennedy was one of nine children born into a wealthy Massachusetts family. His maternal grandfather was a former mayor of Boston. His father served as ambassador to Great Britain at the beginning of World War II. Kennedy graduated from Harvard with honors in 1940 and in 1941, he tried to join the army, but he was rejected because of a bad back. He strengthened his back with exercise and, later the same year, was accepted by the navy. In 1943, he commanded a PT (Patrol Torpedo) boat that was rammed and sunk by a Japanese destroyer. Kennedy led the eleven crew members (out of thirteen) who survived on a four-mile swim to safety, towing an injured crew member by his life jacket strap. After the eleven men were rescued, Kennedy returned to the United States where he was treated for malaria and back problems.

In 1946, Kennedy was elected to Congress. He served three terms in the House of Representatives before being elected to the Senate. He met twenty-two-year-old Jacqueline Bouvier at a dinner party in Washington in 1951. She had attended Vassar, the Sorbonne, and George Washington University, and was working as a journalist for the *Washington Times-Herald* newspaper. Their romance was described as an on-again-off-again affair before they married in 1953. Jackie discovered that being a political wife was difficult because she knew little about politics and her wit was not always appreciated.

In 1955, John Kennedy underwent two serious back operations. While he was recuperating, he wrote the book, *Profiles in Courage*, which was a series of stories about courageous men who later became senators. Sadly, the next year, the Kennedys' first child was stillborn. Two years later, in 1957, Kennedy was awarded the Pulitzer Prize in biography for *Profiles in Courage*. That same year, their daughter, Caroline, was born.

Kennedy wanted the Democratic nomination for vice president in 1956 but did not receive it. Massachusetts, however, reelected him to the Senate in 1958 by a huge majority. In 1960, Kennedy was nominated for the presidency with Lyndon Johnson as his vice presidential running mate. In that same year their son, John, Jr. was born. Kennedy won the election by a very small margin over Richard Nixon. At age forty-three, Kennedy was the youngest president ever elected. With his charisma and charm, his beautiful wife and endearing children, Kennedy was the most popular president of the century.

President Kennedy was in office only a few months before he became involved in the CIA plan to send 14,000 armed Cuban exiles back to Cuba to overthrow the Castro Communist regime. The mission (called the Bay of Pigs invasion) was declared a failure after most of the exiles were captured. The next year, 1962, Kennedy was informed that Soviet missiles were being built in Cuba, thereby compromising U.S. national security. Kennedy demanded the dismantling of the Soviet missile bases, and set up a naval blockade off the Cuban coast, which nearly brought the United States and the Soviet Union into a nuclear war. The Soviets eventually removed the missiles.

President Kennedy established the Peace Corps to aid development in third world countries. He worked to further the cause of civil rights and appointed more Americans of African ancestry to political office than any president before him. Kennedy supported the arts and tried to establish a cultural center in Washington. In 1962, Kennedy issued his "Guiding Principles for Federal Architecture," which helped bring a new sensitivity to urban planning. Both he and his wife encouraged a movement toward historic preservation and toward the improvement of the quality of public buildings in America, seeking dignity and style for new construction of federal buildings, especially on Pennsylvania Avenue, NW, and Lafayette Square.

At the age of thirty-one, Jacqueline Kennedy was a sophisticated, intelligent, and youthful first lady who promoted culture and the arts in America. While living and studying in Paris, she had learned that the laws in France protect historically or architecturally significant structures and she felt the United States should also have such laws. Under her guidance, the historic rooms of the White House were restored and furnished with antiques. Whenever possible, she secured original furnishings that had belonged to the 19th century presidents. In 1962, Jacqueline Kennedy's televised tour of the renovated White House increased her popularity tremendously and her efforts brought attention to the idea of historic preservation throughout the U.S.

In 1963, the Kennedys' third child, Patrick, died only two days after he was born. Three months later, while the Kennedys were traveling on a nationwide tour to gain support for his presidential reelection campaign, Lee Harvey Oswald shot and killed John Kennedy, as he and Jacqueline rode in an open car through the streets of Dallas, Texas. Three days after the assassination, Lee Harvey Oswald was shot and killed by Jack Ruby, a Dallas nightclub owner. President Kennedy was buried in Arlington Cemetery and the two children who predeceased him were re-interred beside his grave. Efforts to establish a memorial to honor Kennedy resulted in the creation of Washington's John F. Kennedy Center for the Performing Arts, which was dedicated in 1972. Gifts from nations around the world decorate the interior of the modern, international-style building designed by Edward Durell Stone.

After her husband's death, Jacqueline chose to reside in the Georgetown neighborhood of Washington, where she and her husband had lived before they moved to the White House. Unfortunately, curiosity seekers constantly invaded Jacqueline's privacy, so she and the children moved to New York City. In 1968, Jacqueline married the multimillionaire, Aristotle Onassis. Seven years later, Onassis died. She stayed in New York and pursued her interest in the arts and writing, becoming a senior editor for a New York publisher. In May 1994, Jacqueline died and was buried next to John Kennedy and her two infant children in Arlington Cemetery.

Reconstructing The Past
With An Eye Toward The Future

During Eisenhower's second presidential term, the General Services Administration (GSA) regarded the construction of new office space for the executive and judicial branches of the government to be a priority issue. Cass Gilbert's 1901 design for Lafayette Square (which would have replaced every historic home with two neoclassical, marble-columned structures) had been overshadowed by a plan for just one modern, office building on Jackson Place. In 1957, a preliminary sketch for a monumental building between Decatur House and Blair House was circulated. By early 1959, the Boston architectural firms of Perry, Shaw, Hepburn, and Dean, along with Shepley, Bulfinch, Richardson, and Abbott submitted their architectural drawings for the modern executive office building, to the Commission of Fine Arts.

In the summer of 1960, Senators John F. Kennedy, Mike Mansfield, and others introduced legislation to designate several of the Lafayette Square homes on both Jackson Place and Madison Place, as National Historic Sites. Although the bill did not pass, the government reacted with a new sense of urgency. Within a few months, GSA announced that not one, but two modern office buildings were to be built on Lafayette Square: one on Jackson Place for the executive offices and one on Madison Place for the U.S. Court of Claims and Appeals (National Courts Building). All of the Lafayette Square buildings were to be razed and replaced, except Decatur and Blair Houses.

When President Kennedy was inaugurated in 1961, he inherited the GSA Lafayette Square building project. The new design placed the two historic Jackson Place homes as anchor buildings for one of the modernist structures. Kennedy suggested an alternative design, which would create a building, predominately faced with brick, between the historic Blair and Decatur Houses, mimicking, on a grand scale, the 19th century, federal architectural style.

Local organizations and influential citizens began to rally against modernism and in support of preserving Lafayette Square's historic residential character. Charles Glover, Jr., who had grown up in one of the houses on Jackson Place, was a strong supporter of preservation. Glover was convinced that "It might be possible to salvage the west side of Lafayette Square by leaving the present houses as a façade."[37] Glover wrote that the houses "are not very deep and the government building could be built in back of them."[38] In another letter, Glover rationalized that if his ideas were followed, "at very small expense, the square could be restored to its appearance of a hundred years ago. Those small buildings could be useful for government purposes and would form a façade for a large government building which would have to be set back a certain number of feet in order to attain height."[39] A local architect, Grosvenor Chapman, translated the idea into a sketch. Glover sent the sketch with his explanation to his friend Janet Auchincloss, Jacqueline Kennedy's mother, who passed the suggestions to Jacqueline, who relayed the idea to her husband.

Although the modern office complex plans for Lafayette Square already had been approved by 1962, Jacqueline Kennedy boldly stated, "the wreckers haven't started yet, and until they do, it [the square] can be saved."[40] Jacqueline worked behind the scenes with a small army of preservation allies to gain support for saving the historic homes on Lafayette Square. Grosvenor Chapman's sketch was shared with David Finley, a motivating force for preservation with both the National Trust for Historic Preservation and the Commission of Fine Arts. Finley suggested that Jacqueline have another architect submit new building designs, using the ideas from Chapman's sketch.

President Kennedy asked John Carl Warnecke, a San Francisco architect, to develop new plans for the disputed government buildings. Warnecke toured the Square and submitted a design that would preserve the historic buildings, integrating them into the project by placing the new structure behind the historic ones. Warnecke commissioned a historic study of the existing 19th century Lafayette Square houses, and he designed a series of new row houses (in the style of the old ones) to replace the four, 20th century, office buildings that had been built on Jackson Place. Warnecke's plan was given to GSA, and was in stark contrast to the Boston architectural firms' design for a modern building fronting on Lafayette Square. After considering both sets of drawings, the GSA eventually yielded to pressure and chose Warnecke's plan.

In mid-September 1962, discussions began in earnest for the design of the two new buildings: the New Executive Office Building behind the Jackson Place houses, and the National Courts Building (as it was later called) near Madison Place. Warnecke proposed that the new buildings should be faced in dark-red brick to match the Renwick Gallery, explaining that the dark color would visually set the new buildings apart from the lighter-colored brick of the houses. "This is the feeling I want: this is the palette I want for these two large buildings. I want them to be a backdrop. They should be dark, darker in tone than the houses, so the houses stand forward," said Warnecke.[41]

The National Courts Building was completed in 1967 to house both the U.S. Court of Claims and the U.S. Court of Customs and Patent Appeals, which merged into the U.S. Court of Appeals for the Federal Circuit in 1982. The Dolley Madison House, the adjacent Cosmos Club building and the Tayloe House were incorporated into the new National Courts Building. The Tayloe House was restored in the 1990s as an adjunct of the National Courts Building, and contains memorabilia from the original house, and a café. The Dolley Madison House was significantly altered many times over a century and a half. The Federal Judicial Center occupied the Dolley Madison House from 1967 until 1992, when it moved to the new Federal Judicial Center Building on Capitol Hill. Offices for the U.S. Court of Appeals for the Federal Circuit then moved into the home.

When construction began in 1964 on the National Courts Building, the Belasco Theater was razed and replaced by the new building's entry courtyard.

Several plaques decorate the walls of the courtyard, two of which were formerly located on the Belasco Theater. One plaque is dedicated to the old Rodgers House, the first building erected on the site. A second plaque, donated by the daughter of Uriah Painter who built the Lafayette Square Opera House (Belasco Theater), boasts of the fireproof nature of the old theater's construction.

In 1967, the National Courts Building was dedicated. Chief Justice Earl Warren, in his dedication speech, related an "ancient story of the wayfarer who was passing a building under construction. There were three workmen on the building. He said to the first one he came in contact with, 'What are you doing here?' His answer was, 'I am following my trade.' He then spoke to the second one and said, 'What are you doing here?' He said, 'I am earning a living.' He then spoke to the third one, asking him the same question. This man, rising to his full height and looking the wayfarer straight in the eye, said, 'Sir, I'm building a temple.' I'm sure that those who have had anything to do with the construction of this building have felt that they were building a temple – a Temple to Justice." Warren explained that "prior to the establishing of the U.S. Court of Claims, a citizen had no right to recover against his Government for a wrong it had done him."[42] Warren also quoted Abraham Lincoln's first message to Congress, which is inscribed on the lobby wall of the National Courts Building: "It is as much the duty of the Government to render prompt justice against itself in favor of citizens as it is to administer the same between private individuals."

GSA Administrator Lawson B. Knott, Jr., noted at the dedication, "The new Lafayette Square, with roots firmly in the past, comes to life today with this dedication," and the building's location is on "one of the most strategically significant pieces of real estate in the world."[43]

In 1969, the New Executive Office Building was completed, rising ten stories to be comparable in height to the Eisenhower Executive Office Building (EEOB) across Pennsylvania Avenue to the south. The modernized Mansard roof was designed to hide the mechanical components of the building as well as to mimic the roofs on the Renwick Gallery building and the EEOB. The upper-story oriel windows are imitative of the bay windows on the 19th century residences. Cass Gilbert's U.S. Treasury Annex and U.S. Chamber of Commerce buildings, built in the Beaux Art-style so popular sixty years before, were ignored in the design process.

In the 1960s, the four 20th century office buildings were razed on Jackson Place, along with the Belasco Theater building on Madison Place. Twenty other buildings were renovated or rebuilt. Thirteen of the houses on Lafayette Square are original. The remainder of the homes were rebuilt as 19th century replicas in order to form a continuous row, filling in the gaps left by the razing of the office buildings. The homes were cut back to be only two rooms deep and three-stories tall, and are occupied by federal agencies or private foundations, except for the Blair House, which is occasionally used as a residence.

Of all the Jackson Place Row Houses, Decatur House at 748 Jackson Place, NW, is the only house not owned by the government. The National Trust for Historic Preservation opened the house as a museum to document the lives of two of the owners, the Decaturs and the Beales. The houses at 744 and 740 Jackson Place (the Decatur House garden lots) are new, and have been used by the White House Historical Association and the Washington Monument Association.

The houses at 736, 734, and 730 Jackson Place are original and used by executive committees, such as the President's Crime Prevention Committee. The house at 722 Jackson Place was one of the most historic homes on Lafayette Square before it was razed in 1932 for the Brookings Institute. The site now is part of the entry to the courtyard of the New Executive Office Building. The house at 718 Jackson Place is new and has been incorporated into the New Executive Office Building.

The house at 716 Jackson Place (Mrs. Blair's rental property) is original and has been used as a residence for former presidents while visiting Washington. The houses at 712 and 708 Jackson Place are original and house the Harry S Truman Scholarship offices and the U.S. President's Commission on White House Fellowship. The last two houses at 704 and 700 Jackson Place are original from the 1850s. The two are now connected to the Blair House and Lee Houses as office and conference space.

W. W. Corcoran first opened the Corcoran Gallery of Art (the Renwick Gallery) next to the Blair House in 1872. Ninety-nine years later, the gallery was given a second life — but not without a struggle. The building was renamed to honor the architect James Renwick in 1965. The gallery was transferred from the government to the Smithsonian Institution, to be operated by the National Museum of American Art, and dedicated to the creative achievements of American designers and craftsmen of the past and present.

For most of its years, however, the Renwick Gallery was used for purposes other than displaying art. From 1899 until 1964, the building housed the U.S. Court of Claims. The gallery rooms and grand salon were parceled into judges' chambers and courtrooms. When the courts moved out, the building was called "a crumbling eyesore." Ninety percent of the exterior ornamental stonework was in ruins. After a decision was made to save the Renwick Gallery building along with the homes on Jackson Place, excavations for the New Executive Office Building caused serious structural damage to the gallery walls. The Renwick's rear wall dropped ten to twelve inches. An urgent meeting was called to discuss the assessed damage with the architects and GSA. Strong arguments were voiced in favor of the complete demolition of the building.

Harold L. Adams, was a young architect representing Warnecke's firm in Washington. He contacted the *Washington Post's* architectural critic, Wolfe Von Eckardt, concerning the Renwick Gallery's impending fate. Von Eckardt immediately submitted an article for publication the following Sunday praising the work and preservation efforts achieved thus far, on behalf of the gallery. GSA's project manager realized that Von Eckhardt's article had served to shift public sentiment strongly in favor of renovation, and against demolition.

Wonderful sources for the preservation work included James Renwick's original pamphlet of architectural "specifications," and Matthew Brady's 1860s photographs of the old gallery, which were discovered in the Library of Congress. Using these resources, the glory of the gallery's interior and exterior were restored, in part, by Hugh Newell Jacobsen, a local architect. The work was described as putting together "the largest jig-saw puzzle in the world."[44] More than 14,000 fragments and shards of ornate metalwork from the roof were reassembled, remade, and replaced. Von Eckhardt described the restoration of the gallery as "a rare exception to our nation's neglect of historical treasures."[45]

The mixing of the new and the old architecture of Lafayette Square was a compromise marrying politics and urban design. The new buildings were criticized because, although they were intended to be backdrops to the Victorian-style homes, the lovely old homes were overwhelmed and overshadowed by the sheer size and the heavy, dark-red color of the bricks and dark mortar of the new federal buildings. However, the new structures were also praised because they were set behind the old, safeguarding history and recreating a sense of neighborhood.

The preservation of Lafayette Square is one of the Kennedys' great legacies. Their ideals of combining art and architecture have been compared to those of Thomas Jefferson, the only other White House resident who truly cared about and worked for cooperation between government projects and artful city planning. Lafayette Square is as old as the city itself and the homes that were saved convey more history than any other single group of homes in the entire country. The most prominent, celebrated, and distinguished people who ever lived in or visited Washington in the 19th and early-20th centuries, were entertained within the walls of the Lafayette Square homes, and these elite individuals played an integral part in the making of local and national politics.

Lafayette Square has survived 200 years of change, and as Benjamin Disraeli noted, "Change is inevitable in a progressive society." The historic homes of Lafayette Square also serve as a reminder that "Plus ça change, plus c'est la même chose" (The more things change, the more they remain the same).

Renwick Gallery of Art

Notes

Stag Parties, Afternoon Levies, And Big Cheeses

1   Arnbeck, Bob, (Lanham, MD: Madison Books, 1991), p.574.

2   Proctor, John Clagett, *Proctor's Washington and Environs* (Washington: written for *The Washington Sunday Star*, 1928-1949), p.363.

3   (Proctor, *Proctor's Washington*), p.363

4   Carrouth, Gorton, *What Happened When* (New York: Harper & Row,1991), p.194.

5   Tayloe, Benjamin Ogle, *Our Neighbors on La Fayette Square*, (Washington: 1872, reprinted by The Junior League of Washington and AIA, 1982), p.20.

6   (Tayloe, *Our Neighbors on Lafayette Square*), p.14.

7   (Tayloe, *Our Neighbors on Lafayette Square*), p.14.

8   Smith, Mrs. Samuel Harrison (Margaret Bayard), *The First Forty Years of Washington Society* (New York: Charles Scribner's Sons, 1906), p.62.

9   Green, Constance McLaughlin, *The Church on Lafayette Square* (Washington: Potomac Books, Inc., 1970), p.7.

10   *American History*, February 1999, p.41

11   *American History*, February 1999, p.42

12   *American History*, February 1999, p.43

13   Beale, Marie, *Decatur House and its Inhabitants* (Washington: National Trust for Historic Preservation, 1954), p.16

14   (Tayloe, *Our Neighbors on Lafayette Square*), p.31.

15   Records of the Columbia Historical Society, Vol. 9, p.180

16   Hutchins, Stilson and Moore, Joseph West, *The National Capital, Past and Present* (Washington: The Post Publishing Company, 1885), p.58.

17   (Proctor, *Proctor's Washington*), p.481

18   Templeman, Eleanor Lee, *The Blair-Lee House* (McLean, VA: EMP Publications, Inc., 1980) p.20.

19   Poore, Ben: Perley, *Perley's Reminiscences*, (Philadelphia: Hubbard Brothers, Publishers, 1886), Vol. I, p.23.

20   (Tayloe, *Our Neighbors on Lafayette Square*), p.27.

21   (Poore, *Perley's Reminiscences*), Vol. I, p.27.

22   (Proctor, *Proctor's Washington*), p.472.

23   Brown, George Rothwell, *Washington, A Not Too Serious History* (Baltimore, The Norman Publishing Company, 1930), p.265.

24.   Works Projects Administration, *Washington, D.C., A Guide to the Nation's Capital* (New York: Hastings House, 1949), p.242.

25.   (Tayloe, *Our Neighbors on Lafayette Square*), p.28.

Holes In The Poles, Rum Punches, and Crushes

1   (Tayloe, *Our Neighbors on Lafayette Square*), p.25.

2   Wilson, Rufus Rockwell, *Washington, The Capital City* (Philadelphia: J.B. Lippincott Company, 1902), Vol. I, p.77.

3   (Wilson, *Washington, The Capital City*), Vol. I, p.377

4   (Wilson, *Washington, The Capital City*), Vol. I, p.378

5   (Poore, *Perley's Reminiscences*), Vol. I, p.250.

6 Ames, Mary Clemmer, *Ten Years in Washington* (Hartford, CT: A.D. Worthington & Co., 1873), p. 193

7 (Ames, *Ten Years in Washington*), p.567

8 Washburn, Wilcomb E., ed., *The Great Design, Lectures on the Smithson Bequest* (Washington: The Smithsonian Institution, 1965), p.97.

9 *Sixteenth Street Architecture* (Washington: U.S. Government Printing Office, 1978), Vol. I, p. 48.

10 (*Sixteenth Street Architecture*), Vol. I, p.44.

11 (Poore, *Perley's Reminiscences*), Vol. I, p.118.

12 Bryant, Wilhelmus Bogart, *A History of the National Capital* (New York: The MacMillan Company, 1914), Vol. II, p.449

13 Walker, Lewis, ed., *Speak for Yourself, Daniel* (Boston: Houghton, Mifflin, Company, 1969), p.247.

14 *The Sunday Star*, Washington, D.C., "The Rambler Writes of Old Corcoran House," December 14, 1919

15 Stevens, William Oliver, *Washington The Cinderella City* (New York: Dodd, Mead & Company, 1943), p.104.

16 (Tayloe, *Our Neighbors on Lafayette Square*), p.35.

17 (*Sixteenth Street Architecture*), Vol. I, p. 35.

18 (Tayloe, *Our Neighbors on Lafayette Square*), p.61.

19 *The Evening Star*, Washington, D.C., "Famed Home on Lafayette Square Known as House of Two Treaties," February 24, 1924.

20 *The Evening Star*, Washington, D.C., "Famed Home on Lafayette Square Known as House of Two Treaties," February 24, 1924.

21 (Poore, *Perley's Reminiscences*), Vol. I, p.87.

22 *The Evening Star*, Washington, D.C., "Famed Home on Lafayette Square Known as House of Two Treaties," February 24, 1924.

23 *The Evening Star*, Washington, D.C., "Famed Home on Lafayette Square Known as House of Two Treaties," February 24, 1924.

24 Gobright, L.A., *Recollection of Men And Things at Washington* (Philadelphia: Claxton, Remsen & Haffelfinger, 1869) p.43.

25 (Poore, *Perley's Reminiscences*), Vol. I, p.267-28.

26 (Tayloe, *Our Neighbors on Lafayette Square*), p.41.

27 (Wilson, *Washington, The Capital City*), Vol. I, p.399

28 (Beale, *Decatur House and its Inhabitants*), p.50.

29 (Beale, *Decatur House and its Inhabitants*), p.51.

30 (Beale, *Decatur House and its Inhabitants*), p.51.

31 (Tayloe, *Our Neighbors on Lafayette Square*), p.33.

32 (Beale, *Decatur House and its Inhabitants*), p.63.

33 (Tayloe, *Our Neighbors on Lafayette Square*), p.34.

34 Eskew, Garnett Laidlaw, *Willard's of Washington*, (New York" Coward-McCann, Inc., 1950), p.27.

35 (Tayloe, *Our Neighbors on Lafayette Square*), p.41.

36 (Poore, *Perley's Reminiscences*), Vol. I, p. 249.

37 Records of the Columbia Historical Society, Vol. 9, p.184.

38 (Brown, *Washington, A Not Too Serious History*), p.278.

39 (Stevens, *Washington The Cinderella City*), p.73.

40   (Wilson, *Washington, The Capital City*), Vol. II, p.87.

41   (Tayloe, *Our Neighbors on Lafayette Square*), p.41-42.

42   (Tayloe, *Our Neighbors on Lafayette Square*), p.41.

43   (Tayloe, *Our Neighbors on Lafayette Square*), p.42-43.

44   (Tayloe, *Our Neighbors on Lafayette Square*), p.39.

45   (*Sixteenth Street Architecture*), Vol. I, p.24.

46   (Tayloe, *Our Neighbors on Lafayette Square*), p.43-44.

47   (Tayloe, *Our Neighbors on Lafayette Square*), p.43.

48   (Proctor, *Proctor's Washington*), p.129.

49   . *The Washington Post*, "Riggs House Razing Revives Old Memories," January 11, 1935.

50   Appelbaum, Stanley, ed., *Abraham Lincoln, Great Speeches* (New York: Dover Publications, Inc., 1991), p. 55 & 61.

Wealth, Women, Scandals, and Favors

1   Jacob, Kathryn Allamong, *Capital Elites* (Washington: Smithsonian Press, 1994), p.90.

2   Raymond, V.L., *Home of the Home Club* (Washington: U.S. Geological Survey, 1915), p.6.

3   Barrett, John, *The Pan American Union* (Washington: Pan American Union, 1911), p.75-76.

4   (Barrett, John, *The Pan American Union*), p.60.

5   Dawes, Anna Laurens, *Charles Sumner* (New York: Dodd, Mead and Company, 1892), p.305.

6   Klapthor, Margaret Brown, *The First Ladies* (Washington: The White House Historical Society, 1975), p. 46.

7   (Poore, *Perley's Reminiscences*), Vol. II, p.349-50.

8   McCue, George, *The Octagon* (Washington: American Institute of Architects, 1976), p.69.

9   (McCue, George, *The Octagon*), p.71.

10   Barry, David S., *Forty Years in Washington* (Boston: Little, Brown, and Company, 1924), p.24.

11   Moore, Charles, *Washington Past and Present* (New York: The Century Company, 1929), p.187.

12   Frank, Sid and Melick, Arden D., *The Presidents Tidbits & Trivia* (New York: Greenwich House, 1982), p.58.

13   Diller, Daniel and Robertson, Stephen, *The Presidents, First Ladies, and Vice Presidents* (Washington: Congressional Quarterly, Inc., 1989), p.49.

14   Torres, Louis, *"To the immortal name and memory of George Washington"* (Washington: U.S. Government Printing Office, 1984), p.89.

15   O'Toole, Patricia, *The Five of Hearts* (New York: Clarkson Potter/Publishers, 1990), p.67.

16   (*Sixteenth Street Architecture*), Vol. I, p.64.

17   (Jacob, Kathryn Allamong, *Capital Elites*), p.12.

18   (O'Toole, Patricia, *The Five of Hearts*), p.141.

19   (O'Toole, Patricia, *The Five of Hearts*), p.192.

20   (O'Toole, Patricia, *The Five of Hearts*), p.197.

21   *The Adams Memorial*, Rock Creek Cemetery brochure, November 1, 1997.

22   (Beale, *Decatur House and its Inhabitants*), p.101.

23   Proctor, John Clagett, *Washington Past and Present* (New York: Lewis Historical Publishing Company, Inc.), 1930, Vol. III, p.3.

24   Goode, James, *Capital Losses*, (Washington: Smithsonian Institution Press, 1979), p.91.

25   Goode, James, *Outdoor Sculpture*, Washington: Smithsonian Institution Press, 1974), p.372.

26   Washburn, Wilcomb E., *The Cosmos Club of Washington* (Washington: The Cosmo Club of Washington, 1978), p.18.

27   (Washburn, Wilcomb E., *The Cosmos Club of*), p.20.

28   (Washburn, Wilcomb E., *The Cosmos Club of Washington*), p.24.

29   Bryan, C.D.B., *The National Geographic Society, 100 Years* (New York: harry N. Abrams, Inc., Publishers, 1987), p.24.

30   (Bryan, C.D.B., *The National Geographic Society*), p.24.

31   (Barry, David S., *Forty Years in Washington*), p.28.

32   (Barry, David S., *Forty Years in Washington*), p.28.

33   Files of Martin Luther King Library, Washington, D.C., "Ingersoll House/25 Madison Place"

34   Files of Martin Luther King Library, Washington, D.C., "Ingersoll House/25 Madison Place"

35   Files of Office of the Curator of the Department of the Treasury, Washington, D.C., "Freedman's Savings Bank."

36   Buckley, Barry, *Washington Old and New* (Washington: Washington Printing Company, 1913), p.60.

37   (Brown, *Washington, A Not Too Serious History*), p.407.

38   (Barry, David S., *Forty Years in Washington*), p.301.

39   (Barry, David S., *Forty Years in Washington*), p.298-99.

40   (Barry, David S., *Forty Years in Washington*), p.69.

41   (Buckley, Barry, *Washington Old and New*), p.60.

42   (*Sixteenth Street Architecture*), Vol. I, p.90.

43   (Buckley, Barry, *Washington Old and New*), p.106.

44   Files of the Martin Luther King Library, Washington, DC, *Houses, 1623 H St., NW*.

45   *The Washington Post* "Potomac" Magazine, Sunday, February 1, 1970, p.14.

Bull Moose, Beaux Arts, and Backdrop Buildings

1   Caemmerer, H.P., *Washington The National Capital*, (Washington: U.S. Government Printing Office, 1932), p.78.

2   (Goode, James, *Outdoor Sculpture*), p.380.

3   Felsenthal, Carol, *Alice Roosevelt Longworth*, (New York: G.P. Putnam's Sons, 1988), p.104.

4   National Park Service/Department of Interior brochure, *Theodore Roosevelt Island*, p. 1

5   *National Geographic Magazine*, November 1951, Vol. C, No. 5, p.569.

6   *The Washington Post*, "She Painted the Town Pink," March 29, 1999.

7   Weeks, Cristopher, *AIA Guide to the Architecture of Washington, D.C.*, (Baltimore: Johns Hopkins University Press, 1994), p.150.

8   (Wilson, *Washington, The Capital City*), Vol. II, p.142.

9   *The Evening Star*, May 20, 1942.

10   The Washington Board of Trade, *The Book of Washington*, (Washington: Cleland C. McDevitt, 1927), p.462.

11   Charlick, Carl, *The Metropolitan Club of Washington*, (Washington, Judd & Detweliler, Inc., 1965), p.68.

12   (Charlick, Carl, *The Metropolitan Club of Washington*), p.70.

13   (Charlick, Carl, *The Metropolitan Club of Washington*), p.71.

14   (Felsenthal, Carol, *Alice Roosevelt Longworth*,), p.67.

15   (Diller, Daniel, *The Presidents, First Ladies, and Vice Presidents*), p.64.

16   (Klapthor, Margaret Brown, *The First Ladies*), p.68.

17   (Klapthor, Margaret Brown, *The First Ladies*), p.68.

18   *Washington Flyer*, November-December 1997, p.57.

19   *The Washingtonian*, April 1984, p. 173.

20   (Klapthor, Margaret Brown, *The First Ladies*), p.70.

21   *Architectural Record*, Vol. 21, No. 1, January 1909.

22   *The Washington Post*, "Woodies, in the Beginning," August 17, 1995.

23   (The Washington Board of Trade, *The Book of Washington*), p.212.

24   *The Washington Post*, October 7, 1909.

25   National Capital Planning Commission, *Downtown Urban Renewal Area Landmarks*, (Washington: U.S. Government Printing Office, 1970), p.59.

26   (Carrouth, Gorton, *What Happened When*), p.807.

27   (Weeks, Cristopher, *AIA Guide to the Architecture of Washington, D.C.*), p.110.

28   Files of the Department of the Treasury, "Treasury Annex," Letter to the Superintendent, August 12, 1924.

29   (Brown, *Washington, A Not Too Serious History*), p.226.

30   United States Chamber of Commerce, information brochure, "A Tour of the Main Floor of the U.S. Chamber of Commerce."

31   *The Evening Star*, "AFL Planning to Build," April 4, 1947.

32   (Proctor, *Proctor's Washington*), p.127.

33   (Raymond, V.L., *Home of the Home Club*), p.11.

34   (Raymond, V.L., *Home of the Home Club*), p.11.

35   Washington Daily News, February 21, 1957.

36   *The Evening Star*, July 15, 1940.

37   Levey, Jane Freundel, ed., *Washington History*, Vol. 8, No. 1, Spring-Summer 1996, p.27.

38   (Levey, Jane Freundel, ed., *Washington History*), p.27.

39   (Levey, Jane Freundel, ed., *Washington History*), p.28.

40   (Levey, Jane Freundel, ed., *Washington History*), p.28.

41   *Blueprints*, "Tales of Trustees," Vol. XI, no. 4, Fall 1993, p.15.

42   Files of the Department of the U.S. Court of Claims, "Dedication of the new Court of Claims," dedication speech by Supreme Court Chief Justice Earl Warren, September 20, 1967.

43   Files of the Department of the U.S. Court of Claims, "Dedication of the new Court of Claims," dedication speech by Mr. Lawson B. Knott, Jr., Administrator of GSA, September 20, 1967.

44   *Washington Post Potomac Magazine*, Sunday, February 1, 1970, p.16.

45   *Washington Post Potomac Magazine*, Sunday, February 1, 1970, p.23.

Bibliography

Adams, Henry, *The Education of Henry Adams*. Boston, Houghton Mifflin Company, 1918.

Ames, Mary Clemmer, *Ten Years in Washington, Life and Scenes in the National Capital*. Hartford, A.D. Worthington & Co., 1873.

Appelwhite, E.J., *Washington Itself*. New York, Alfred A. Knoff, 1981.

Barrett., John, *The Pan American Union*. Baltimore, Munder Thomsen Press, 1911.

Barry, David S., *Forty Years in Washington*. Boston, Little, Brown, and Company, 1924.

Bryan, Wilhelmus Bogart, *A History of the National Capital, Volumes 1-2*. New York, The MacMillan Company, 1914.

Brown, George Rothwell, *Washington, A Not Too Serious History*. Baltimore, The Norman Publishing Company, 1930.

Buckley, Barry, *Washington Old an New*. *Washington*, Washington Printing Company, 1913.

Caemmerer, H.P., *Washington The Nation's Capital*. Washington, U.S. Government Printing Office, 1932.

Carr, Roland T., *32 President's Square*. Washington, Acropolis Books Ltd., 1975.

Charlick, Carl, *The Metropolitan Club of Washington*. Washington, Judd & Detweiler, Inc 1965.

Commission of Fine Arts, *Commission of Fine Arts, A Brief History, 1910-1984*. Washington, 1984.

Commission of Fine Arts, *Massachusetts Avenue Architecture, Vol. I*. Washington, U.S. Government Printing Office, 1973.

Commission of Fine Arts, *Sixteenth Street Architecture, Vol. I*. Washington, U.S. Government Printing Office, 1978.

Commission of Fine Arts, *Sixteenth Street Architecture, Vol. II*. Washington, U.S. Government Printing Office, 1988.

Eberlein, Harold D., and Courtlandt, Van Dyke H., *Historic Houses of George-town and Washington City*. Richmond, The Dietz Press, Inc., 1958.

Ellis, Dr. John B., *The Sights and Secrets of the National Capital*. Chicago, Jones, Junkin & Co., 1869.

Eskew, Garnett Laidlaw, *Willard's of Washington*. New York, Coward-McCann, Inc., 1954.

Ewing, Charles, *Yesterday's Washington, D.C.*, Miami, E. A. Seemann Publishing, 1976.

Federal Writers Project, *Washington City and Capital, American Guide Series*. Washington, U.S. Government Printing Office, 1937.

Fensenthal, Carol, *Alice Roosevelt Longworth*. New York, G.P. Putnam's Sons, 1988.

Gobright, L.A., *Recollection of Men and Things at Washington, During the Third of a Century*. Philadelphia, Claxton, Remsen & Haffelfinger, 1869.

Goode, James M., *Capital Losses, A Cultural History of Washington's Destroyed Buildings*. Washington, Smithsonian Institution Press, 1979.

Goode, James M., *The Outdoor Sculpture of Washington, D.C.* Washington, Smithsonian Institution Press, 1974.

Green, Constance McLaughlin, *Washington, A History of the Capital, 1800-1950*. Princeton, Princeton University Press, 1962.

Guilford, Martha C., ed., *From Founders to Grandsons*. Washington, Rufus H. Darby Printing Company, 1955.

Gutheim, Frederick, *Worthy of the Nation*. Washington, Smithsonian Institution Press, 1977.

Hearing and Markup before the Subcommittee on Government Operations and Metropolitan Affairs of the committee on the District of Columbia House of Representatives, Ninety-seventh Congress on H. Res. 532 to Preserve and Restore Rhodes Tavern, Washington, U.S. Government Printing Office, 1983.

Hutchins, Stilson, and Moore, Joseph West, *The National Capitol Past and Present*. Washington, The Post Publishing Company, 1885.

Hutchinson, George, *The History of Madison Place, Lafayette Square, Washington, D.C.* Washington, the Federal Circuit Bar Association, 1998.

The Charles Sumner School, Rededication, 1986, District of Columbia Board of Education, D.C.

Public Schools, 1986.

Jacob, Kathryn Allamong, *Capital Elites*. Washington, Smithsonian Institution Press, 1995.

Kayser, Elmer Louis, *Bricks Without Straw, The Evolution of George Washington University*. New York, Appleton-Century-Crofts, 1970.

Kousoulas, Claudia D. and George W., *Contemporary Architecture in Washington, D.C*. New York, John Wiley & Sons, The reservation Press, 1995.

Klapthor, Margaret Brown, *The First Ladies*. Washington, National Geographic Society, 1985.

Lockwood, Mary S., *Historic Homes in Washington, Its Noted Men and Women*. New York, Belford Company, Publishers, 1889.

Logan, Mrs. John A., *Thirty Years in Washington or Life and Scenes in Our National Capital*. Hartford, A.D. Worthington & Co., 1901.

Maddex, Diane, *Historic Buildings of Washington, D.C*. Pittsburgh, Ober Park Associates, Inc., 1973.

Moore, Joseph West, *Picturesque Washington*. Cedar Rapids, G.W. Lyon, Publisher, 1889.

National Capital Planning Commission, *Downtown Urban Renewal Area Landmarks, Washington, D.C*. Washington, U.S. government Printing Office, 1970.

Netherton, Ross and Nan, *Fairfax County in Virginia: A Picture History*. Norfolk, The Donning Company Publishers, 1986.

O'Toole, Patricia, *The Five of Hearts*. New York, Clarkson Pottor/Publishers, 1990.

Poore, Ben: Perley, *Perley's Reminiscences of Sixty Years in the National Metropolis*, Volumes 1-2. Philadelphia, Hubbard Brothers, Publishers, 1886.

Proctor, John Clagett, *Proctor's Washington and Environs*. Written for the Washington Sunday Star (1828-1949), 1949.

Proctor, John Clagett, *Washington Past and Present, A History*, Volumes 1-5. New York, Lewis Historical Publishing Company, Inc., 1930.

Records of the Columbia Historical Society, Washington, D.C., Volumes 3,9,11,31-36.

Scott, Pamela and Lee, Antoinette J., *Buildings of the District of Columbia*. New York, Oxford University Press, 1993.

Sadler, Christine, *Children of the White House*. New York, Putnam's Sons, 1967.

Seale, William, *The President's House, A History*. New York, Harry N. Abrams, Inc., 1986.

Smith, Margaret Bayard, *The First Forty Years of Washington Society*. New York, Charles Scribner's Sons, 1906.

Stevens, William Oliver, *Washington The Cinderella City*. New York, Dodd, Mead & Company, 1943.

Tayloe, Benjamin Ogle, *Our Neighbors on Lafayette Square*. Washington, privately printed 1872, reprinted by Junior League of Washington, 1982.

United States Department of Justice, *Attorneys General of the united States 1789-1985*. Washington, U.S. Government Printing Office, 1985.

Walton, William, *The Evidence of Washington*. New York, Harper & row, Publishers,1966.

Washburn, Wilcomb, *The Cosmos Club of Washington*. Washington, The Cosmos Club, 1978.

Washington Board of Trade, *The Book of Washington*. Washington, 1927.

Weeks, Christopher, *AIA Guide to the Architecture of Washington*, D.C. Baltimore, The Johns Hopkins University Press, 1994.

Wilson, Rufus Rockwell, *Washington The Capital City and Its Part in the History of the Nation*. Philadelphia, J. B. Lippincott Company, 1902.

Index

Book 1: <u>**Proximity To Power - Neighbors to the Presidents Near Lafayette Square**</u>

Book 2: <u>**Two Hundred Years - Stories of the Nation's Capital**</u>

<u>**Note Cards:**</u> Sets of five cards each reproducing a line drawing by artist **Edward F. Fogle** of historic buildings and homes in Washington, DC described in brief, lively essays by historian Jeanne Fogle

Please specify how many of each set:

___**Set 1: Washington Views**   ___**Set 5: Galleries**
___**Set 2: Historic Buildings**   ___**Set 6: Downtown Buildings**
___**Set 3: Georgetown Buildings**   ___**Set 7: Sites Around the Capitol**
___**Set 4: Capitol Hill Buildings**   ___**Set 8: Assorted Christmas cards**
                                                            (6 cards)

Postal orders: A Tour de Force   (*Please make check payable to:* **A Tour de Force**)
                         P. O. Box 2782
                         Washington, DC 20013

Please send the following:

___ copies of **Proximity To Power** .... $ 19.95 ea./ (total)$_____
___ copies of **Two Hundred Years**............................. $ 14.95 ea./ (total)$_____
___ sets of **Washington Note Cards** (as listed above) (no S&H)
                                                            $ 5.00 ea./ (total)$_____
Sales tax: Add 4.5% for books shipped to Virginia   VA tax $_____

Shipping: Add $4.00 for the first book; $2.00 for each additional book.
                                                            S&H $_____

                                                    TOTAL: $_____
Send to:
Name_____

Address_____

City_____ **State**_____ **Zip**_____

Visit our website at: www.ATOURDEFORCE.com   /2000